The Rescripted Self:
Attaining Competency and Wellbeing

By

Robert Kayton, Ph.D.

Bethesda Communications Group

Copyright © Robert Kayton, Ph.D., 2019

Published by Bethesda Communications Group
4816 Montgomery Lane
Bethesda, MD 20814
www.bcgpub.com

ISBN-13: 978-1-7321501-6-4
ISBN-10: 1-7321501-6-8

Robert Kayton can be reached by email at drrobertkayton@gmail.com.

To my family for their unwavering support while I completed this book and to the many colleagues and patients who taught me how to apply theory to rescripting techniques

Table of Contents

Tables and Diagrams 7
Acknowledgements 8
Foreword 9
About the Author 10
Prologue 11
Introduction: The Emergence of Affects, Scripts and Self: The Co-evolution of Brain, Body, Affect, and Mind 13
    The Dynamics of the Nervous System 16
    Neural Structures 17
    The Neuroscience of the Affect System 20
Part I: The Functional Self 23
    Chapter 1: The Affect System 27
        The Individual Affects 27
        The Affect System and the Emergence of the Mind 31
    Chapter 2: The Cognitive System 36
        Learning 37
        Memory 39
        Language and Communication 40
        Thinking 41
        Explicit and Implicit Thinking 42
    Chapter 3: The Emotional System 45
        Emotions and Moods 48
        The Negative Emotions 50
        The Positive Emotions 55
    Chapter 4: The Behavioral System 58
        From Inscripts to Behaviors 58
        Behavioral Learning 59
        Conclusion: Self-Will and Behavior 64
    Chapter 5: The Script System 66
        The Formation and Structure of Scripts 68
        Types of Complex Scripts 72
        Ideoaffective Cost-benefit Scripts 73
        Ideological Scripts 74
        Defensive Scripts 75
        Diagnostic Scripts 77
    Chapter 6: Function-Focused Rescripting 78
        Rescripting Affects 80
        Rescripting Cognition 85

- Rescripting Emotions 94
- Rescripting Behavior 96

Part II: The Emergent Self: Integrative Rescripting and Wellbeing 102

Chapter 7: The Self and its Self-Scripts 104
- The Composition of the Self 106
- The Functional (Structural) Self 107
- The Emergent (Integrated) Self 108
- The Functions and Properties of the Self 109
- The Formation of the Self: Development and Emergence 110
- Stages of Self Development 111

Chapter 8: Integration and the Emergent Self 117
- The Emergent Self 122
- The Autobiographical Self 122
- The Selfother Self 126

Chapter 9: Emotional Wellbeing and the Integrated Self 130
- Factors Related to Wellbeing 131
- Competency in Functioning 132
- Temperamental Predisposition 132
- Autobiographical Memory 133
- Context 135
- Aging 136
- What Is Wellbeing? 138
- Wisdom, Self-Agency and Willpower 141

Chapter 10: Integrative Rescripting 145
- Rescripting the Autobiographical Self 153
- Rescripting the Selfother-Self 154

Chapter 11: Disorders of the Self 155

Appendices 165
- Appendix 1: Affect Recognition Worksheet 166
- Appendix 2: Graduated Desensitization Worksheet 167
- Appendix 3: Diaphragmatic Breathing 168
- Appendix 4: Progressive Muscle Relaxation 169
- Appendix 5: Basic Autogenic Training 170
- Appendix 6: Defensive Beliefs 171
- Appendix 7: Maladaptive Styles of Thinking 172
- Appendix 8: The Practice of Mindfulness 173
- Appendix 9: Affirmation Self-Statements 174
- Appendix 10: Anxiety Inoculation 175
- Appendix 11: Reframing Worksheets 176
- Appendix 12: Disputation Exercise 178

Appendix 13: Counter-Thinking 179
Appendix 14: Narrative Rescripting 180
Appendix 15: Daily Log 181
Appendix 16: Wellbeing Questionnaire 183
Appendix 17: Brain-Body-Mind Integration Techniques 184
Glossary of Terms..186
References..195

Tables and Diagrams

Diagram A   The Triune Brain..18
Diagram A1 The Four Lobes of the Brain 19
Diagram B   The Left-Right Hemispheres 19
Diagram C   Profiles of Neural Findings 21
Diagram D   ANS Profiles of Affect Activation...22
Diagram E   The Scene 25
Table 1-A   The Innate Affects 27
Diagram 1-A Reciprocal Affect Changes 35
Table 2-A   Procedural vs. Declarative Learning 37
Table 2-B   Forms of Memory and Thinking 43
Table 3-1   Secondary Emotions...47
Table 3-2   Cognitive-Memory-Emotion Table 48
Table 3-3   Secondary Emotions and their Secondary Cognitions 50
Diagram 5-1 The Self 70
Table 5-1   Reordering of Scripts 71
Diagram 5-2 Development of a Depressive Script 72
Table 6-1   Affect-Focused Rescripting Techniques 82
Table 6-2   Primary Affective Schemas 86
Table 6-3   Cognitive Rescripting Techniques 90
Table 6-4   Behavioral Rescripting Techniques 98
Table 7-1   Composition of the Self..107
Diagram 7-1 Linear vs. Nonlinear Changes in Time..111
Diagram 8-1 The Integrative Self 121
Table 9-1   Attributes Associated with Wellbeing..139

Acknowledgements

I would first of all like to extend my gratitude to the late Donald Nathanson, M.D. founder and director of the Silvan S. Tomkins Institute. His teaching and encouragement were essential to my study and understanding of Tomkins comprehensive model of human functioning. In addition, I want to thank Victor Kelly, MD. whose guidance and support, as Assistant Director of the institute, added enormously to my tutelage.

I would also like to thank Ken Sachs, Ph.D. who was the first psychologist to read my manuscript and provided me with the necessary support and encouragement to continue finishing this manuscript. To Bruce Pickle, Ph.D. whose knowledge of Tomkins' theory was the most advanced and who agreed to write the foreword group to this book. In addition, I would like to thank those members of the Tomkins Study Group in Bethesda where I had the honor of being the organizer and director.

To my family who provided not only support but helped in the editing of this book. To Drs. Bruce Pickle and Ken Sachs who read an early draft and encouraged me to continue writing this book. To my son Bradley who provided the initial set of edits and comments, and whose endorsement of the material helped motivate me to finish and publish the manuscript; and to my youngest daughter Brittany, whose feedback and comments helped shape the narrative. Most of all to the many patients I have seen over the years who not only taught me how best to help them, but inspired me to continue the clinical model that is herein contained. And finally to Debbie Lange, President of the Bethesda Communications Group, for editing and formatting this manuscript and bringing it to fruition; I especially appreciate her diligence and celerity in moving this project forward.

There are two caveats that I would like to make. First, some ideas or text may not have been properly credited to the appropriate source. If so, I deeply apologize; it was completely unintended. I would encourage anyone to notify me of problems and I will correct the error as soon as possible.

Secondly, although this book is primarily written for the mental health professional, it is also accessible to the general public. For example, Chapter 6 on function-focused therapy delves into many self-help techniques that are apropos for most readers who are just interested in treatment strategies. In addition, several non-professionals with degrees in other fields, such as business, have indicated that they were able to understand most of the material. Like any complex writing, it is best to first read through the text without trying to fully understand the content; it is then best to reread the material more comprehensively. I did this when trying to understand the author of the affect-script model. I was fond of saying that reading Silvan S. Tomkins was like "trying to nail jelly to a wall;" I would understand the material for a moment, only to feel it slip away in the moment after that. It was only after I slowly and meticulously reread the material that I was able to truly grasp this comprehensive theory. To simplify and clarify this complex information is the best way to understand it. I trust that I have succeeded in this endeavor.

Read and enjoy,
Robert Kayton

Foreword

I use the concepts in Dr. Kayton's book every day in my clinical practice. I am grateful for the clarity and practicality of such profound insights into living successfully and well. Here is a breadth and depth rarely encountered on the subject. Dr. Kayton's work is multidisciplinary, an inquiry which is historical, scientific, philosophical, psychological and human. He knows that a viewpoint is 'a view from a point' and so gives us an integrated picture from many points. And he succeeds in tying detail to design, addressing the parts while holding the whole as greater than their sum.

He accomplishes this with openness and curiosity, yet precision and rigor, and with a clinician's heart to help us heal and be whole. He lives and breathes a creative, life-enhancing, evolutionary accommodation and assimilation, graciously considering other's ideas while solidly grounded in his own.

I respect his courage and integrity in not resting on his considerable and well-earned laurels, not becoming doctrinaire--he does not have a 'hardening of the categories'--but instead, pressing forward in the excitement of genuine curiosity toward the discovery of applied scientific truth. As such, he builds bridges between many schools of thought in science, humanities and psychology in a way which helps us become a human fully alive.

I am so glad to commend Dr. Kayton's life-changing work to you, the reader, and trust it will become a treasured guide on your journey of success and well-being. Enjoy in good health.

Dr. Bruce Pickle
Clinical Psychologist

About the Author

Robert Kayton is a retired clinical psychologist who practiced psychotherapy for over 40 years. In addition to his private practice he was a consultant to many agencies, was Director of several mental health centers, and held such academic positions as: Associate Clinical Professor at the George Washington University Medical School, faculty member at the Washington School of Psychiatry, and a Lecturer in Psychology at the University of Maryland in College Park.

He received his M.S. and Ph.D. at the University of Massachusetts at Amherst in 1969, did his clinical internship at the Northwestern University Medical School, and a post-doctoral at the Illinois State Psychiatric Institute in Chicago.

Dr. Kayton was Director of the Center for Anxiety and Stress in Bethesda Maryland, and Co-Director of the Center for Depression in Washington D.C. At the Prince George's County Mental Health Department, he was, Chief Psychologist, Director of the Outpatient Clinic, and Director of Research. He held licenses in clinical psychology from Maryland, Virginia, and Washington D.C. In addition to his private clinical practice, he was among the first psychologists in the nation to have a private hospital practice as an Attending Psychologist at the Psychiatric Institute of Washington D.C. He also testified at the Maryland congressional hearing on mental health as both Assistant to the Director at the Prince George's Health Department and as a registered lobbyist for the county's Mental Health Association. He has also appeared on local and national television and has published numerous articles in various magazines. He has given many talks on Affect Rescripting to professional organizations around the country, and has taught a course on this subject at the Washington School of Psychiatry.

He was originally trained as a psychoanalyst, and was a supervisor of psychoanalysis at the George Washington University Medical School, Department of Psychiatry. An eclectic at heart, he began training in many other clinical approaches; these included Jungian Therapy, EMDR (Eye Movement Desensitization Reprocessing), Interpersonal therapy, hypnosis, and Cognitive-Behavioral Therapy. In 1991, he began studying Silvan S. Tomkins' Affect-Script theory at the Thomas Jefferson Medical School in Philadelphia and was the organizer and leader of the Silvan S. Tomkins Institute study group in the Washington-Baltimore area. This launched his intensive study of neuroscience, which ultimately led to this book.

Robert Kayton can be reached by email at drrobertkayton@gmail.com.

Prologue

The *rescripted self* refers to a person who has achieved both competency and success in life, and who has attained a state of being that is characterized by happiness and wellbeing.

Rescripting therapy is my method for achieving this, first by changing the parts that make up the self, and then changing the self as a whole. We will use *function-focused rescripting*[1] to change the component parts of the self, and *integrative-rescripting* to change the self as a whole. Competency and wellbeing are the primary goals in life; by rescripting the self we improve our ability to function successfully in life, while also attaining a state of emotional wellbeing and fulfillment.

Affects underlie our emotional and psychological life. What we feel when emotional is essentially the physical sensations associated with affects. The rapid heartbeat and labored breathing when scared is that of the affect *fear-terror*, while the relaxed feeling of calmness is based on the affect *enjoyment-joy*; in other words, affects make up the physical experiences of an emotion. They are innate neurobiological functions and are often referred to as the basic inborn emotions. Emotions are combinations of both affect (feeling) and cognition (thinking) and, rather than being inborn, are based on learned experiences.

Through natural selection, affects evolved to give us a greater capacity to adapt and cope in an ever-changing world. Affects did so by giving us a wider range of innate abilities as compared to the simpler stimulus-response (S-R) reactions found in instincts, such as danger-escape, food-eat. Humans (and mammals) evolved six negative affects that were genetically programmed to deal with danger, and two positive affects necessary for the fulfillment of our basic needs. However, since we no longer live in nature, affects have come to play a deleterious role in our lives. Consequently, adaptation is now largely based on our ability to efficaciously regulate and control these very same affects. The mechanism for doing so lies with scripts. Scripts are patterns of thinking, feeling and doing that operate much as does a written script. They are learned sets of rules that organize and govern our lives in the service of both affect-regulation and self-regulation. Scripts emerged as the mind evolved, and provided us with a higher cognitive level of regulation and, therefore, a greater ability to successfully adapt to the world.

The two essential dynamics leading to competency and wellbeing are, respectively, *affect-regulation* and *affect-integration*. Affect-regulation is the fundamental process underlying our capacity to function competently in life. At its core is the regulation of two essential processes, excitation and inhibition in which brain and mental functions are either turned-on or turned-off. This *excitation-inhibition* polarity operates at all levels, from the cellular to the neurophysiological to the psychological. This dynamic is the essence of affect-regulation, namely to balance levels of excitation with countervailing levels of inhibition that can then lead to optimal functioning. Too much excitation or too much inhibition will interfere with adaptive functioning.

As affect-regulation is essential for successful functioning, affect-integration is essential for wellbeing. At the brain level this requires that synaptic neural circuits connect structures top-down, left and right, as well as interior-exterior. Since brain structures perform certain functions, their integration is essential to function competently, to feel competent, and to attain wellbeing. Such integration applies to the neural functions that make up the mind, and how the mind then directs behavior. We could only imagine the chaos that would ensue if these systems were not integrated, each operating independently of one another. Psychoneurobiological integration is

---

[1] Originally rescripting therapy was functional in nature and was called *Affect Rescripting Therapy.*

essential for developing an integrated self, the prerequisite for living life in a state of emotional wellbeing.

The principle function of the *self* is to regulate and organize its component scripts into an integrated self-system. In script formation, there is a hierarchy of scripts based on increasing levels of complexity, from the relatively simple *affect-scripts* that directly regulate affects, to *self-scripts* that organize these affect-regulating scripts into a more cohesive and coherent whole. As affect-regulation follows the dynamics of excitation and inhibition, self-scripts follow the *convergence-divergence* principle that looks instead at the ratio between degrees of similarity and degrees of difference. For integration to take place, there needs to be far greater degrees of similarity than there are differences among self-scripts.

In general, then, we can say that there are two primary goals in life, the first to function competently in the world, the second to live life with emotional wellbeing. To function competently in life is essential for survival, safety and security; it is also essential for wellbeing. However, just because one functions well does not necessarily mean that one feels well; although affect-regulation is a necessary component for wellbeing, the necessary *and* essential factor is the integration of the self.

Introduction: The Emergence of Affects, Scripts and Self: The Co-evolution of Brain, Body, Affect, and Mind

How life evolved from a simple collection of molecules into the complexity of a human being is an extraordinary story. What is equally astounding is that the basic properties that explain the dynamics of molecular physics are fundamentally the same properties that underlie our thoughts, feelings, and behaviors. Consequently, by understanding and appreciating the interwoven fabric of our existence, from the molecular level to the macro-level, helps determine how our physical-self and mental-self operate.

Why do we need to understand our evolutionary past? The answer is that the past is still present and will help carry us into the future; as the saying goes, *past is prologue*. Knowing how molecules and cells work provides the knowledge neuroscientists need for understanding how the brain and body work. Since the mind is a function of the brain, this knowledge is invaluable for understanding how and why we function the way we do. This information is also critical in developing medications and psychotherapy treatments for the many problems that plague untold millions of people worldwide.

There are two, among many, important principles of evolutionary law. One is that evolution is parsimonious, efficient, and very practical. Rather than discarding older structures for newer ones, existing structures are instead typically used to accommodate new and more adaptive functions. This often entails modifying the form of the organs to be changed, such as increasing its size or borrowing from adjacent structures. This leads to the second principle, namely that *form follows function*. The brain is organized according to what is needed to successfully function internally and to successfully adapt to the world we live in. People walk, birds fly, and fish swim. Our different brains are structured to accommodate these functions. In other words, the formation and organization of these brain structures was predicated on how well they operated in the service of adaptation and natural selection. Nevertheless, it should be noted that there is actually an interactive system between form and function whereby each is simultaneously influencing the other.

Life began as unicellular organisms that over time evolved into ever-increasing complexities of cellular colonies. These colonies then evolved into multi-cellular organisms, which later divided into two major morphologies, plants and animals. Plants are stationary, animals move. Movement involves a two-way communication between the moving organism and its ever-changing environment. This requires a mechanism that detects and processes internal and external data to then calibrate and drive the animal toward nutrients and safety, and away from danger. This mechanism is the nervous system.

The evolved nervous system is divided into two systems, the *Central Nervous System (CNS)* and the *Peripheral Nervous System (PNS)*. The CNS consists of the spinal cord and brain, while the PNS consists of the Somatic Nervous System and the Autonomic Nervous System. The brain of the Central Nervous System is the processor of data that is sent to it via the spinal cord, and by the Peripheral Nervous System in the body. The PNS's somatic system detects external stimuli, while the Autonomic Nervous System transmits to the brain the sensory-motor impulses that make up our internal sensations.

This, however, was not the nervous system of our earliest ancestors.[2] Our evolutionary journey began soon after plants and animals differentiated, to the time when unicellular

---

[2] Largely taken from Bloom & Lazerson, (1988) and Allman (2000)

bacterial organisms first emerged. These simplest of mobile organisms had to solve the problem of seeking resources and avoiding toxins and danger. Although bacteria lack a nervous system, they exhibit rather complex behavior. They sense their environment through a large number of receptors and store this elaborate sensory input in the form of brief memory traces that they use to produce adaptive behaviors. In other words, bacteria integrate sensory data and modify behavior to adapt better to the changing environment. Thus, bacteria contain some of the basic functions of the brain: sensory integration, memory, decision-making, and the control of behavior. Bacteria have also been found to contain the basic rudiments of society and the interrelationships among other similar bacteria. It has been found that when bacteria are confronted by predators or toxins, they will congregate together to form a chemical film that acts as a shield. Other studies have identified differing social activities among different types of bacteria in terms of cooperation and adaptation.

Sight and hearing, along with touch, taste and smell, were significant in the evolution of the Somatic Nervous System. Many neuroscientists argue that the development of several central nervous system structures was initiated by the need for greater functional sophistication, especially of the sensory system. Again, form follows function.

Unlike unicellular organisms, multicellular organisms are encased in a unit, a body that provides a wall between the internal and external world, thus allowing it to better control its chemical environment and the flow of information. The chemical information is regulated by channels, located in the membranes of cells, that control the passage of specific ions, such as sodium and potassium. Information is compartmentalized so that different cells evolved to take on different functions.

Neurons are specialized cells for processing information. Like their unicellular cousin bacteria, neurons have receptors that signal and integrate diverse information. In bacteria the sensing of a nutrient, without sensing a toxin, results in seeking behaviors, while if instead it senses just a toxin, the consequent behaviors will be to avoid or escape. These approach-avoid behaviors are called *action **tendencies***. Neurons develop *action **potentials***, which precede activity; thus, the neuron can inhibit its tendency to fire when activated. Although bacteria can suppress an action tendency, it does so by the relative amount of nutrients vs. toxins present at that moment, while neurons have action potentials, the seeds for the development of anticipatory control; thus, unlike bacteria that largely live in the moment, neurons have the ability to prepare for future happenings and then act accordingly. This capacity to predict provides animals with an extraordinary evolutionary advantage.

This capacity to anticipate means there is memory. To expect some outcome is based on previous outcomes that get stored as memory traces within the molecular structure of the neuron, and most importantly in the communication network among neurons. This tells us that the temporal factors so important to our mental functioning are already set within the nuclei of the brain.

The evolutionary development of the brain can be traced from these simple unicellular organisms to the simplest organism that possess a rudimentary nervous system, namely jellyfish, to the earliest vertebrate fish and their descendants, and then to the amphibians and reptiles, and finally to warm blooded animals.

With the advent of mammals, brain development truly escalated. Co-evolving with increased brain development was the brain's mental functions. Mental functions, such as knowing, judging, and deciding, make up the higher and more complex neural system we call the mind. In essence, the mind evolved as the brain's master regulator and organizer of the brain's mental functions. The mind evolved in humans (and primates, elephants, porpoises, crows and parrots) to form a state of mind we call the self.

The emergence of the mind was truly transformative in propelling birds, mammals, primates and especially human beings to dominate the earth.[3] The emergence of the mind, from the brain, seems apparent when we consider that our mental functions are analogs of many of the basic functions we see in neurons. As stated by Silvan S. Tomkins, "The gene is to life as the neuron is to mind."

Neurons can learn and process data, possess memory, anticipate and plan for the future, and execute these plans. Neurons, as analogs of bacteria, are constituted at a higher and more organized level; consequently, its neuronal functions are magnified to a far greater degree of complexity when we refer to the mind.

The complexity of our mental functions is exponentially augmented when compared to the data processing functions of the neuron. Complexity itself is partially based on the analog principle. The more removed an analog is from its original source, the more complex that analog becomes. Each increasing stage of complexity represents greater degrees of separation and distance from the original source; yet, however changed and complex an analogical function becomes, it will still maintain many of its original functions.

An analog is a near duplication of its progenitor. The analog concept provides a very broad and overarching philosophical and scientific principle. Duplication exists at all levels and among all mediums, from the molecular level of DNA reproduction to the macro level of human reproduction, as are the patterns of neural connections to the patterns of interpersonal relationships, life will imitate life in analogous ways.

The analog principle is embedded in evolutionary development. This is evident in the process by which older structures are retained, and when modified enough, become new and different structures. This *is* the analog process.

Mirror neurons help explain how one person's emotions get analogically replicated in another person. These neurons were discovered in studies on monkeys, giving credibility to the proverbial "monkey see, monkey do." A person's movements sensitize the same neuromuscular activity in the observer; this is the basis of empathy. We know, however, that internalized mirrored experiences are not identical. This is because an analog is not an exact copy. If analogs were pure duplications, nothing would change; everything would simply be a clone of its original; each of us would then be able to read the minds of others. In truth when we speak of duplication and similarity, there is by fiat its counterpart, variance; thus, we duplicate that which is constantly changing. Accordingly, although an analog is a replication, it is nevertheless a replication of that which is dynamic and constantly in flux. Therefore, even though an analog is a copy, there is also enough that is different to allow for variation. It is the design and aim of evolution to capture that, which is both similar and dissimilar at any given moment of time, a task of such enormous complexity that it is better understood through nonlinear dynamics. This is because changes in complexity are not sequential and predictable, such as X causes Y; instead, complex changes take places through the dynamics of quantum mechanics. We shall return to nonlinear analysis and the analog principle in a myriad of ways throughout this book, and especially when we discuss the integration of the self in Part II.

The mind generally reflects not the functions of a single neuron,[4] but the totality of multiple neurons whose functions are exponentially magnified by the entire neural network.

---

[3] alongside insects and plants

Mental functions are synchronic with the broad expanse of the neural-networking activity in the brain. We, therefore, usually look at functioning in terms of patterns and systems rather than as individual and static units, such as the single neuron.

It is important that we examine both the dynamical and structural foundation of the brain so as to better understand the dynamics and structure of the mind. Our basic assumption is that the structural dynamics of the mind evolves from, and thus corresponds to, the structural dynamics of the brain; thus, the mind is an analog (or *mental representation*) of the brain. This is what neuroscience, and especially cognitive neuroscience, is all about. We shall now examine how the development of the mind parallels the development of the brain.

The Dynamics of the Nervous System

We shall begin with the dynamics of the brain, since it is through these neural processes that the structures and functions of the brain and mind develop. The anatomical structure of the brain consists of massed clusters of billions of neurons that coalesce through neural activity. Each neuron grows through the expansion and branching of its (dendritic) fibers that extend to other neuronal projections. It is through this connection with other neurons, in multiple combinations called *neural networks*, that these basic units come to play a vital role in brain functioning.

As the renowned neuropsychologist Donald O. Hebb once stated, "Neurons that fire together wire together." This is *potentiation,* namely the "enhancement of one agent by another so that the combined effect is greater than the sum of the effects of each alone."

This neuronal enhancement takes place through *synaptogenesis,* the growth of new neural networks and connections. Synaptogenesis plays a fundamental role in the way the brain develops and changes. Significant in synaptogenesis, as well as neurogenesis,[5] are increases in neuronal mass, which leads to the growth and development of new and different brain structures. "Plasticity and *neurogenesis* allow an organism to adaptively respond to changing environments...learning involves a physiological modification of the inherited brain mechanisms." (Bloom, F.L & Lazerson, A. 1988, p. 267) Thus plasticity of the brain is critical for adaptation and regulation. Learning impacts on the brain, and changes synaptic clusters. The impact of new data modifies existing synaptic connections. It usually expands through synaptogenesis, the growth of new synaptic connections and contracts by pruning out older and less essential synapses. Learning can therefore be thought of as a neural process entailing a choreography of synaptogenesis, neurogenesis, and pruning that leads to the state of having been learned.

This *having been learned* process is how memory develops. What are retained in memory are experiences that form into an organized pattern of data entry (disparate and dissociated data becomes *information* only when they become organized). The verb *memory* entails the process of laying down information, while the noun *memory* refers to the patterned change of information. This is what learning is, namely changing synapses.

---

[4] There is evidence that some single neurons do possess important functions. For example, there have been discoveries that facial recognition of a famous face can reside in a single neuron (e.g. *Holly Berry Neuron*). However, these singular neurons are only part of the matrix of mental functioning.

[5] It was, until recently, believed that we are born with a given number of neurons, period, and that throughout life this number decreased through neuronal death, i.e. pruning. We now know that new neurons can generate from stem cells in the brain, a process called neurogenesis.

Obviously, we can draw the conclusion that this pattern of data provides a variety of dimensions and profiles. This suggests that learning and memory do not lead to neural profiles, but that neural profiles underlie learning and memory. *Neural profiles* are being used in this context to mean patterns of synaptic activity that are increasing, decreasing or constant. Affects are based on these neural profiles, which speaks to their significant role in learning.

Synapses refer to specialized junctions through which neural signals are transmitted from one neuron to another neuron. The transmission of signals along neural fibers is electrical[6], while its transfer across the synaptic gap takes place through the chemical activity of neurotransmitters. In short, synaptogenesis refers to the growth of new neural networks and connections, and plays a fundamental role in the way the brain develops and changes. The creation of new synapses leads to neurons interconnecting and communicating more with each other, and is thus the basis for neural integration. [Conversely, the pruning of synapses leads to disintegration]

The neurotransmitter activity in synaptogenesis is not only the basis for integration, but also underlies affect-regulation. Neurotransmitters help regulate brain activity by signaling some neurons to fire and others to hold their fire, so that the excitation or inhibition of neuronal firings make up the basic mode for all neural communications. Neural firings vary according to both the rate and density of firings. Patterns of neural firing also vary according to whether these firings are accelerating, decelerating, or maintained at a relatively steady rate and density. When increasing, there is more excitatory than inhibitory neurotransmitter activity; when decreasing there is more inhibition than excitation; and when steady and level, there is a relative balance between excitatory and inhibitory functions.

These patterns of neural firings determine which affects get triggered, how they get expressed, and what feelings are experienced. Affects are made up of physical sensations, which gives us the experience of the affect itself, i.e. the *felt-feel* of an emotion. The transformation of neural sensations to emotions and feelings is processed by affects, and is why Tomkins regarded affects as "the bridge between the brain and the mind."

Neural Structures

The formation of brain structures entails the synaptogenic integration of neurons. We could also say that the structures of the brain and mind operate in similar ways. Perhaps the best way to understand the co-evolution of the brain and mind is to look at the structures of the brain from an evolutionary point of view. Essentially, we can look at brain evolution as being bottom-up, right-left, and interior-exterior. From both evolutionary and developmental perspectives (called *evo-devo*), the development of an individual person's brain follows a sequence that corresponds to the evolution of the human brain itself, as described by the adage that *ontogeny recapitulates phylogeny* [i.e. individual development replicates species development].

The most direct and useful application of the recapitulation theory is represented in Paul McLean's *Triune Brain*, as illustrated on the next page. Since development co-evolves with evolution, it is bottom-up, namely progressing from the lowest level reptilian brain to the more midlevel paleomammalian (early mammals) brain, and then to the higher and more

---

[6] Recently, some neuroscientists are suggesting that in addition to electrical transmission, information is also transmitted by wave oscillations. *Scientific American Magazine,* 2018.

advanced neomammalian brain. As is the case in evolution, older structures are not discarded for newer ones, but instead parsimoniously accommodate and add new and more adaptive functions.

Diagram A The Triune Brain

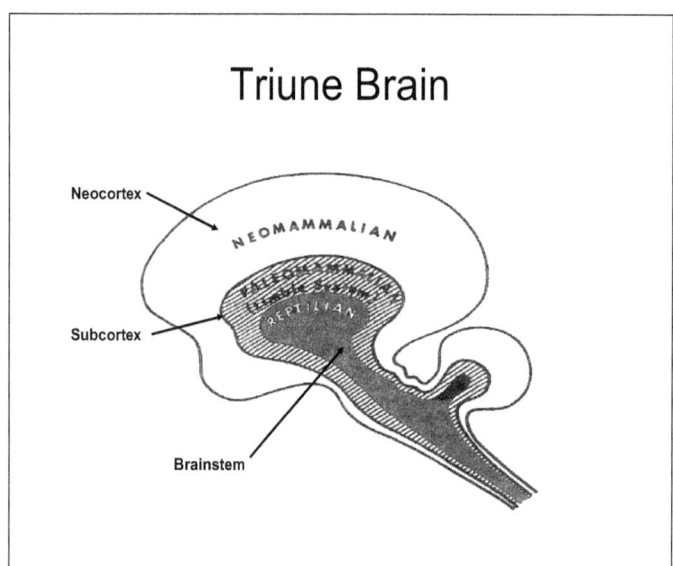

The lowest level reptilian brain is the brain stem, which is fully developed at birth and controls many important functions, such as the production of neurotransmitters, the regulation of bodily homeostasis, and the processing of the innate affects. Next is the paleomammalian brain, or subcortex, which is where the limbic system resides. The highest level is the neomammalian brain, or neocortex. As the limbic system represents the emotional part of the brain, the cerebral cortex represents the cognitive part of the brain. It is particularly in the prefrontal areas (behind the nose ridge) that higher-level reasoning and other executive mental functions are processed.

The brain is divided into four lobes, as illustrated in Diagram A1 on the next page. The frontal lobe is important for cognitive functioning and for the control of voluntary movement or activity. The occipital lobe is primarily responsible for vision, while the temporal lobe processes vision. The parietal lobe processes information about temperature, taste, touch and movement. The parietal lobe is also considered by many neuroscientists to be the region of the brain where the self is processed, where self-awareness and the cohesion of subjective feelings are integrated.

Diagram A1
The Four Lobes of the Brain

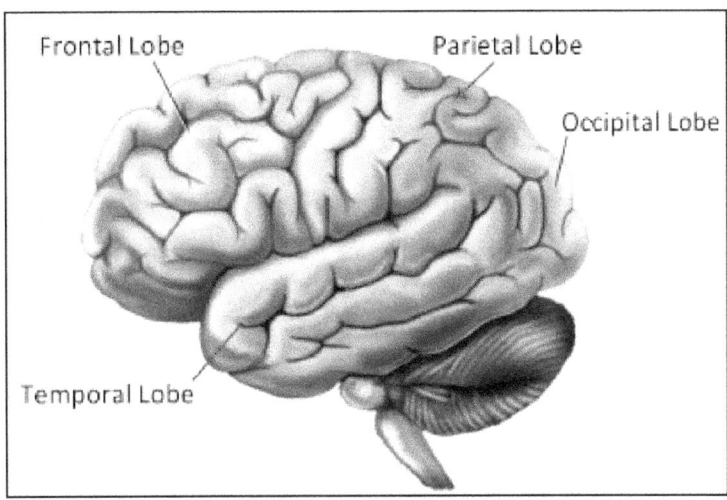

In addition to the triune brain and cerebral lobes are the two cerebral hemispheres, as depicted below, in Diagram B. These two hemispheres evolved from a unicameral brain, which bifurcated with the evolution of the left hemisphere. This is replicated in individual development, whereby during the first two years of life, the right hemisphere has a growth-spurt while the left hemisphere remains relatively dormant.

Diagram B The Left-Right Hemispheres

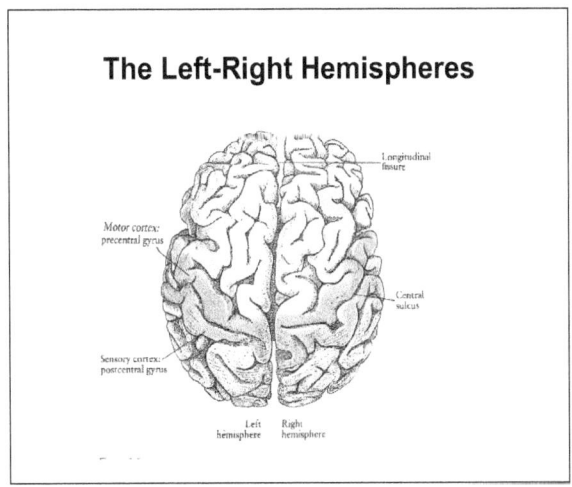

At around two years of age this growth spurt shifts to the left hemisphere; consequently, the two hemispheres at first function independently and then gradually gain coordination and integration through experience-dependent learning. The right hemisphere is biased toward negative emotions, and is more involved in lower-level cognitive processing, while the left hemisphere is biased toward positive emotions, and is more involved in higher level cognitive processing.

The Central Nervous System consists of the brain and spinal cord. A sister system, the Autonomic Nervous System, and especially its Peripheral Nervous System (PNS), play a significant role in the way we internally experience affects. The PNS is the brain's vehicle that governs the body, and is the body's source for communicating with the brain. The primary function of the Peripheral Nervous System is to transmit sensory-motor signals in the body to the Central Nervous System. The PNS conducts sensory signals to the central nervous system from sensory receptors in different parts of the body, and conducts motor signals away from the CNS to muscles, glands and organs that are capable of action (*effector organs*). The CNS receives, stores, and analyzes these sensory signals from the peripheral nervous system.

The Peripheral Nervous System is divided into the *Somatic Nervous System* (SNS), the *Autonomic Nervous System* (ANS), and the *Diffuse Enteric System*. This latter system acts specifically on the digestive tract. The SNS is that part of the PNS that deals with the external world through sensory receptors. For our purpose, however, it is the Autonomic Nervous System that is especially of interest. The ANS is divided into the sympathetic and parasympathetic nervous systems. In general, the *Sympathetic Nervous System* is excitatory and carries signals that help organize, mobilize and energize resources during periods of real or perceived threat. The *Parasympathetic Nervous System* is the inhibitory and energy conserving system of the ANS, which carries signals that act to conserve energy during periods of rest. The interaction between these two systems plays a critical role in affect regulation, as we shall soon discuss.

The Neuroscience of the Affect System

The affect system is part of the brain-body system. Affects are processed in the reticular activating system located in the upper part of the brain stem. Since the bulb of the brain stem rests adjacent to the limbic (emotional) system, it makes neuroanatomical sense that affects underlie emotions.

Affects are activated by specific patterns of neural firings that are experienced in, and expressed through, the body. Although neurobiological in nature, affects underlie both our mental and behavioral systems. They are the physiological component in emotions. By understanding affects, we will gain a better understanding of the dynamics involved in both doing well and feeling well.

Affect-regulation largely governs optimal functioning; when regulated and managed judiciously, the more competent one will be. Although affect-regulation is necessary for emotional wellbeing, it is the integration and organization of the self into a higher and more complex configuration that makes up the essential factors underlying the emergence of wellbeing.

Affects, as stated, are the link that connects the brain and the mind. This linkage takes place as affects move from the neurobiological realm to the psychosocial realm. It is through experiential-learning that affects come to shape our thinking, underlie our emotions, and motivate our behaviors.

The neurotransmitters involved in each affect determine whether an affect is excitatory or inhibitory. As to the positive affects, the affect enjoyment-joy is processed by inhibitory neurotransmitters, such as acetylcholine, while interest-excitement is modulated by the excitatory transmitter dopamine. Surprise-startle and fear-terror are processed by both norepinephrine and epinephrine, while both anger-rage and distress-anguish are mediated by epinephrine. Acetylcholine is the primary neurotransmitter for shame-humiliation, while serotonin[7] is likely the primary neurotransmitter in disgust/dissmell.

The basic affects[8] are activated by specific neural profiles whose rate, speed and density (number of neurons) of neural firings are increasing, decreasing, or steady. These three neural patterns replicate the dynamic stimulus patterns taking place in the external world.[9] Thus, unlike the simple stimulus-response equation replicated in our sensory-motor system, affects replicate the more nuanced patterns of stimulus change. This is what helped give us the more sophisticated and nuanced "knowing" and experiencing of the dynamic and changing world we live in. Thus, affects are analogs of neural profiles, which in turn are analogs of the external world.

Diagram C on the next page illustrates these three patterns of neural firings. The left graph shows that surprise-startle has the steepest incline, fear-terror the next, and interest-excitement the least. It is evident that changes in the degree of incline will lead to corresponding changes in affect. The middle graph shows the decreasing rate and density of neural firings that leads to the enjoyment-joy affect, while the graph on the right side displays the non-gradient and level affects of anger-rage and distress-anguish. As you will note, anger-rage is far denser than is distress-anguish. The affects with increasing rates of neural firings are experienced as arousing and stimulating; enjoyment-joy, with decreasing rates of neural firings, is calming and relaxing; while the non-gradient negative affects of anger-rage and distress-anguish are experienced as tension and pressure.

Diagram C Profiles of Neural Findings[10]
Taken from Silvan S. Tomkins

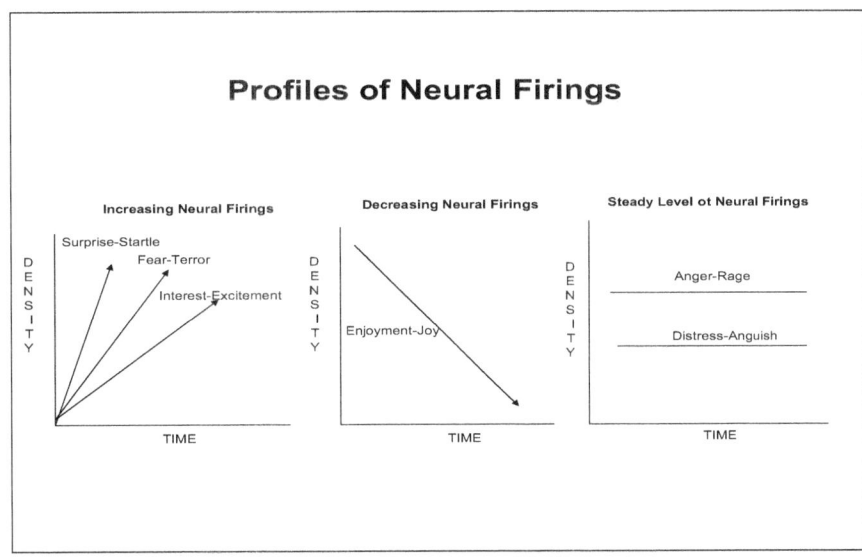

---

[7] Norman Rosenthal, M.D, (personal communication)

[8] Shame-humiliation and disgust/dissmell are not considered basic affects, but auxiliary affects that developed with social learning. We shall discuss this in Chapter 1.

[9] As Nathanson so often declared, this was one of Tomkins' most brilliant insights.

[10] Although each profile is depicted as a straight line, in truth each profile is undulating.

Another caveat relates to changes in the rate or density of neural firings. These changes occur when a different affect becomes dominant, thereby displacing the current profile. When we look at the gradient profiles, we primarily look at the changing rates of neural firings. When we consider the non-gradient affects of distress-anguish and anger-rage, we instead focus on the density of neural firings, since the rate of firings is relatively steady. When distress-anguish or anger-rage escalate, it is because of the increased number of neurons that are firing at any given moment. Neural profiles are also replicated by patterns of activity in the autonomic nervous system, thus extending this analogic progression to the body. In the coming chapters, we shall extend this analog beyond the body to encompass both the mind and behavior.

Diagram D on the next page illustrates the three profiles of neural firings in terms of the excitatory sympathetic nervous system and the inhibitory parasympathetic nervous system. The top graph displays the non-gradient affects of distress-anguish and anger-rage. There is an antagonism between the excitatory and inhibitory systems whereby parasympathetic inhibition is more dominant in distress-anguish, while sympathetic excitation is more dominant in anger-rage. This tension is responsible for the pressured build-up of feelings we experience from these two affects

Unlike the sympathetic-parasympathetic antagonism seen with the non-gradient affects, the gradient affects display a corresponding balance between sympathetic arousal and parasympathetic de-arousal. When looking at the lower-left graph you will notice that there are increasing levels of sympathetic activity and decreasing parasympathetic activity. The right-hand graph shows the decelerating profile of enjoyment-joy, whereby sympathetic activity is decreasing while parasympathetic activity is increasing.

Diagram D ANS Profiles of Affect Activation
Robert Kayton

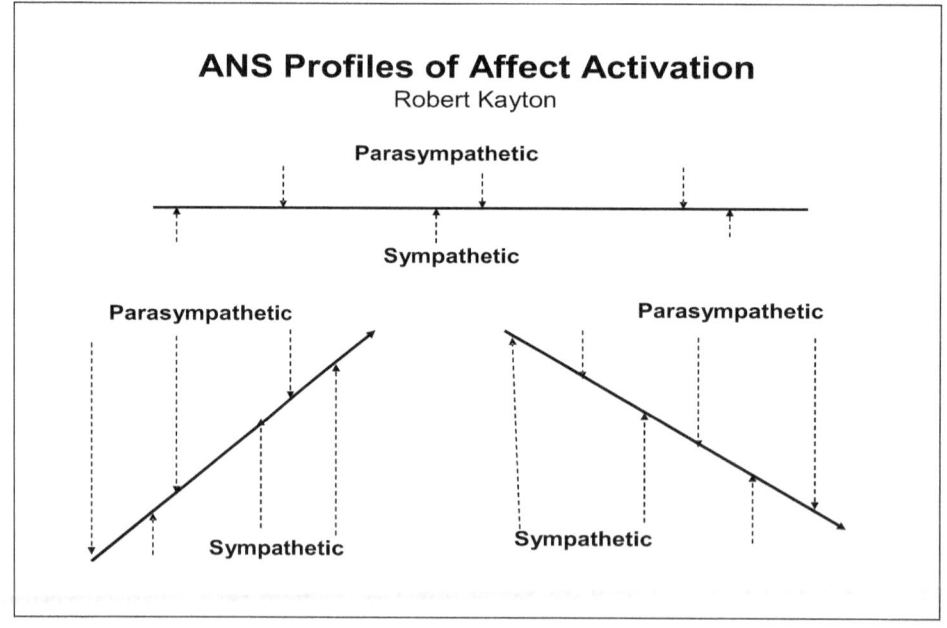

Part I: The Functional Self

Competency and Success via Function-Focused Rescripting Therapy

Affects underlie our mental and behavioral functioning as based on their regulation; thus affect-regulation is the essential factor determining how well we function in life. At the genetically programmed level, an affect is activated by a profile of neural firings that is an analog of its triggering stimulus; thus, a sound that is increasing in volume at a very high rate will activate a very high rate of neural firings, just like a very low level of light will lead to a very low level of neural firings. The synchronization of external stimuli with its corresponding patterns of neural firings is also replicated in bodily patterns which, in turn, will trigger the given fixed action pattern that is inscripted into each affect.

These inscripted action patterns are more complex than a reflex, yet simpler than an instinct, and make up the most basic level of affect-regulation. For example, the inscripted reaction in fear-terror is to escape, which then reduces that fear, while in enjoyment-joy the inscript is to relax, which enhances pleasure. The prescribed goal in affect-regulation is to reduce negative affect and enhance positive affect, as articulated in the Johnny Mercer lyrics, *accentuate the positive, eliminate the negative, latch onto the affirmative, don't mess with mister in-between.*

Inscripted action patterns played a significant role in the life of our distant ancestors, and especially in terms of their ability to adapt and survive. As affect regulators today, however, they are very limited in their efficacy, given their lack of flexibility to an ever changing and complex world. Adaptation is based on our ability to modify our actions according to changes in our environment. This largely depends on experiential-learning rather than on inscripted fixed-action-patterns. It is through the interplay between changes in our environment and changes in our learned experiences that give us the tools and strategies to better adapt. Scripts provide this mechanism for adapting and regulating affect in a changing world.

Scripts evolved from their inscripted action patterns through experiences that both cognified and socialized affects. Cognification[11] developed with the development of memory and the mind, and it did so within the context of our social experiences. Scripts are codified patterns of functioning similar to what some call personality styles. They are learned cognitive sets of rules and schemas that order and govern our lives in the service of affect-regulation (and later, self-regulation).

We could say that the first scripts were actually *protoscripts,* which consisted of inscripted fixed action patterns. As earlier stated, these innately fixed action patterns are more than simple reflexes, yet simpler than the more complex instinctive behaviors. The first level of learned scripts are the *affect-scripts*. These are scripts whose fundamental purpose is to directly control and manage their underlying affect; thus, negative affect-scripts help manage negative affects, while positive affect-scripts help govern positive affects. With increasing development, these basic affect-scripts become more complex and operate more indirectly in their regulation of affects. Most often this entails a regulatory system that essentially weighs both the costs and benefits necessary for adaptation. Since our prescribed goals (to increase positive affect and decrease negative affect) are often unattainable, it

---

[11] Cognification is the analogical transformation of affects into cognition, as when the affect fear is cognified into fearful thoughts.

becomes necessary to compromise the benefits gained from positive affect by allowing the costs, due to negative affect, to take place in order to adapt, if not survive, in society. These *cost-benefit scripts* are mostly defensive scripts based on inhibiting negative affect and minimizing negative affect scripts, often at the expense of the positive. These defensive negative scripts may come to form the scripts we classify as mental disorders. For example, anxiety disorders (anxiety is the emotion that is based on fear-terror) are scripts that function to minimize fear, although there is a cost in terms of the loss of positive consequences that may accrue by engaging in the feared activity, such as avoiding an interview that may lead to a job. At the highest and most complex level are *self-scripts* whose function is to organize and regulate these cost-benefit scripts.

Most often, when we speak about how we live our life, we look not to affects but to scripts. As the mind evolved, affects took on a more implicit role, as cognition and emotion became more prominent. Just as our heart, lung, and endocrine systems continuously operate subliminally, so too do affects. And like these biological functions, which come out of the shadows when they malfunction, affects come to our attention when there is dysregulation in our functioning. For example, when engaged in a task, it is likely that one's attention is focused on that task, rather than the feelings one is having; however, if an affect amplifies to the point of consciousness, our attention will shift away from that task to our emotions and cognitions, as when one feels she has had "enough of this," or says, "I'm screwing things up." What this says is that in our everyday life, scripts play a more apparent role than just the affects from which scripts are based on.

We shall discuss the script system at greater length in Chapter 5. For now, we will look at the basic unit of a script, the *scene*. As depicted in the Diagram E on the next page, a scene consists of a cause-effect linear sequence whereby an event triggers patterns of activity in the brain and body that then excites an affect, which in turn activates the cognitive-emotional system that finally leads to behavior. Overall, the event activates the neurophysiological system, which then activates the cognitive-emotional system that then initiates a behavioral response. In looking specifically at how this event impacts the cognitive-emotional system, we can see that an event kindles basic affective schemas, which in turn activate learned schemas that determine both our perception and thoughts about that event; this will then trigger the emotional and behavioral reactions.

As an example, let us take an event whereby one runs into their standoffish boss at a social gathering. In the diagram we would look at the top line which depicts an explicit set of happenings, namely: **Event** [meeting boss at social gathering] → **Physiological reaction** [fear-terror] → **Cognitive-Emotional Reaction** [anxiety and worry] → **Behavioral Reaction** [avoidance]. When we look at what is implicitly going on in that person we will note the following: **stimulus input** [meeting boss at social gathering] → **core affective schemas** [fear-terror embodied reaction] → **learned affective schema** ["this is scary and embarrassing"] → **interpretation** ["she's going to say or do things that will shame me"] → **thoughts** ["I better stay away"] → **avoidance**. Of course, we could also find the opposite reactions when meeting the boss: **interest-excitement → "what a great opportunity" → enthusiasm → approach and engagement with boss.**

Diagram E The Scene
Robert Kayton

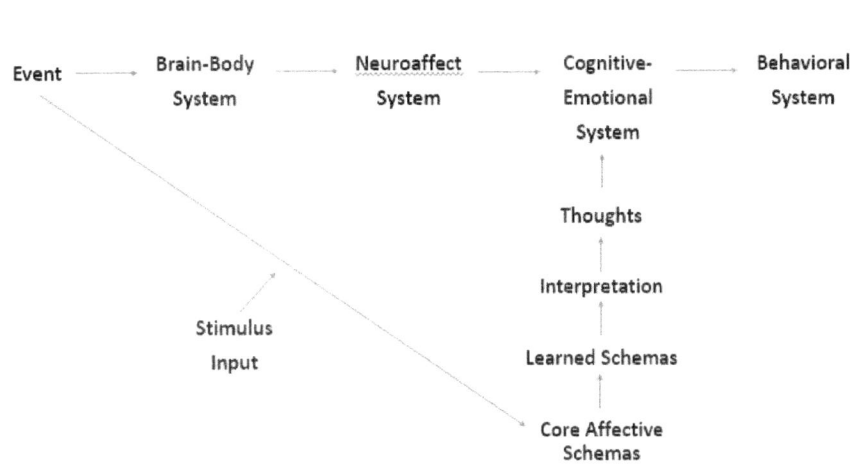

The cognitive-emotional system is essentially what makes up the mind. As learned experiences modify affects, they will also modify their accompanying cognitions. In so doing, affects get transformed into emotion through the filter of its cognition; this is the *cognification of affect*. Although we tend to dichotomize cognition and emotion, just as we do with the brain and mind, they are in truth two forms of the same mental operation. In cognition one thinks, while in emotion one feels. We can thus look at cognition as the conduit through which affects get socialized through experience.

The development of the cognitive system is related to the evolution of the triune brain whereby an older system is modified and added onto by new functions. This is illustrated in Diagram E above in its bottom-up linear depiction under the cognitive-emotional system. This topographical depiction illustrates that affective schemas represent the earliest primary cognitive system that underlies higher levels of thinking, and thereby continues to play a prominent role in one's present functioning. This speaks to the role of the unconscious and its implicit operation in current affairs.

Affective schemas are protoscripted, fixed action patterns that reflect the body's sensory-motor experiences. These physiological experiences are expressions of the affect's innate "feel." For example, the schematic feel of fear is exemplified by the harrowing experience associated with fleeing from an event that is interpreted as dangerous, while that of interest relates to the allure and fascination experienced while moving toward an event that is interpreted as new and enticing. These schemas form the cognitive framework for our learned beliefs and expectations, which then acts as the prism through which we assess and judge events. The resulting thoughts are based on one's interpretation of the event, which may be or may not be explicit; importantly, behavior is activated not by affective schemas, but by one's perspective of the event. For example, let us say that you receive a congratulatory letter from your friend that has a few witticisms and humorous anecdotes. If some of these shared experiences remind you of the good times you had together, it will trigger enjoyment-joy schemas; however, if a few incidents instead tap into shame schemas, your interpretation may be tinged with shame-anger; the consequent response may be one of gratitude mixed with sarcasm.

Chapter 1: The Affect System

There are eight innate affects[12] as seen in Table 1-A below. As based on their feel, two are positive, one is neutral, and five are negative. The two positive affects are enjoyment-joy and interest-excitement; the neutral affect is surprise-startle; and the five negative affects are fear-terror, distress-anguish, anger-rage, shame-humiliation, and disgust/dissmell. The first six affects mentioned constitute the *basic affects*, basic both because their origins go back further into our evolutionary past and because they are activated by neural firings. Shame-humiliation and disgust/dissmell, however, are not activated by neural firings, but instead are triggered by other variables. Consequently, these affects are identified, not as basic affects, but as *auxiliary affects*. Nevertheless, they still function the same way as do the basic affects.

Distress-anguish is the earliest observed affect expressed by an infant. The second is interest-excitement followed by enjoyment-joy, which is then followed by fear-terror and anger-rage. It is later that the auxiliary affects of shame-humiliation and disgust/dissmell emerged.

The Individual Affects

As discussed, affects are analogically activated by discreet patterns of neural firings that simulate patterns of neuromuscular and tissue changes in the body (see Diagram C on page 21). These physiological changes and their sensations, whether perceived or not, make up the affects themselves. Although neurologically activated, affects are located in the body.

Table 1-A The Innate Affects

The Innate Affects

<u>The Positive Affects</u>
Enjoyment-Joy
Interest-Excitement

<u>The Neutral Affect</u>
Surprise-Startle

<u>The Negative Affects</u>
Fear-Terror
Distress-Anguish
Anger-Rage
Shame-Humiliation
Disgust/Dissmell

---

[12] There are actually nine innate affects. Technically disgust and dissmell are separate affects, although they share many features. Each evolved from biological systems, disgust from the gustatory (taste) sensory system, and dissmell from the olfactory (smell) sensory system. In addition, both are aversive affects. Consequently, and for purposes of clarity, I have combined them as disgust/dissmell.

Of the eight affects, six are negative. This discrepancy fits Darwin's theory of natural selection. It is likely that our hunting and gathering ancestors needed more negative affects than positive affects to survive the many dangers in the wild. When threatened by a predator, fear-terror would motivate one to flee. If trapped, to attack with anger-rage; anger-rage not only served the function of protection from enemies, but also contributed significantly to a hunter's success, since a good shot of adrenalin and sympathetic arousal certainly makes one's muscles taut and dense, which helps give one the energy sources and motivation to attack. Distress-anguish may be an outgrowth from microphysical pain, inducing a hibernation response when injured or ill; this, in turn, can lead one to lie down and remain inactive, thus lessening the exposure to predators. Shame-humiliation would display contrition and likely evoke a sympathetic reaction in others, thus staving off certain death if exiled from the protection of the tribe. As an aversion affect, disgust/dissmell helps avoid exposure to another who is experienced as toxic and distasteful.

In addition, we are usually more aware of negative affect than of positive affect, especially when both occur concurrently. Fear-terror has a greater rate and density of neural firings than interest-excitement, and will produce a more intense sensation that will more likely get our attention. This is essential for our survival. If focused on eating a meal while some danger approaches, you had better be attuned to the source of that fear than to the food you are eating. In regard to the steady and non-gradient affects of distress-anguish and anger-rage, the absolute density level of stimulation in anger-rage will prevail over the inhibitory and less dense affect of distress-anguish. Anger-rage will also trump the enjoyment-joy affect that depends on a reduction of stimulus density.

This innate bias toward negative affect helps explain why so many of us have psychological problems in the modern world we live in. When we look at child rearing, we see that negative behaviors are most likely to get a parent's attention. Our society no longer requires us to depend so heavily on these negative affects, yet they still govern much of our lives. Unfortunately, our affect system has not yet evolved the genetic modifications that would allow for a better fit with today's civilization.

The use of binary affect labels indicates the density differences within an affect, the first label being the least dense and the latter the densest; thus, fear is less dense than terror, anger less than rage, distress less than anguish, enjoyment less than joy, interest less than excitement, shame less than humiliation, and disgust less than dissmell. We shall retain this bimodal labeling to distinguish affects from emotions, and use a unimodal label, such as fear or terror (rather than fear-terror), or enjoyment or joy (rather than enjoyment-joy) to differentiate an emotion from an affect.

As stated, shame-humiliation and disgust/dissmell do not have a specific neural profile pattern because they are not really the "basic" innate affects that evolved through natural selection. The six basic affects evolved for the purpose of coping and adapting better to the natural world by internally replicating the external world's sensory patterns, thus forming the blueprint from which we get to "know" the outer world. Shame-humiliation and disgust/dissmell are auxiliary affects. Shame-humiliation is triggered by the partial interruption of positive affect, while disgust/dissmell is activated by noxious stimuli. In other words, they are not analogs of external stimuli that get triggered by differing rates and densities of neural firings, but are activated by other variables, especially those that relate to the social world. As such these auxiliary affects evolved in social mammals, and thus can be thought of as making up the social and moral affects.

Unlike emotions, affects are purely physiological and, when activated, last no longer than a few seconds. When maintained longer, affects enter the realm of emotions. Often this takes place when affect expression is inhibited, thus blocking its release. Emotions that are derived directly from their affective base are primary emotions; from enjoyment-joy comes the primary emotions of enjoyment or joy, and from anger-rage, there is anger or rage. These primary emotions maintain the essential elements that are embedded in an affect's neurophysiology and in its innately inscripted expression.

Enjoyment-joy is triggered when there is a decrease in the density and rate of neural firings; the decrease in physiological arousal is experienced as pleasurable. Enjoyment-joy is a positive affect because it feels good, and the steeper the gradient the more intense will be the good feelings. It is also positive because it both enhances social bonding and expedites memory consolidation. These positive functions are partly due to the salutatory role that familiarity and similarity play in reducing neural firings. These factors do not mean, however, that enjoyment-joy is always beneficial; feeling too much of anything, including this affect, can lead to deleterious results, such as the unbridled hedonism we see in addictions.

Interest-Excitement is the other positive affect and is activated by an "optimal" increase in neural firings. Unlike familiarity, which is basic to enjoyment-joy, novelty is basic to interest-excitement. Curiosity and creativity are also directly based on this affect. Like enjoyment-joy, interest-excitement is essential for early bonding, as well as for early learning. There is a great deal of research that strongly suggests that interest-excitement is the basic affect involved in constructive learning; there is also evidence that enjoyment-joy is the basic affect involved in the storage and consolidation of what is learned into longer term memory. However, like enjoyment-joy, too much interest-excitement can become maladaptive, leading to the disorder of Mania, or to high risk-taking behaviors.

Surprise-Startle is activated by a sharp and extremely sudden increase in the density and rate of neural firings. The innate behavior is the freeze response. Surprise-startle is considered a neutral affect because of its brevity and transitory nature; some neuropsychologists, however, consider startle a reflexive reaction rather than an affect.

The principle role of surprise-startle is to clear and reset the limbic-orbitofrontal circuit in order to refocus attention quickly from that which is occupying one's consciousness at the moment, to the stimulus that suddenly interrupts it. We see this in a grazing animal in the wild that suddenly stiffens when capturing a different odor or sound; at that moment, it immediately freezes and refocuses attention from eating to determining whether there is danger. This adaptive function is obvious, to eat or be eaten. Surprise-startle can also incur negative consequences; in trauma, this is the initial affect that is activated, and like its freeze reaction, the event or scene becomes "frozen" in both time and memory.[13]

Fear-Terror is an arousal affect like interest-excitement or surprise-startle, whose level of increasing neural firings is less than surprise-startle, but more than interest-excitement. Fear-terror is the most toxic of all the affects. It is an emergency response to danger that may have life and death implications at its core. Because there is such energy cost to the body, its duration is limited, since exhaustion would set in if maintained over too long a period of time. Fear-terror is the underlying affect in anxiety and worry.

---

[13] In association theory, the greater the stimulus and the closer in time it is to the response, the stronger the S-R bond.

There is a kinship among the three-increasing gradient affects. These arousal affects are somatically characterized in our breathing: in surprise-startle, our "breath is literally taken away," in fear-terror we are "suffocating" and cannot catch our breath, while interest-excitement is said to be "breathtaking." In addition, because these three affects share a similar profile of increasing firings, their interaction is most apparent, since increases or decreases in firings will activate a different affect. An example of the interactions of these three accelerating affects is presented on page 35 in the next section.

Distress-Anguish is one of two non-gradient affects that is not based on increases or decreases of neural firings, but by the relative constancy of neural firings. Distress is often mistaken for anxiety. As stated, anxiety is about fear, is sympathetic[14] (excitation) dominant, with a profile of increasing neural firings. Distress is about stimulation overload, a constancy of neural firings, and is parasympathetic (inhibition) dominant. The pressure we feel in distress is due to an antagonistic tension between sympathetic excitation and parasympathetic inhibition, although parasympathetic activity is dominant when distress-anguish is activated.

Distress-anguish is an analog of chronic, unyielding sameness; stress is its context. Stress comes from the need to maintain homeostasis or sameness. Since distress is an analog of the constancy in the rates and densities of neural firings, then change is necessary to get out of the distress of sameness. Distress may be triggered by the pressure of too much sameness that can then become a trigger to change. This would create oscillating cycles of seeking sameness until that state creates distress or anguish; distress-anguish can then motivate one toward change.

Too much change however, can trigger fear. This fear may then motivate one back toward the safety and security of sameness and familiarity. This follows the laws of periodicity. Cycles of sameness and change may underlie, if not parallel, separation and attachment problems; thus, intimacy anxiety (fear of too much attachment) may be triggered by too much familiarity and closeness, while separation anxiety may be activated by too much change and loss. As we shall see, too much sameness can lead to depression, while too much change can lead to anxiety. These differences can often be boiled down to a matter of perspective and context; as Carlos Castaneda, the hippie anthropologist, philosopher and author of the 1960's said, "to see is sameness, to look is change."

Anger-Rage is the other non-gradient affect that can be activated by such factors as elevations in the neural profiles of distress-anguish or fear-terror, or triggered as a defense against shame-humiliation. And like distress-anguish, anger-rage is characterized by the relatively constant antagonism between excitation and inhibition, although unlike distress-anguish, it is sympathetic dominant.

Anger-rage is the affect that presents society with its greatest problems, since its inscript is to attack; it is the affect underlying aggression. Next to fear-terror, anger-rage is the second most toxic affect yet, of all the affects, including fear, it is the most urgent; this urgency exists because anger-rage is the affect most likely to self-amplify;[15] in other words anger-rage begets more anger-rage in ever-escalating cycles that can ultimately lead to violence. Of

---

[14] This refers to the Sympathetic Nervous System, which is the excitatory part of the Autonomic Nervous System. The inhibitory part is the Parasympathetic Nervous System.

[15] As we will discuss later, self-amplification takes place only through the amplification of its source, which then further amplifies the affect itself. Anger-rage does not directly amplify more anger-rage; instead, anger-rage intensifies and further vilifies the antagonist, which then further amplifies anger-rage.

course, attack behaviors can occur instantaneously when cognition is overwhelmed by the intense and acute amplification of anger-rage.

Shame-Humiliation is not activated by a given neural profile, but is instead triggered whenever positive affect is partially interrupted; we say "partially" disrupted because for shame-humiliation to be triggered there still needs to be some value and worth placed on the activating source; when positive affect is completely absent, there will be no shame-humiliation. To be ignored or rejected by someone who is still esteemed and valued, at least at some level, will lead to shame-humiliation; to be ignored and rejected by someone who is not important, will lead to a "don't care" reaction. It is important to note that we are not talking about the commonly held psychosocial meaning of shame and humiliation, but shame-humiliation as *solely* a neurobiological process.

Shame has often been called the "master emotion" because it is critical in both the development and definition of one's self, as well as in determining and governing interpersonal relationships. Critical in understanding how shame operates in our everyday life is to understand shame within the context of the events and situations that occur, and particularly how these experiences are perceived. When shame is coassembled with distress there is self-pity, with anger there is humiliated-fury, with disgust self-depreciation, and with fear shyness or guilt. Anger is most often a defense against shame-humiliation, which is usually the case when the context is interpersonal.

Disgust/dissmell, like shame-humiliation, is not activated by a profile of neural firings. It is instead an innate defensive reaction to biological drives related to hunger, thirst and the need for oxygen. Disgust is the affect associated with getting rid of its once valued, but now noxious source, whether it be a person, idea, or thing, while *dissmell* leads to complete and unequivocal detachment from its source.[16] Dissmell is far more severe than disgust; once disconnected, rapprochement is unlikely. In couples' therapy, I would often shift the treatment focus to that of separation or divorce therapy when dissmell was the dominant affect for at least one partner, let alone both.[17]

These aversive affects, so called because their inscript is to move away from their source, are prominent among those who are deeply bigoted and prejudiced. When extreme, dissmell in particular underlies genocide. When these affects coassemble with shame, we have self-disgust, when coassembled with anger we have contempt.

The Affect System and the Emergence of the Mind

There are several features of the affect system that play a significant role in the development of the mind. Affects make up our motivational system and underlie our psychological needs; motivation provides both the energy and goals that help lead to the fulfillment of our needs. As an impetus, affects are analogs of neural firings that either excite or inhibit motivation. To attach or succeed involves excitation, to relax or avoid involves inhibition. Of course, both excitation and inhibition may operate together to better attain one's goal; for example, to succeed entails not only excitatory proactive behaviors, but the inhibition of aggressive self-destructive behaviors.

---

[16] Disgust emerges from the need to vomit-out noxious foods, while dissmell emerges from the need to defecate. Tomkins discusses this process of association in Volume 2.

[17] This was first articulated by Victor Kelly and Donald Nathanson, Directors of the Silvan S. Tomkins Institute.

Affects are also programmed with three innate *prescripts*, namely to maximize positive affect, minimize negative affect, and maximize the expression of all affects (whether positive or negative). These strivings and yearnings form the building blocks of our psychological needs, and can be thought of as prescripted motivational goals. Thus, self-efficacy, attachment, and control are prescripts that are geared to fulfill these inscripted strivings which evolve into goal-directed images, mental representations and schemas. We shall see in the upcoming chapters, prescripts come to shape cognition, emotion and behavior.

Affects are also essential for awareness; no matter what is going on within or outside one's self, an affective reaction is required to get one's attention. The transition from biology to psychology takes place at that point in which an affect is amplified to the point of awareness. Since affect amplification is necessary for awareness, then only those perceptions, thoughts, images, emotions and behaviors that are affect-laden are likely to gain entrance into that narrow band of consciousness we call awareness.[18] And when affects amplify at the same time, one becomes aware of that which is most amplified, most urgent, and most salient. This is one of the evolved functions of affects, namely to amplify a stimulus so that it enters our consciousness and awareness, thus giving us the added benefit of higher level cognitive-cortical functioning.

Affects are likely processed in many implicit neurological systems. What activates an affect is the increase in its amplification level. At a basic neuropsychological level, a triggering affect is largely made up of kinesthetic, olfactory or gustatory sensations; these "embodied" sensations are what then gets amplified into awareness. This is evidenced by the newborn, whose perpetual-motion gestures and facial expressions belie the prominence of these sensory-motor sensations. With further neurological development, affect-based images begin to correspond to auditory and visual sensations as well; these images are of a higher order of complexity than are the basic sensations, and are therefore capable of being transmuted into words and pictures.

Affects are expressed primarily in the face, voice, and body, and function as signal communicators to others; it is also through their expression that we get the *felt-feel* experience of an affect. This takes place when sensory-motor feedback-signals occur in the skin tissues and muscles of the face, voice and autonomic system. In addition, the expression or display of affect plays a critical role in nonverbal communication. Thus, affect expression acts as a communication signal to others, as well as to one's self. Although communication does take place through the autonomic nervous system, such as through sweating or muscle twitching that leads to self-awareness; however, it is mainly through the face, voice and bodily posture that affective information is conveyed to others.

Built into each affect are fixed action patterns I call *inscripts*.[19] Inscripts evolved from reflexes and instincts and, through social learning developed into more general behavioral patterns. Each affect has a different inscript. For example, the inscript for enjoyment-joy is to engage and smile, interest-excitement to move toward and to attend, surprise-startle to freeze, fear-terror to escape, shame-humiliation to hide, distress-anguish to whine and cry, anger-rage to attack, and disgust/dissmell to avert and move away. These inscripts are the earliest

---

[18] I differentiate awareness from consciousness as follows: Consciousness is more of a sentient, experiential and feeling state of mind, while awareness relates to a mindful, alert and cognizant state of mind. Consciousness is more of a general state, while awareness is more focused. It is like the difference between seeing and looking, or hearing and listening, of seeing the forest or the trees.

[19] Tomkins labeled these inscripts as *innate affect scripts*.

forms of affect regulation, since negative affect is reduced when one escapes, moves away, or attacks, while positive affect is increased when one engages and moves toward its source.

Affect expression is thus very important, not only in sending signals to one's self in terms of feelings, but in sending signals to others. As discussed earlier, both negative and positive affect has a built-in tendency to express its inscripted fixed-action pattern. However, there are a variety of factors that may inhibit such expression; in fact, the process of socialization entails the inhibition of affect that helps channel its expression through socially appropriate scripts.

As an inscript, the urge to express affect is genetically programed, and since optimal functioning is based on optimal affect-regulation, we work to control affects by intervening in their expression. This means modifying its activators by inhibiting negative affect and/or amplifying positive affect. Most often, however, affect inhibition targets negative affects, whose expression feels negative, whose actions are negative, and simply because they are expressed more frequently.

Affect inhibition needs to be well-balanced so that there is not too much or too little inhibition. If there is too little inhibition then one's social relationships will me marred (through too much narcissism). If there is too much inhibition, the urge toward affect expression can create a tension state of longing or yearning for fulfillment, especially when inhibited too much and for too long.

However, even when affect is expressed, it is not always expressed directly. In most societies, the socialization of affect may lead to pseudo-affective expressions, or *backed-up affect.* (Nathanson, 1992) This is particularly observed in the facial expression of the *stiff upper lip,* or in suppressed vocalizations when one bites their lips. Tomkins believed that the inhibition of affect is what makes up *stress*, and that such backed-up affect leads to a host of psychosomatic illnesses. In the framework of the excitation-inhibition polarity, it is the excitation of affect expression, which when inhibited leads to the state of backed-up affect.

Negative affect that is denied expression, or affect inhibition that is maximized rather than minimized, will generate a power strategy to break through the constraints that are enforced. This could lead to a host of maladaptive scripts; this can include positive affects as well, such as the joy of addiction or the excitement of mania.

As neural and motoric analogs of their triggering stimulus pattern, affects help synchronize our reactions to events. The sudden noise that triggers a sudden increase in neural firings will, in turn, trigger a sudden change in body tone and posture, while a slow decrease in a sound will trigger a correspondingly slow decrease in neural firings that, in turn, activates a slower change in facial, vocal, and bodily expression. By way of this analogical simulation, affects make up the glue that binds a stimulus to a response; this is the basic process in learning.

At birth, there are individual differences in affect-sensitivity levels. This is what makes up our inborn temperament. Affects dominate the newborn's psychological life. Unsocialized, an infant's facial, vocal and bodily expressions will display affects that are pure and uninhibited, such as the broad grin and *goo-goo* sounds of a newborn experiencing enjoyment-joy, or the crying and flailing of arms and legs associated with distress-anguish. As the brain's capacity to store and process data develop, these innate affects come to play a major role in the development of cognition, emotion and behavior.

Affects have the capacity to *cognify*, which takes place when patterns of bodily sensations are transformed into embodied images. These bodily images come to form the foundation of cognition, and ultimately of scripts; in other words, as learning and memory develop, affects become both psychologized and socialized. This is most apparent in emotions, which are essentially cognified affects. Information is *amplified* by affect and *transformed* by cognition. Thus, when an affect is amplified, its arousal is increased and, as an *analog-amplifier*,[20] will amplify its triggering source as well. If a person feels fearful about giving a talk, that fear may turn to terror as one peruses the audience. The increase in affect arousal amplifies its source (audience) and correlatively increases the activation of fearful thoughts ("they look hostile"), as affective data is transformed into cognitive data. Thus, affect amplification is required for cognification to take place.

This transformational function is critical since cognition acts as a communication system, a higher-level evaluating system, and as a more organized governor of behavior. The transmutation of affect into cognition takes place at a primary level in the form of cognitive schemas. [See Diagram 6-2, p.151]. For example, in the fear-terror schema the theme is "what is going to happen is dangerous;" in shame-humiliation, "I am undesirable;" and in enjoyment-joy, "this is pleasurable."

In addition to these characteristic features of affects, there are several principles that govern their dynamics. As an analog-amplifier, an affect will indirectly amplify itself by amplifying its source. When fearful of one's boss, this fear will intensify as one dwells on all the bad things that could happen, just as our excitement about our lover increases as we think of his or her wonderful qualities.

Each person also has different set points for the activation and amplification of an affect. First of all, there is a level of affect intensity set at birth that makes up one's inborn affective temperament. Secondly, there are the many life experiences that may inhibit or enhance these innate sensitivity levels. Finally, there is the context in which an affect is activated. We know that there are times when we are more sensitive than usual. This may be due to a myriad of contextual circumstances, such as one's mood or physical health, work or relational issues, as well as social, cultural and political influences.

Affects operate as an interactional system in which the dynamics of one affect will impact on the dynamics of other affects. Thus, the activation or amplification of one affect can reciprocally inhibit, activate or amplify other affects. Consequently, when a dominant affect (i.e. the affect which is most salient, intense and urgent) is activated and amplified, the subordinate affect will be inhibited. On the other hand, if a dominant affect is reduced, the subordinate affect will correspondingly amplify. In fact, the speed, magnitude or aggregate amount of change in one affect, will proportionally modify and influence the degree of change in other affects.

For example, as illustrated in Diagram 1-A on the next page, if while walking down a street at night while you are deeply immersed in thoughts about a work project, and you suddenly notice someone walking quickly toward you, there will be a sudden increase in the gradient of neural firings as to activate surprise-startle. By so doing, your brain will likely wipe out your thoughts about your work project and instead propel you to focus on that approaching shadowy figure. If that person is familiar and known as a friend, there will be a

---

[20] Affects act as analog amplifiers by amplifying its source, such as making a scary dog even scarier; this in turn will amplify the fear-terror affect even more, so that it appears as though affects are self-amplifying. As Nathanson describes it: "…each affect is an analogue of its triggering stimulus in that it more or less feels like the situation that incited it…a rush of ideas makes an affect that makes the rush more; the analogy is the *feeling* of "rush." (1992, p.67)

reduction in the highly elevated level of neural firings, thus triggering the affect of enjoyment-joy. If, however, that person is unknown, the increasing rate will continue as that person is further assessed. If this stranger looks ominous, there will likely be a slight reduction in the steepness of the surprise-startle gradient, triggering fear-terror. If he looks non-threatening, the steepness will decline even further to the level that instead will activate the affect of interest-excitement.

Diagram 1-A Reciprocal Affect Changes
Robert Kayton

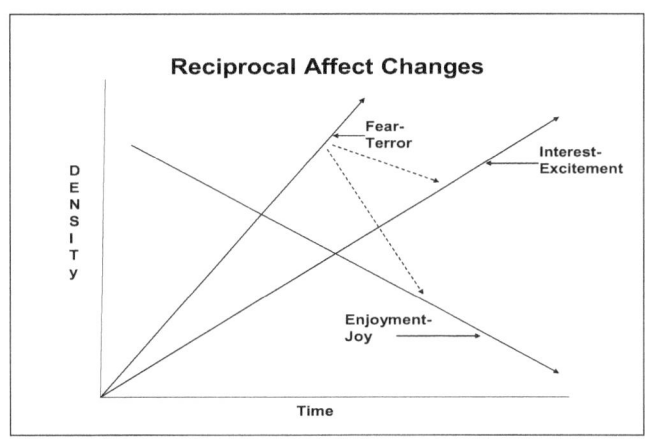

Another principle is that the reduction of any negative affect is rewarding and will likely activate a positive affect. On the other hand, the interruption and reduction of positive affect is punishing, and will likely activate a negative affect. Of great importance, especially when applying these principles to the regulation of affects, is that the ratio between or among affects is more significant than the specific level of any singular affect. An example of this principle is risk-taking. Risk takers have both fear-terror and interest-excitement. The action taken depends, not on the absolute level of one affect or the other, but on the relative ratio between the two. Thus, if a person whose interest-excitement level is 6, compared to a fear-terror level of 8, is more likely to take a risk than if interest-excitement is 2, and fear-terror is 6.

A third axiom is that when two or more affects compete for consciousness, that which is most salient, intense and urgent will win out. For example, when there is a large increase in the constancy of stimulation, anger-rage rather than distress-anguish will more likely be felt because it is the more urgent of the two. Thus, when a parent comes home from an extremely difficult and stressful day at work and is unexpectedly and immediately set upon by overly excited children, anger-rage may well trump the distress-anguish harbored from the workday.

Affects also combine with each other through fusion and co-assembly. When affects merge, they establish such primary emotions as guilt, which is shame-humiliation plus fear-terror, or contempt, which is anger-rage plus disgust. When affects co-assemble and are sequentially connected, we have such sequences as fear-terror followed by shame-humiliation that is evidenced in social anxiety, or the anger-rage that acts as a defense against shame-humiliation. We could also point to bipolar disorders, which displays swings between the distress-anguish of depression and the mania of interest-excitement.

Chapter 2: The Cognitive System[21]

Cognition evolves when affects are inhibited, and when affects are inhibited, affect-regulation is momentarily impeded; it is from this state of dysregulation that cognition begins to take over as the regulator of affects. When an affect-image is maintained,[22] stored and later consolidated in the mind, we have the development of memory and cognition. Memory provides the information necessary for anticipation, which is a critical function of cognition.

The advantages of cognition over affect is well stated by Tomkins: "cognitions coassembled with affect become hot and urgent. Affects coassembled with cognitions become better informed and smarter." Affects provide abstract and general information; cognition provides more specific and defined informational content. Sedgwick and Frank, with equal loquaciousness state: "Reason without affect would be impotent, affect without reason would be blind. The combination of affect and reason guarantees man's high degree of freedom."

Cognition, along with its affective component emotion, makes up the mind. The mind is the summation of many integrated neural systems. Cognition and emotion represent higher levels of knowing as compared to the sensorial and affective modes of knowing. Cognition consists of the perceiving and conceiving part of the mind, while emotion is the affective "experiencing" and "feeling" part of the mind. As implied earlier, the "...neuron proves to be a cognitive system in miniature...the most elementary neurons exhibit all of the essential properties of the whole cognitive system." (Tomkins (IV, pp.37-38))

The neuron is the most basic information-processing mechanism for nervous system transmission. As such it is possible to delineate fundamental distinctions between cognition as structure and cognition as process. Its most general cognitive mechanisms are represented through the reception and translation of data. The neuron, therefore, is not only a sensitive receiver of information but has its own code or language through received impulses that are systematically transformed and expressed into its own inherited language. This is akin to *translation*, since translation preserves information in one language and expresses it in another language.[23]

Like the neuron, cognition is a very dynamic system with a variety of functions, each with a purpose. Cognition processes information, sends and receives information, correlates messages, encodes them, keeps information parceled and separate, and mediates inhibitory and excitatory information. These neuronal and cognitive attributes can be generalized to the entire brain-mind system.

Affects intervene between the neuron and cognition. Cognition is shaped by these innate neural affects.[24] Their neural profiles are genetically activated as analogs of external events,

---

[21] As earlier discussed, cognition and emotion are part of the same cognitive-emotional system. However, for purposes of discussion and understanding, and for the sake of clarity, I will continue to artificially divide the two.

[22] Think of the after-image that occurs when you close your eyes after seeing a bright image.

[23] My use of neurological terms to help describe psychological functioning, is called *neurologizing* (which some have derided). This is a form of translation-through-metaphor, the intent being to better understand the significant fact that psychological functioning is imbedded and interwoven within the nexus of neurological functioning, so that what is happening in one modality is replicated in the other modality. We will discuss this integrative theme throughout this book, and especially in Part 2.

such as the excitement at a rock concert or the enjoyment of listening to the soothing sounds of a gurgling brook. Cognition can also activate neural firings as a *secondary* activator. This is evidenced by increases in negative or positive feelings as we think negative or positive thoughts.

Just as affects are analogs of their activating stimuli, images, language and speech are analogs of their underlying affect. This is apparent when we say that cognition is "cognified affect." As earlier stated, affects that are excitatory will lead to cognitions that are excitatory, while affects that are inhibitory will lead to cognitions that are inhibitory.

There are a number of critical brain functions that make up the mind; these include learning, memory, perception, language and thinking. In addition, there are different topographical levels of cognition, such as conscious and unconscious (or implicit and explicit), as well as different developmental levels, from the most elementary and primary to the most complex and recent. We shall explore each in turn.

Learning

Cognition takes place through learning and memory. Learning involves the acquisition of information, while memory entails the storage of that information. There are two basic forms of learning, procedural and declarative. Procedural learning is implicit; it is thus a bottom-up process. Information is acquired, not through cognition, but through action, which some call "muscle memory." It is the first mode of learning; it begins in-utero and continues throughout life. Declarative learning is top-down, takes place explicitly through the use of symbols and syntax, and is mostly a learned cognitive process; it includes semantic (factual) and episodic (autobiographical, event-based) processing, and requires conscious attention. Most academic learning takes place declaratively.

Table 2-A
Procedural vs. Declarative Learning

Procedural	Declarative
Begins in-utero	Begins at about two-years of age
Bottom-up process	Top-down process
Implicit	Explicit
Subconscious	Requires conscious attention
Action (sensory-motor) based	Based on symbols and syntax
Experiential	Instructional
Muscle memory	Cortical memory
Affect-based	Cognitive based
	Types: semantic & episodic

We could also identify several levels of cognition, namely the primary, secondary and complex. Primary cognition is the earliest form of thinking. It is processed in the right hemisphere at the lower amygdala-hippocampus limbic circuit. Primary cognition is the most

---

[24] I suspect that the direct activating source of affects take place in the somatosensory cortex, and lies either in the reticular activating system or in the upper brain stem.

primitive, non-logical, proto-cognitive, non-cortical level of thinking. All memory at this level is implicit and consists of embodied images. Cognition at this basic level is highly *affect laden* and codified in sensory-motor images via touch, smell or taste. Sensory data gets stored at cellular levels in the muscles and tissues of the body; this is the neurophysiological basis of "muscle memory." Because these images are so primal, they form the foundation for all higher levels of mentation. It is at this level that non-semantic schemas, which underlie our core beliefs, begin to develop.

It is also from these early sensory images that models and images of the external world form. When affect is present, these images get formed according to the basic prescripts, namely to maximize positive affect, minimize negative affect, and maximize the expression of all affects. These become what Tomkins called *general images*. Often, an overarching general image develops that says that all prescripts must be fulfilled completely and at all times; when this image persists, say due to sensory deprivation or over-stimulation, it will become an idealized image of the world. In reality, of course, these prescripts are seldom fully satisfied since positive affect is often inhibited, negative affect enhanced, and their expression constrained. Consequently, many general images, and in particular idealized general images, conflict with reality.

Schemas cognify basic sensory images and, therefore, represent the earliest cognitive-based images that effect affect-regulation. These generalized images and schemas determine our core beliefs and expectations, a basic element in the composition of emerging scripts. The degree to which these themes are actualized determines the development of realistic or unrealistic thinking. However, because prefrontal cortical development, especially left hemispheric, is relatively undeveloped at the primary level, cognition is mostly dominated by the striving to consummate these themes. This then leads to distortions in thinking that develop at the next stage of cognitive development.

Secondary cognition evolves with the developing orbitofrontal cortex, and combines both implicit-procedural and explicit-declarative learning and memory. Instead of the language of embodied images, there now begins to form the verbal language of signs and symbols. Early secondary cognition extends from early childhood to about 8 years of age and consists of relatively irrational, distorted and faulty reasoning that is processed in concrete, rigid, bi-modal (all-or-none) terms.[25] This is the level people will regress to when mental and emotional problems dominate.

As cognition grows through the developing left-hemisphere and prefrontal cortices, thinking moves to a higher secondary-level of cognition that extends through middle adolescence. Cognition is more reasoned, logical, and realistic allowing for greater variance, flexibility, and abstraction in thinking. We can see that the emotions associated with secondary cognition are more affective at the earlier level, and more cognified at the later level.

Complex cognition, which extends from late adolescence through adulthood, is the highest mode of cognition. Learning and memory are declarative and processed at higher prefrontal and frontal levels of the brain. Thinking is objective and open to corroboration. Semantic language, realistic judgment, and analytic thinking are hallmarks of this higher cognitive mode. Complex emotions are the most cognified. They consist of one's feelings about an event, rather than feelings embedded in the event; for example, "I was so enthralled

---

[25] This mode of thinking was first described by Harry Stack Sullivan as *parataxic thinking*.

and happy to give this talk" as opposed to "my heart was pounding with excitement." Emotions at this level are relatively cerebral and expressed as a narrative.

Learning can be thought of as a cognitive process and as a behavioral response; usually it is both. Interestingly, although cognitive theory postulates that behavior is activated by the mind, there is sufficient evidence that the mind is instead activated by behavior (as well as by affect). Remember, the brain evolved because of movement, and without movement, even micro-movements, there is no brain activity.[26]

Memory

Learning underlies memory, while memory is the retention of what was learned. Affects are critical in this retention function as based both on the frequency and duration that an affect is activated, as well as by the degree to which expression is denied. Repeated activation will more likely lead to both the development of associational learning and the storage of that learning into memory. Retention is critical for storage and relies on extended periods of time through the inhibition of affect expression. We can, thus, hypothesize that when an affect is frequently and continuously activated, while its expression is blocked, cognition will become a *secondary affect activator* that then maintains the memory of the triggering event. For example, if someone receives an award, their thoughts will likely be positive and thus amplify positive affect, just like a reprimand will likely elicit angry or hurtful thoughts, and therefore amplify its negative affect.

Memory is of the past, yet memory underlies anticipation. Tomkins calls this process *postication*, "the linking of the past with the future." (Tomkins (IV, pp37-38)) Remembering, which is involved in the development of anticipation, must be compelling in the here and now, thus connecting the past and the future with the present. Actually, the evolutionary purpose of memory is to retain learning for use in the future: "Any experience that sparks fear or passion, any situation that is truly novel, anything you put in your mouth that tastes foul or delicious - each has a high probability of being retained as an event important for the future." (Fields, Scientific American Mind, Feb,30)

In this regard, affects can be thought of as the basis underlying transference.[27] Thus, when an affect gets activated in the present, or in anticipation of a future event, its link to past events can elicit earlier related scripts. Simply put, transference takes place when a current situation activates an older script.

The recollection of past events does not necessarily, or even typically, evoke the same affect, since alterations occur through sensitization, desensitization and habituation. Even if the same affect is triggered, the intensity and density of neural firings is likely different from the original experience. In fact, a totally different affect may be evoked as when the shame of a previous event can instead activate anger when recalled. In truth, memories are never the same. This is partly because the context, in which a memory is elicited, will be different from not only the original memory, but from every subsequent memory. In addition, there is ample

---

[26]. The brain responds to sensory-motor activity and remains "alive" as long as there are micro-muscular movements going on in the body.

[27] Transference takes place when a person transfers their feelings about one person onto another person. Freud coined the term *transference neurosis* to describe the phenomenon whereby a patient will unconsciously transfer childhood feelings toward a parent onto the analyst; expressing these feelings in the therapeutic relationship provides an opportunity to resolve them in the present.

evidence that memory is stored and reconsolidated differently than the way it was initially recalled due to neurochemical changes in its protein synthesis.

In essence, memories consist of increased neural networks that are created at synaptic junctures by way of associational processes, whereby "neurons that fire together wire together." (Hebb, 1949) We can distinguish three kinds of memory: working memory, short-term memory, and long-term memory. Working memory takes place while one is thinking in order to hold thoughts together for a moment; it is fleeting and does not get stored. Short-term memory is of longer duration, though still relatively brief; these memories get stored for a limited time in the hippocampus, though they can become consolidated when they change the neural structure of the hippocampus. Long-term memory takes place when new structural changes permanently strengthen synaptic connections; unlike the locus of short-term memory being in the hippocampus, long-term memories are dispersed throughout the cerebral cortex.

Interestingly, there is ample evidence that, "Scent memories pack a more potent emotional wallop than recollections triggered by sights, sounds and other sensory cues." (Jerome, 2019) Neuroscientists refer to "odor-evoked autobiographical memories," that highlight the significance of smell in evoking early childhood memories. Although some of these odor-produced memories are negative, most often they are positive. One of the reasons why smell is so evocative is that odors are directly sent to the olfactory bulb, which is linked directly to the limbic system's hippocampus and amygdala, unlike other sensory modalities, which are routed to the limbic system via the thalamus.

There are two major modes of memory, implicit memory and explicit memory [Table 2-B, page 44]. These types of memory also translate into modes of thinking. As is apparent, implicit memory takes place at lower brain levels than explicit memory and is present at birth, unlike explicit memory, which develops after two years of age. As we shall see, implicit memory is where the protoself and early forms of the self begin their development. Finally, it is the interaction of both implicit and explicit memories that is critical in the evolution of the emergent self.

Language and Communication

"Language is an extreme instance of [complex] duplication, with maximal informational and minimal energy ...transformation..." (Tomkins). Most language transformations are based on societal and cultural convention. This means that the duplication process in conventional language entails *transformational representations*, such as signs, symbols and words; thus, more advanced language entails several progressive layers in the duplication of symbolic informational transformations.

The earliest language was dictated more by its analogic mode of duplication than through convention or through complex symbolic representations. It is likely that affect expression was the first mode of communication; this would be through bodily movements, and particularly hand gestures, and facial and vocal displays. As cognition evolved, these physical expressions morphed into higher and more complex forms of cognition, such as seen in dance and song.

With further evolution, pictorial images developed, such as those found in cave dwellings or in ancient Egyptian hieroglyphics, whereby the picture itself became the word for something. This duplication was more representative of the external stimulus than the more abstract meanings found in conventional words. However, even spoken language follows the progression from analogic duplication to more complex language transformation.

As Nathanson (1992) points out, language can simulate the sound of its affect; this is the phonics of language, which technically is called *echoic* or *onomatopoeic.*

At higher levels of cognition, words transform into abstract symbols that show little commonality with their affective origins. Based on convention, context, and the variety of forms of language, including the language not only of society but also of science (math) and art (abstract paintings), the original analogical connection no longer represents the original. Although a sign is a concrete representation of the original, the symbol is an abstract representation of the original.

In the brain, language is dominated by left-hemisphere functions, although the right hemisphere is capable of processing language as well. As taken from Siegel and Hertz, right-hemisphere functioning is nonlinear, holistic, and visual-spatial. It specializes in auto-biographical information and sends and perceives nonverbal signals. It processes the awareness of the integrated body map [see Appendix 17, p.182], and plays an important role in social cognition. Left-hemisphere processing is linear, logical, and linguistic, and processes both syllogistic cause-effect reasoning and right-versus-wrong thinking.

The capacity for language provided an exponential leap in our ability to communicate, thus providing humans with a significant advantage in the socialization of relatively large numbers of people. This helped lead to the development of more complex societies that culminated in the complex cultures and civilizations of today. Language, both verbal and scientific, also gave us a wealth of knowledge about our world that provided the essential tools for the human domination of the earth (for better and worse).

Thinking

Thinking takes place largely in the language of pictorial and auditory imagery. Auditory images represent the language of sound that gets transformed into symbols and images, words and sentences, thoughts, ideas and beliefs. Visual images are more stable than are the images of sound. These relatively fixed and steady images provide a mental model for transforming visual and auditory thoughts into written language; it also enhances memory and affords greater accessibility for recall.

The complex combination of talking and writing have become our conventional modes of communication with others. In this regard cognition has largely supplanted affectation,[28] which is a primary way of communicating among animals and early humans. Human communication is therefore dominated, at least conventionally, in transmitting thoughts and complex ideas to others.

Tomkins identified two fundamental styles of thinking, *variant* and *analogic*. The former looks at that which is different, the latter at that which is similar. Variant thinking looks at differences and is more related to *interest-excitement,* while analogic thinking looks at similarities and is thus more related to *enjoyment-joy,.* Each style developed in the service of affect-regulation. In general, variant-thinking is associated with a more humanistic and liberal perspective, while analog-thinking is associated more with a normative and conservative belief system. In many ways, we could also re-label analog-thinking as invariant-thinking since there tends to be a fixed, all-or-none mode of thinking. We will return to this division between humanist and normative when discussing ideological scripts and cognitive styles of thinking in Chapter 5.

---

[28] Affect-expression, nevertheless, plays a critical role when talking.

Although specific thoughts evolved from experience-dependent learning, they nevertheless began as analogs of affect, whereby each thought was a verbal analog of its triggering and underlying affect. This is illustrated when we look at the diagram of a scene on page 87, in which we could see how each affect determines its cognitive response to a given event. For example, *enjoyment-joy* is the affect of decreasing activation that leads to comforting and pleasant thoughts, a wishful and dreamy perceptual style that tends toward optimism, and a positive way of interpreting events as enjoyable, satisfying and sometimes humorous. *Distress-anguish*, the non-gradient affect, will lead to negative and cynical thoughts such as "life sucks," and a perceptual style that internalizes issues and sees life as hopeless.

These thoughts and perceptions represent extrapolations of our cognitive schemas. As discussed, schemas form in early development and represent the primary cognitive structure from which all thoughts, images, and beliefs are derived; as such they function implicitly. Initially their formulation of the world was adaptive, but with time many of these beliefs failed to change and adapt; these initial schemas, therefore, became maladaptive and unrealistic, and operated as protective defense mechanisms. In cognitive rescripting our goal is to change these unrealistic schemas into realistic schemas by using a variety of cognitive-behavioral strategies.

Explicit and Implicit Thinking

Topographically, thinking takes place at both explicit and implicit levels. At the explicit level, we are conscious and aware of our thinking. In consciousness, we could be aware of something, and also be aware that we are aware of something. This direct mode of awareness is triggered by an affective experience in which the observation of awareness is a cognified experience. This suggests that higher levels of awareness are coupled with more complex levels of cognition. Since more complex systems are also more organized, they provide an enhanced level for regulating affect that promotes more adaptive and successful functioning. The functions of both implicit and explicit memory and thinking can be seen in Table 2-A on the next page.

Table 2-B Forms of Memory and Thinking

FORMS OF MEMORY AND THINKING Siegel & Hertzel

IMPLICIT MEMORY
    Present at birth
    No sense of recollection present when memories recalled
    Includes behavioral, emotional, perceptual, and bodily memory
    Includes mental models
    Conscious attention is not required for encoding
    Does not involve the hippocampus
    Includes procedural (behavior based)
 	
EXPLICIT (Declarative) MEMORY
    Develops during the second year of life and beyond
    Sense of recollection present when recalled
    If autobiographical, a sense of self and time are present
    Includes semantic (factual) and episodic (autobiographical) memory
    Requires conscious attention
    Involves the hippocampus
    If autobiographical, also involves the prefrontal cortex

The subconscious operates at a deeper and more implicit level than does the preconscious, and so awareness is generally lacking. If there is any hint of awareness it is so vague that it is unavailable for top-down processing. Making the subconscious conscious is a bottom-up, emergent process; it also requires a larger affective reaction than do preconscious thoughts.

As to the unconscious, there is controversy over its nomenclature. This is largely due to Freud, who at times referred to the unconscious as anything not conscious, while at other times referred to it as the repository of repressed thoughts. Some theorists such as Demos (1995) use the term *nonconscious* to refer to all thoughts that are not conscious or preconscious, and reserve the term unconscious to the *repressed unconscious*. To avoid confusion, I shall maintain the conventional use of the term *unconscious* to mean both, namely that which is not conscious, and will only distinguish the terms in the service of clarity.

Theorists like Freud and Tomkins argued that the mind is largely unconscious; this is supported by neuroscience research. The amount of information available for consciousness is limited to a given number of "bits" of information, while the unconscious is relatively limitless. Given that many of our core cognitions operate below our level of awareness means that they will continue to influence our thoughts, emotions and behavior.

Many of you may be familiar with the Freudian dictum to make the "unconscious conscious." This is essential for adaptation because until we become aware of our thoughts, there is little we can do to rescript them. Conscious thoughts take place in the prefrontal cortex. However, cognition can also take place in parts of the limbic system, such as the hippocampus. Although there is not a simple one-to-one relationship, we can generally say that the lower the level of cognitive processing, the less conscious we are of its activity.

The defensive unconscious consists of implicit, long-term memories that are associated with negative affect. These emotional memories were stored and consolidated both as defensive beliefs and as distorted cognitive-perceptual styles. These irrational and maladaptive cognitions need to be changed via. cognitive rescripting (see Chapter 6).

Chapter 3: The Emotional System

Emotion is socialized affect, whereby the innate and automatized nature of affect is transformed, through experiential learning, into emotions, which make up the cognitive-emotional complex, or more technically the *ideoaffective complex*. To further complicate matters, emotion is also movement, as evidenced by the root word *motion* when we remove the letter "*e*." Consequently we can say that emotion is a highly complex mental process that incorporates all functions. Just as we need to consider the affective/emotional component when discussing cognition, so too should we keep in mind that emotion is part of a greater complex of functions, including behavior.

The development of emotion from affect and cognition can be illustrated by the following; when fear-terror is triggered, its experience is in the body, which will then activate fearful thoughts that will, through secondary feedback signals, amplify the fear-terror affect; however, this amplification of affect will be filtered and colored by learned experiences, which will then modify the original cognition.

The "felt-feel" of an emotion is the experience of the affective sensation itself;[29] when cognified, the experience is more that it "feels-like" a given affect. One's "evaluative feel" of an angry thought will feel heavy, just as a pleasant and enjoyable thought will feel light; yet its "feel" will in turn influence its activating cognition and perspective. For example, the excitement felt while riding a roller coaster could amplify to fear-terror when that sensation is elevated by a sudden acceleration in speed during a sharp turn; this affective sensation can elicit fearful thoughts until the roller coaster's speed and direction levels out, thus re-triggering exciting thoughts. In the first scenario, the change in affect changes the cognition, while in the second scenario the change in cognition modifies (as a secondary affect activator) the emotion.

Affect, cognition, and emotion serve a number of important functions. All present different kinds and different levels of information processing and transmission, each being processed at different neurological levels. We have already discussed the functions of affect and cognition. Emotions integrate the functions of both by duplicating some, modifying others, and evolving new functions. Affect and emotion share some features and differ from others.

Among these differences are that affects are innately fixed programs, while emotions are learned through experience. Thus, affects will have the same "feel" regardless of its source, while the emotional feel will be far more nuanced and dependent on its triggering source. Unlike the inborn fixed nature of affects, emotions are learned reactions that can be modified and unlearned; affects can only be regulated.

Affects are distinct and specific, while emotions are variant. The latency and duration of affects and emotions differ as well. Affects get activated more quickly and for a briefer moment of time than emotions; estimates range from milliseconds to seconds for affects and minutes to days for emotions. This is partly due to differences between their activating agents; for affects, the trigger is the discrete profile of neural activity, while emotions are elicited by cognition.[30]

---

[29] Crick and Koch (Gazzangia (2018)) call this state *qualia*, "the subjective character of experience, the feeling of red."

[30] This brings to mind LeDoux's finding of two pathways for fear, one directly from the thalamus, the other

Among their similarities, affects function as motivators as do emotions. Affects send signals to other people, and so do emotions. Affects send signals to one's self, as do emotions. Affects set up an innate fixed-action pattern, while emotions activate a behavioral sequence. Affects elicit neurophysiological feeling experiences as does emotion, although the felt-feel in emotion is more varied and changeable.

We can see similarities and differences with cognition as well. Cognition helps control affect, so does emotion. Cognition processes information, as does emotion. Cognition evaluates information, so does emotion. Cognition helps us care about something important, so does emotion. Cognition helps us know what is happening, so does emotion. Cognition has memory, so does emotion.

The many differences between affect and cognition are obvious. Fundamentally, there are greater differences between cognition and emotion than there are between emotion and affect. Cognition is largely embedded in mental processes and is far more structural in composition, while emotions are more rooted in biology and is more dynamic in its operation. Of course, there are essential differences in their neurological systems; cognition is processed at higher levels of the brain than is emotion.

Emotions serve additional functions when compared to affects or cognition. Emotions are typically the direct trigger for our behavior; emotions help integrate affect and cognition, and are thus important determinants in our decision-making. As such, emotions help manage various motives.

Commensurate with the three levels of cognition, are three analogical levels of emotion. Often these levels emerge when affects combine into more complex levels of organization. At the primary level, emotions clearly approximate their underlying affect. Quite likely, the "felt-feel" of a primary emotion such as fear,[31] will nearly duplicate the "felt-feel" of the affect fear-terror. At the affective level, fear-terror is related to the immediate present, when danger *is* immediate, such as an infant suffocating on an overdose of milk. When stored in the body, fear can be triggered by both memory and anticipation; thus, unlike affects, which are innate, reflexive-like, and solely in the "now," emotion is learned, cognitively processed, and includes past (memory) and future (anticipation).

Primary emotions are the earliest to bifurcate from their affective base and come into being as *embodied* images. This takes place between birth and three months of age. The primary emotions are: fear, terror, distress, anguish, anger, rage, surprise, startle, enjoyment, joy, interest, and excitement. Shame, humiliation, disgust and dissmell (not the affect, but the emotion) likely appear a bit later when socialization takes place.

Most often we are not conscious or aware of our primary emotions. Given that primary emotions are mostly embodied images stored in the muscles and tissues of the body and therefore lack syntax, they often remain implicit. Like affects, however, when intense and urgent they will enter into awareness. Because of the physiological basis to these primary embodied images, many of the innovative body-focusing techniques we will discuss later are designed to deal with the nonverbal (biological) level of emotion.

Most often, however, we are aware of our secondary emotions. Secondary emotions are further differentiated from their underlying affect by the multi-faceted nature of secondary

---

through the prefrontal cortex. The direct thalamic circuit may account for the affect *fear-terror*, while the thalamic-prefrontal circuit may be the basis for the emotion "anxiety." Perhaps these direct and indirect circuits will be found for all affects and emotions.

[31] Remember that we use the singular word for an emotion and the bi-label for affect.

cognition. Some differentiate earlier than others; for example, distress-anguish may differentiate into *sadness* (due to loss) or *frustration* (when a goal is blocked) relatively early; although very similar to the profile and "feel" of distress-anguish, there are clear differences between these two primary emotions. Others, such as shame-humiliation, can evolve later into remorse or embarrassment.

The myriad of secondary emotions, as seen in the Table 3-1 below, is typically what emotion theory deals with, and is usually what we refer to as emotions. Unfortunately, this is also the emotional level from which many of our problems lie, since the triggering cognition, especially at the early secondary level, is likely distorted. Like secondary thinking, secondary emotions are what psychotherapists most often deal with. Emotions at this level are more readily manageable than are affects or primary emotions.

At the early secondary level, emotions are based more on implicit cognition, while those at later stages are based on explicit thinking. Thus, early implicit secondary emotions are linked to its cognitive precursor at the primary level, while the more advanced explicit-based secondary emotions will be connected to a higher and more complex level of functioning. Adaptively, these higher-level secondary emotions serve important functions for affect regulation and overall adaptation.

Table 3-1 Secondary Emotions
Robert Kayton

Secondary Emotions

Enjoyment-Joy	Happy, pleased, loving, ,calm, relaxed, contented, comfortable, satisfied, likes, appreciates.
Interest-Excitement	Interested, excited, thrilled, inspired, engrossed, curious, delighted, turned on, engaged, absorbed, captivated, engrossed. enthusiastic exhilarated, eager, zealous, engaged, inspired.
Surprise-Startle	Surprised, startled, shocked. stunned, amazed, astonished, incredulous, bombshell, revelation astonished, astounded, unanticipated, unexpected.
Fear-Terror	Fearful, frightened, terrified, dread, nervous, scared, worried, threatened, imperiled, jeopardized. tormented, intimidated, afraid, apprehensive, anxious, panicked, timid, dreadful, terrible, gruesome, disturbing.
Distress-Anguish	Distressed, sad, anguished, despairing, lonely, alone, bored, unhappy. sorry, pained, agony, miserable, needy, troubled, tense, chagrined, grieved, tormented, troubled, bothered, disturbed, irritable, frustrated, upset, exasperated down dejected, unhappy, agitated.
Anger-Rage	Angry, annoyed,, irritated, aggravated, resentful, furious, outraged, indignant, riled, mad, piqued, irate, infuriated.
Shame-Humiliation	Shamed, ashamed, guilty, humiliated, embarrassed, rejected, unimportant, bad, defective shy, foolish, dumb, hurt, disappointed,, wounded. chagrined, contrite, remorseful, mortified, disgraced, regretful, pitiful, belittled, nothing, ashamed, put down, ridiculed.
Disgust/Dismell	Disgusted, repulsed, contemptuous, revolted, repelled. bitter, nauseated, offended, sickened, distasteful, loathing, abhorrent, repugnant.

Secondary emotions are likely processed in both the auditory and visual sensory modalities when compared to the kinesthetic, olfactory and gustatory modalities found in primary emotions. Thus, the experience and felt-feel of these emotions will differ to the degree from which their sensory modality is most active. Keeping in mind that primary cognition is in the body, while secondary and complex cognition entails visual and auditory processing, then their felt-feel would be different than what would be expected. In primary or early secondary emotions, the feel is more likely in terms of the body; in late secondary processing, the emotional feel is more symbolic and expressed in verbal (auditory) or pictorial (visual) language. Table 3-2 below compares each cognitive mode with its corresponding memory system and its related emotional level.

Table 3-2
Cognitive-Memory-Emotion Table
Robert Kayton

Cognitive Mode	Memory System	Emotions
Complex Mode Thinking is abstract, flexible, logical and realistic	Explicit Memory	Complex Emotions
Secondary Mode Thinking is rigid, absolutistic, fixed, concrete, and self-centered	Implicit-Explicit Memory	Secondary Emotions
Primary Mode Thinking is in bodily images related to feel, taste and smell	Implicit Memory	Primary Emotions

At the highest level, complex emotions relate to one's feelings *about* an event, not one's feelings embedded in that event. At this level, emotions are experienced as more cognified and detached from its affect. For example; if one feels threatened at the primary level one might say "I feel immobilized and cannot breathe;" at the secondary level one might say "I feel like running away;" while at the "intellectualized" complex level, "I feel like the time when I had to face my boss without completing my project."

Emotions and Moods

An emotion can develop into a mood. A mood is an extended emotional state. (Nathanson) This often occurs when a current emotion is tied to a past emotion that has not yet been resolved. A mood can be based on any affect. We can be in an angry mood, a distressed mood, a fearful mood, a shameful mood, an excited mood, or a serene and happy mood. We speak of mood as being positive or negative, of high or low. Unlike an affect or emotion, moods are less differentiated and discrete and have a broad, all-encompassing "feel" to them. Most often a person does not know the source of their feelings. A mood can actually be thought of as a script since there often is a given pattern of thinking and doing tied to the mood. What we call the mood disorders, however, usually address moods based on distress-anguish as in depression, interest-excitement as in mania, or fear-terror as in anxiety. Anxiety and depression are the two most ubiquitous moods. It is also important to point out that a mood is body based; when ill, distress and depression will be one's constant companion.

Anxiety is sometimes confused with distress or anguish.[32] Philosophers talk of "existential" anxiety as *angst,* which is the German word for anguish. Many symptoms associated with anxiety disorders are actually symptoms related to distress. In other words, the predominant mood is of tension and pressure, not excitation. It is likely that many emotional moods will, over time, co-assemble with distress, given the steady-state nature of this emotion. People often talk of feeling stressed-out when moody.

The cognition most associated with anxiety is worry. When a person worries it is because that person anticipates impending danger, catastrophe, or misfortune. In generalized anxiety[33] worrying can become a near obsession occupying much of a person's time and energy. When it reaches this level of severity there are a number of cognitive distortions we call superstitious thinking. These include the underlying belief that worrying will prevent danger, which is reinforced because seldom does the worst happen. Or, one might believe worrying will better prepare oneself for the impending catastrophe; unfortunately, it does not, and in fact can render one less capable of handling the event, since anxiety becomes more sensitized and therefore more likely to interfere with rational planning and judgment.

Depression personifies a mood, and is in fact classified in the Diagnostic & Statistical Manual as a mood disorder. Unlike the incessant worrying about the future found in anxiety, depression is characterized by perseverative ruminations about how awful and hopeless life is or was.

There are two primary depressive states, one is vegetative, the other agitated. These states are physiologically due to the antagonistic barrier between sympathetic and parasympathetic nervous systems. In the vegetative state, parasympathetic inhibition is so dominant that there is a shutdown of all systems, the physical, mental and behavioral. In an agitated state, sympathetic excitation is so intense that it places ever-increasing pressure on parasympathetic activity; if sympathetic excitation breaks through it may lead to mania as interest-excitement takes over.

Often anger and shame are emotions evident in depression. Anger may come up when the level of distress-anguish amplifies to the point where the density of neural firings triggers the anger-rage affect. Shame frequently makes its appearance in depression because distress inhibits and interferes with positive affect, and thus triggers shame; as discussed, anger is often a defense against shame.

Table 3-3 on the next page lists several common emotions. For some people, they occur from time-to-time, while for others they seem to dominate their lives. If this is the case, then these emotions come to characterize a major script.

As you will notice, each of these emotions emerge from a given affect, or from a combination of affects. As expected, there are far more negative emotions than positive. Keeping in mind the diagram of a script's scene (page 25), it is through the filter of cognition, based on an affect's schema, that determines which emotion will emerge. From this sequence determines the way we interpret an event.

---

[32] In fact, two anxiety disorders are labeled as stress disorders, Post-Traumatic Stress Disorder and Acute Stress Disorder.

[33] Generalized Anxiety Disorder is the mood disorder while others are labeled as phobias or Obsessive-Compulsive Disorder.

Table 3-3
Secondary Emotions and their Secondary Cognitions
Robert Kayton

The Emotion-Cognition Connection			
Emotion	**Affect**	**Cognitive Theme**	**Thought/Interpretation**
Anxiety	[fear-terror]	Danger/Threat	Something bad is going to happen
Stress	[distress-anguish]	Too Pressured	I cannot stand it
Depression	[distress-anguish]	Hopeless, trapped	Nothing will change
Sadness	[distress-anguish]	Loss	I miss that person or thing
Disappointment	[distress-anguish]	Unmet expectations	I should have gotten that
Frustration	[distress-anguish]	Blocked	My goal is obstructed
Anger	[anger-rage]	Unfairness	That was wrong or unjust
Resentment	[anger-rage]	Injuriously insulted	How dare s/he
Contempt	[anger-rage +disgust]	Derisive disdain	S/he is abhorrent
Embarrassed	[shame-humiliation]	Faults publicly exposed	Others think I'm a fool or stupid
Guilt	[shame-humiliation + fear-terror]	Wrongdoing	I shouldn't have done it
Hurt	[shame-humiliation]	Emotionally wounded	I'm unimportant to her/him
Envy	[shame-humiliation + distress/dissmell]	Wants what another has	I am powerless without that
Jealousy	[shame-humiliation + distress/dissmell]	Another is favored	I am less important than another
Regrets	[distress-anguish + shame-humiliation]	Dissatisfied with decision	I should have done it differently
Happiness	[enjoyment-joy]	Fulfilled	I feel good and contented
Love	[interest-excitement + enjoyment-joy]	Adoration	S/he or it is wonderful
Pride	[interest-excitement + enjoyment-joy]	Self-respect	I did a terrific job

The Negative Emotions

Sadness

Sadness is an emotion based on distress-anguish that gets activated by a real or imagined loss of someone or something that is deemed valuable and important. Sadness is clearly parasympathetic dominant. When mild it is more on the distress side and described as sorrowful, sad, grieved, dejected; when intense it is on the anguish side associated with agony, torment, and despair. Many complex feelings, such as loneliness and aloneness are related to sadness. Shame can co-assemble with sadness when loss is attributed to some defect in oneself. Sadness is not depression but can become a part of depression when prolonged.

Disappointment

Disappointment also stems from distress-anguish and is based on unfulfilled expectations. As such, disappointment can be associated with sadness when the failure to attain what was desired is perceived as a loss. Disappointment can also be related to shame when hurt feelings are elicited. To expect with certainty, is to guarantee disappointment. Expectations often lead to what Albert Ellis called the *tyranny of the shoulds;* these are the unrealistic expectations that can lead, not just to disappointment but also to anguish when accompanied by feelings of suffering. We shall discuss this problem at length in our chapter on cognitive restructuring.

Frustration

Frustration is another distress-anguish based emotion which is activated, not by loss, but when one's intent or goal is blocked or thwarted. Unlike parasympathetic-dominant sadness, frustration is exemplified by the antagonistic damned-up tension caused by high levels of sympathetic arousal, with countervailing high levels of parasympathetic inhibition. Frustration, and its lesser forms of irritation and annoyance, can lead to anger when the density of neural firings reaches the anger-rage level as though a dam has broken;[34] this is especially true when one continues to unsuccessfully pursue their goal. All of us have had the experience whereby too much frustration leads to the expression of anger; for many this is a frequent occurrence when working on a computer.

Hurt

Hurt is the emotion we feel when wounded, injured, damaged, harmed, disappointed, or wronged. There are two types of hurt; there is the physical hurt related to physical pain, and the emotional hurt that is related to distress-anguish or shame-humiliation. Distress is the innate, affective reaction to pain. Like the *pressured* feeling of chronic pain or the *searing* feeling of acute pain, distress has analogs of both sudden upset, and chronic dissatisfaction and disappointment.

Hurt can also be activated by shame-humiliation. This is most often evident when we say our feelings *are* hurt, rather than our feelings hurt. In this respect feelings come to represent the self; this is the pain of shame that comes from feeling invalidated by another person. Many people refer to their shame as feeling wounded or burned.

Anger

When feeling hurt or disappointed it is because shame was activated, and because shame is such a painful emotion, it is often defended against by anger. The ubiquity of the shame-anger response lies with the fact that most situations are interpersonal and therefore more likely to elicit shame. Benjamin Franklin once said, "Whatever begins with anger, ends with shame." (Washington Post, August 2, 2018); in truth we could say that anger not only ends with shame, but begins with shame. In addition, the shame-anger script is a very strong script because there are far more benefits than there are costs. Shame is painful, anger is not; shame

---

[34] Freud in fact postulated that frustration is the *damning up of psychic energy*. Dollard and Miller developed their *frustration-aggression* hypothesis from their work with rats who displayed increased aggression when they were blocked from getting food.

leads to feelings of helplessness, while anger leads to feelings of power and dominance. Neurophysiologically, the high density of sympathetic arousal in anger will inhibit the parasympathetic inhibition of shame.

The schematic theme in shame-anger is based on the belief that one is being treated unjustly, and to be treated unjustly is to be invalidated as unworthy. Shame-anger is largely based on the schema some call the *fairness fallacy*. Most people believe there is a universal truth as to what is fair and what is not fair. Unfortunately, this could not be further from the truth. Fairness is in the eyes of the beholder, and follows what could be described as the reverse golden rule; instead of *do unto others as you would like others to do unto you,* the fairness fallacy instead says, *others should do unto me as I would do unto them.* According to this formulation, it is not your own behavior that is being judged, but others for whom you believe should behave as you would. This fallacy is a major contributor to interpersonal, if not international, conflicts. When we reframe our view of fairness, and recognize that others do not have to live up to our own expectations, we are more likely to undo the shame, and thus the anger.[35]

Although shame is most often the major emotion underlying anger, it is not the only one. Genetically, anger is a reaction to fear, as in the fight-flight survival paradigm. In this situation anger is most often the affect or primary emotion; however, it can also act as a defensive secondary response to anticipated threat. This is characterized by the saying that "the best defense is a good offense." As discussed earlier, anger can also be a primary emotion in reaction to increased levels of distress, as discussed under the emotion of frustration.

Resentment

Resentment is an emotion defined as "a feeling of bitterness, animosity or hostility elicited by something perceived as insulting or injurious." (APA Dictionary, 1993) As noted, bitterness and hostility, insult and injury help define its underlying affects, namely shame-anguish, anger-rage and disgust/dissmell. Often there is righteous indignation that can catapult this emotion into a brooding mood when related to the object of one's scorn.

Resentment is a *damage-repair* script in which the hurt has not yet been repaired. The insult and injury are so personal and deep that it strikes at one's sense of self-integrity. Like most moral emotions (especially shame), the anger and contempt generated by resentment festers and grows as one becomes preoccupied with the hurtful event. Like Freud's *repetition compulsion*, one attempts, via fixated obsessing, to find the "reason" behind the insult as though that will resolve the damage; instead it amplifies the damage considerably, leaving open wounds and an escalated feeling of antipathy.

Much damage has been sown by this emotion. It certainly plays a major toll on relationships. It is sometimes said that women never forget and men never remember, suggesting that resentment is an emotion more often found in women; however, there is no evidence to this belief. It is plausible that for women, who appear more prone to shame issues revolving around interpersonal exclusion and rejection, resentment is more pronounced in intimate relationships. For men, however, whose shame themes relate more to competency and adequacy, resentment can be a major component when a man's power or capability is

---

[35] In anger-management training, we ultimately need to undo the shame; however, since anger is the "'hot" emotion, we need to begin therapy by using physical relaxation and calming techniques.

believed to be challenged. There are ample examples of powerful men who can hold deep resentment to anyone challenging their "machismo."

Contempt

Contempt is an "emotion characterized by negative regard for anything or anybody considered to be inferior, vile, or worthless." (APA dictionary, 1993) Contempt is the fusion of disgust/dissmell with anger-rage. Anger is associated with attack and aggression; however, when blended with disgust, it becomes hostile, cruel or even sadistic, and has as its goal the elimination or removal of its source. It is important to keep in mind that contempt can also be turned inward; self-hatred can be the basis for suicide, and may take on a particularly grisly picture. Cruelty holds little bounds when contempt is present.

Guilt

Guilt is a "...conscious emotion characterized by a painful sense of having done (or thought) something that is wrong, and often by any readiness to take action to undo or mitigate this wrong." (APA dictionary, 1993) In this definition guilt is characterized by the awareness of wrong action (real or imagined) and is considered to be a moral emotion. Freud related guilt to the superego; the harbinger of what is right or wrong. Pine (1990) made the distinction that guilt is about one's behavior, while shame is about one's self.

Guilt is based on the melding of shame and fear. In guilt, we feel both shame about our self, and fear that our behavior might lead to retribution. One can distinguish which emotion is most pronounced by simply recalling an event that evoked guilt, and examining whether shame about oneself was most prominent, or whether fear of its consequences was most apparent.

Jealousy and Envy

Jealousy is a ".... negative emotion in which an individual resents a third-party for taking away (or likely to take away) the affections of a loved one." ((APA dictionary, 1993)) Jealousy requires three people: the one who is jealous, a partner with whom the jealous individual desires, and the rival who represents a preemptive threat to these desires. Romantic relationships are the prototypic source of jealousy, but any significant relationship is capable of producing it. It differs from envy in that three people are always involved; we call this *triangulation*.

Envy is a. "...negative emotion of discontent and resentment generated by desire for the possessions, attributes, qualities, or achievements of another." (APA dictionary, 1993) Unlike jealousy, which shares a number of similarities, "...envy involves only two people, the envious person and the person envied." ((APA dictionary, 1993))

Both jealousy and envy are based on shame and contempt, the former toward the "splitter" in a triangle (jealousy), and the latter because it is "unfair" that the other person has what one covets (envy). Both involve shame because there is an interruption of positive affect in obtaining the other person or object, and contempt toward the source of one's jealousy or envy. By turning the source into disgust, one disowns and removes oneself from this noxious or evil source; this negative response to another person acts as a defense against one's own feelings of shame or self-disgust.

Regrets

Regrets are the emotional response to the remembrance of a task, state, condition, or experience that one wishes were different. Regrets are secondary emotions related to sadness, and are thus based on distress-anguish. The cognitive theme is related to feeling disappointed at unrealized expectations.

These expectations are often compensatory idealized-images based on the inhibition of shame-humiliation. As we know, shame-humiliation is activated by the interruption of positive affect. The greater the intensity of the positive affect that is interrupted, the greater will be the shame-humiliation; and if the positive affect is interest-excitement, instead of enjoyment-joy, then shame-humiliation will be further amplified. [36]

Regrets are imbued with unfulfilled expectations. An expectation can exist at the primary level, when one's bodily sensations become activated in anticipation of a positive affect, or at the secondary level with thoughts or pictures of success, adoration, and achievement. These cognitions, together with their idealized prescriptive images, form expectations that are helpful when realistic, disappointing when not.

Often regrets are based on the belief that one should have done something different and better. Not living up to these expectations can easily lead to shame. This failure to live up to one's standards of worthiness can certainly disrupt any positive fantasies tied to these idealized expectations, thus triggering the shame-humiliation response.

Regrets can serve a useful purpose when cognified, allowing the person to objectively learn from his or her experience for the future; most often regrets are costly and painful, and serve no meaningful benefit. When shame is a large part of regret, it is often associated with one's failure to act, which can then be transformed into guilt about the actions one did or did not take in the past.

Regrets are fallacious distortions of reality because we apply today's reality to the reality that existed at that time we performed the regretful action (or inaction). Hindsight is 20/20, meaning that we could always look back and see that we should have done something differently. We must remember that most of us do something for reasons that appeared to be the best at the time the decision was made. It is hard to imagine a person purposely deciding to do something because there are negative consequences. Given the information we had at the time, and the context in which it took place, most of us would make the most reasonable choice afforded at that time; if we knew the outcome would be negative, we likely would have made a different choice. We make decisions with intended consequences in mind and do not, or cannot, see the future through the lens of unintended consequences; thus, we make decisions based on the reality and information we had available at that time. In regrets, we apply a standard that is based on the reality of the present to the reality of the past; this is what makes regrets a fallacy. What makes regrets foolish is that the deed has already been done.

---

[36] This is largely due to the fact that interest-excitement is an excitatory affect, while enjoyment-joy is an inhibitory affect, meaning that the energy interruption will be far greater for the increasing gradient affect than the decreasing gradient affect; this will have a reciprocal and proportional effect on the affect's intensity level. In addition, the yearning to fulfill one's expectations is motivated mainly by interest-excitement.

The Positive Emotions

Happiness

To be happy is "to be favored by good fortune, successful, pleasure in or contentment with one's circumstances... pleased...glad...satisfied...a pleasant spirit of harmony and mutual goodwill," (Oxford Dictionary) and as: "an emotion of joy, gladness, satisfaction, and wellbeing." (APA Dictionary, 1993)

Happiness, at least its pursuance, is said to be a right of all men (and women), as so declared in Jefferson's Declaration of Independence. Happiness is equal to the rights of life and liberty. Many a hedonist has taken up this banner to justify behaviors that make one happy. However, in the 18th century, happiness was not just equated with an emotion, but with fulfillment. Thus, Jefferson was advocating the right of all men to have the opportunity to achieve success. This also means that happiness is a state that is attained when one's psychological needs, and affective prescripts, are actualized.

The emotion happiness is primarily based on the affect enjoyment-joy. It is the *feel-good* emotion. Neurophysiologically it entails such neurotransmitters as dopamine, oxytocin, and the endorphins. It is often equated with optimism, which we now know has many beneficial effects, not only on one's mental wellbeing, but also on one's physical wellbeing as well. Happiness has been shown to improve one's immune system and lead to a longer life; it is the epitome of "living life well" in developing a sense of wellbeing.

Love[37]

Love is a complex yet basically integrated emotion, involving strong feelings of affection and tenderness for the loved object, pleasurable sensations in his or her presence, devotion to his or her wellbeing, and sensitivity to his or her reactions to oneself....All love is based on the experience of positive affect...the part of love that is exciting and makes the heart pound owing to its power of interest-excitement; the part of love that makes us feel calm, safe, relaxed, and untroubled owes its power to enjoyment-joy." (Nathanson, 1992, p. 241) Thus, to be *in love* entails high sympathetic-dominant excitement; while *to love someone* is based largely on parasympathetic-dominant enjoyment. The greater the ratio between these two positive emotions, the greater will be the intensity and degree of romantic (excitement) over platonic (joy) love, (or vice-versa).

Love is probably the most discussed emotion with a plethora of different definitions. The Greeks defined several types of love:[38] *Eros,* the sexualized passionate love between two people, *filios,* the love among family members, and *agape*, the platonic love between good friends. Love can vary from the deeply emotional and sensual "romantic" love, to the more complex emotion associated with the love of ideas or things. Its descriptive synonyms include adoration, infatuation, passion, admiration, respect, kindness, affinity, attachment, admiration, appreciation, fondness, admire, adore, cherish, appreciate, idolize; its antonyms include hatred and disgust, contempt and disdain.

Love represents the amount of positive affect and emotion that is attached to another person, thing or idea. Idealized love is when all affective prescripts are fulfilled. At the primary level, love is experienced as very deep and passionate, while at the more complex

---

[37] Largely taken from Donald Nathanson, *Shame and Pride, 1992*

and intellectualized level it is expressed as the love of ideas, pursuits, or interests as a complex emotion. It is primary when it speaks from the body; this may include sensory expressions, such as eating food or listening to music, and the biological drives of sex or appetite. At the emotional level, there is the experience of joy and excitement.

Love at the primary level is where the interest-excitement of romantic love takes place, and is characterized when one feels the "right chemistry," a biological bond with another person. At the complex level is platonic love, the enjoyment-joy shared between two people, a love that is deeply affectionate. This is evident when two people share the mutualization of maximized positive attunement, and the minimization of negative misattunement. This is the kind of love between best friends, the kind of love one feels towards one's sports team during a game, or the love of music and art. Although there may well be passion, it is a craving based on joy.

Passionate or romantic love is evident when there is a mutualization of *maximized positive affect attunement,* and a *minimization of negative affect misattunement* that is associated with both interest-excitement and an amplified sexual drive. One can, however, be in love with sex and not the other person, or in love with the person but not sex. So-called "true love" takes a relatively longer period of time in which there is sexual and emotional attachment to each other.

"Pure love" is altruistic love, an ongoing state of high positive regard toward another person which manifests itself in concerns for the others welfare, pleasure in his or her presence, and a desire for his or her approval. Together with unconditional love[39], pure love is potentially attainable by those who have an integrated self

Shame is an intricate component of love: "Shame always looms in direct proportion to the degree of pre-existing positive affect that it has restrained." (Nathanson, 1990) The more we love, the more vulnerable we are to being shamed. Although seemingly opposites, shame and love are intricately interwoven, each with the other. The more we can expose ourselves to the potential shame of rejection, and instead receive affirmation and validation, the greater the degree of trust, and therefore the greater the feeling of love; in other words, by risking shame, the bond of love is both tested and strengthened.

Pride

Pride is defined as "having a high opinion of one's own worth or importance, the pleasure or satisfaction derived from some action that does one credit." (Oxford Dictionary) In the APA Dictionary, pride is categorized as a "self-conscious emotion that occurs when a goal is attained and one's achievement has been recognized and approved by others," making it a complex emotion. Synonyms include esteem, self-efficacy, dignity, worth, and respect. It is an affiliative emotion, based on both positive affects.

In his book on this topic, Nathanson speaks of the *"shame/pride"* axis. Pride is not the absence of shame; if it is then pride is usually called "false pride," which is an overcompensated defense against underlying shame. What he calls "healthy pride" is "the basic feeling of pride [that] stems from a pleasure we achieve in a moment of competence." Healthy pride requires three primary conditions: first, there must be a "purposeful, goal-directed, intentional activity undertaken under the influence of the affect interest-excitement;" secondly, "this activity must be successful in achieving its goal;" and finally,

---

[39] Unconditional love, like pure love, are ideals that we strive toward, rather than ideals that are fully attainable.

"the achievement of that goal suddenly releases the individual from the preceding effort and the affect that accompanies and amplifies it, thus triggering enjoyment joy."

Pride begins soon after birth through the process of autosimulation. Thus, when an infant mimics the innate affect display of sucking the breast by sucking its own thumb, and then does so through his own initiative with directed intentionality, he is experiencing a sense of prideful competence. This is the prototype for both pride and the efficacy of achievement, and marks the beginning of self-agency and willpower, attributes essential not just for functioning well, but for the integration of the self and the consequent attainment of wellbeing.

In false pride, such as seen in the sociopath, the hubris displayed is of a disdainful and hurtful arrogance toward others. What is important in the shame/pride axis is the counterbalance between these two emotions, with pride situated at the non-shame pole of this continuum. "Shame, of course, is the polar opposite of pride. Where pride allows us to affiliate with others, shame makes us isolate ourselves from them...pride is capable of acting as an antidote for what amounts to a chronic sense of shame." (Nathanson, 1992, p.83) Even posturally, shame and pride are recognized by their opposite behaviors; in shame, one's posture is constricted and face bowed downward as if to hide from others; in pride one puffs out their chest to direct others attention toward oneself.

Chapter 4: The Behavioral System

Like the evolution of the brain and mind, behavior developed from affect-based inscripts. These inscripts are manifest at, or soon after birth, and immediately become modified by experience. Through social learning, these action patterns change from being fixed to being adaptive and flexible. By two to three months old, when implicit memory is operative, these modifications become different enough from their innate inscript to become newly learned behavioral patterns, triggered by emotion rather than by affect.

From Inscripts to Behaviors

Behavior began as micro-muscular movements. The most primary movement is both the simple and the complex reflex. (Bloom and Lazerson, 1988) A simple reflex is the "automatic response to a stimulus by a part of an organism's body." It is purely a stimulus-response paradigm as epitomized by the *knee jerk* response. The complex reflex requires "processing interneurons between the sensory and motor neurons." This means that the complex reflex entails intermediary synapses that we are not born with, but develop automatically in concordance with the development of the brain; thus, complex reflexes are epigenetic and appear during critical stages of brain development.

At a somewhat higher level of reflexive behavior are fixed-action-patterns (FAP). Fixed-action-patterns refer to an automatized sequence of specific movements, a fixed set of reflexes that represent a furthering of motor sequencing actions. At an even more complex level are instincts, which can be thought of as a combination of a "series" of fixed-action-patterns. It is generally agreed that humans do not have instincts; this is likely because we did not need instincts to survive. Our advanced learning and memory abilities, which requires an extensive childhood, and our successful ways of dealing with the natural world, has provided us with the ability to make the world adapt to our needs (which is partly why there is so little diversity among the human species); consequently, instincts likely dropped out because of their disuse. In fact, instincts may well have interfered with learning by, for example, reducing the need for higher-level complex activity. The necessity to learn makes learning the "mother of invention."

Inscripts are essentially fixed-action-patterns that are innately programmed within each affect. As earlier stated, some neuropsychologists believe the freeze inscript in surprise-startle is actually a reflex. An inscript, however, is more complex than a reflex, but simpler than an instinct; as explained above, this provides for greater flexibility, allowing inscripts to modify through learning and therefore evolve into behaviors.

Let us begin by describing the inscript for each affect. Enjoyment-joy is characterized by approach and involvement with its source, and is innately identified by the smile of enjoyment or the laughter of joy. Interest-excitement also entails a moving toward, seeking out, and proactive approach. The neutral affect of surprise-startle is instead identified by a frozen, paralyzed and immobilized behavioral response. Fear-terror is characterized by the innate behavior to escape a dangerous triggering source; when this affect evolves into the emotions of fear or terror, and is now governed by anticipation, the behaviors of avoidance and hyper-vigilance develop. Distress-anguish is distinguished by crying, whining, and complaining; when highly parasympathetic dominant, there is lethargy, apathy, inactivity, avoidance and lack of communication; if there is a strong sympathetic antagonism, the behavior is agitation, tenseness and a need to pace back-and-forth. Anger-rage is represented by attack behaviors, unlike shame-humiliation where there is an innate need to hide and avert one's eyes or face. And finally, there is disgust/dissmell, where the innate reactions are to move away and avoid the aversive-triggering source.

From these inscripts develop several basic behavioral patterns. Karen Horney, the eminent psychoanalyst, identified three directions, moving-toward, moving-away, moving-against; we could also add immobilization to this list. Thus, the positive prosocial emotions prompt moving towards others; fear, distress, shame, disgust and dissmell entail moving away; anger prompts moving against; startle to immobilization. From these basic patterns develop a plethora of behaviors that have become so diverse that behavior has come to be the most difficult of all modalities to predict. For example, a person who is anguished is likely to have very dark, possibly suicidal thoughts, and despairing emotions; yet it is often difficult to predict what that person will do. There are too many variables involved, such as the individual's inborn temperament, vacillating affects and emotions, current, past and anticipated experiences, the availability and willingness to seek out support, and social and cultural factors. In addition, behavior is more directly activated by thoughts and emotions that can then mediate the response to its triggering event.

Unlike the mind, which is a function of the brain, behavior is a function of the body. And like the mind's capacity to influence and change the brain, behavior can influence and change the body. We can abuse it or use it. Obviously, if you punch a hole in a wall your hand will be injured and hurt, or if you exercise healthfully, you build muscle and improve metabolism. Given that the brain is part of the body, and that this anatomical structure began with movement, it is not too much of a leap to see the direct and profound importance of behavior in changing not just our body, but our brain as well (which reciprocally changes behavior).

Although behavior is directly derived from inscripts, it is analogically connected to all other modalities. This parallel in developmental-processing demonstrates the interconnection among all functional systems: in other words, there is a synchrony of mutually interactive growth among body, brain, mind and behavior. This analogic maturation is critical for both affect-regulation and affect-integration. When something goes wrong with any one component during development, all other systems are likely to be impacted. This analogical principle is critical in epigenetics, the interdependence between nature and nurture, and demonstrates that what is genetically innate is also dependent on the environment.

Behavioral Learning

Inscripts are evident among newborns, but is seldom seen in children and adults. Through social learning, each inscript gets modified quite early in development, as emotions (rather than affects) become the primary source to activate behavior. Some behaviors are combinations of inscripts, such as seen in social anxiety whereby the avoidance of social situations is a combination of both fear and shame.[40] Behaviors also become a part of a script and therefore of a greater level of complex organization, which we will discuss in Chapter 5; in fact, behavior is considered the most complex of all modalities making up a scene.

---

[40] This is not guilt, which is the fusion of fear-terror and shame-humiliation, rather than a co-assembly of both emotions

Like all learning, behavioral learning can be described as the socialization of inscripts. This brings us to the evolutionary principle called *self-organizing complexity*. Accordingly, evolution moves toward greater levels of adaptation. The behavioral expression of an inscript provides an immediate means for regulating affect; therefore, moving toward another person satiates positive affect, while moving away or against another person reduces negative affect. Like mental functions, behavior provides a greater and far more adaptive level of affect-regulation. Behavior is learned and thus is more adaptive in the social world we live in; thus, when angry, rather than attack another person physically, one can revert to irony or sarcasm.

Learned behavior, when activated by an emotion, becomes associated and connected to its activating stimulus event. Behavioral learning can thus be both procedural and declarative, and therefore implicit or explicit. Implicit learning is stored as procedural memory that becomes consolidated in the body by way of pre-limbic and lower limbic areas of the brain. This learning is based on neuromuscular activity and its sensory feedback; its behavior is implicitly expressed through affects or primary emotions. On the other hand, explicit declarative-learning, such as instructional learning, activates behavior at the secondary and complex cognitive levels, and is likely based in the hippocampal-prefrontal areas. Unlike the automatic unconscious behavior that is elicited by implicit memory, explicit memory leads to more calculated and mentally directed behavior.

When explicit learning is consistent and frequent, it becomes integrated top-down through implicit functions that over time become processed and activated at lower centers of the brain. This is evident in learning to dance or ride a bicycle. It may begin with instructional and declarative learning, but when coupled with hands-on procedural learning, will now come to be processed at more implicit levels. Thus, instructional declarative-memory is initially processed at higher centers, but with further practice and procedural use, become integrated, stored and processed at lower brain-mind centers. What once required active and calculated consciousness now becomes more automatized and unconscious. These behaviors become habits and appear as automatic as a reflex or fixed-action-pattern.

Learned unconscious habits, such as crossing the street or tying one's shoes, reflect relatively complex behaviors. This provides great adaptive benefits in that we need not divert our energy and attention to details as we carry out these adaptive behaviors. However, just as they were learned, they could be extinguished. Although we can modify and reduce a reflex, we cannot, with the exception of injury or medical intervention, extinguish a reflex. By withholding reinforcement over long periods of time, a habit will ultimately extinguish.

Both affective and emotional expressions act as a communication mechanism whose expression is highly modified by the particular social demands placed on it. The few times we see the pure innate affect script displayed is soon after birth, or when a young child, and in some cases adult, *breaks down* and *loses it;* in other words, they are overwhelmed with affect because the higher-level, socialized prefrontal cortex *breaks down*. Yet no matter how far afield our behavior develops from these inscripts, we can trace the core of our behavior to their inscripted origins.

We know that behavior is based on experience-dependent learning, and thus, is subject to many social and cultural prescriptions and proscriptions. Temperament, however, is another significant factor shaping one's behavior. Temperament refers to one's inborn level of affect sensitivity; this essentially relates to threshold levels in which an affect gets both activated and amplified to the degree in which an inscript is expressed.

One of the leading authorities on temperament, Jerome Kagan (2004) has categorized two basic dispositions, the inhibited and uninhibited. This fits the excitation (uninhibited type) and inhibition (inhibited type) polarity and suggests that these propensities are inborn. Those considered inhibited are more parasympathetic-dominant, and their behavioral displays are more reserved, passive and perhaps avoidant. The uninhibited are born more active and more sympathetic-dominant, take more risks and are more likely to engage in approach behaviors.

We know that every newborn expresses their inscripts facially, vocally and bodily in similarly programmed patterns, unlike behavioral displays that vary enough so as to lead to differences in excitable and inhibitory behaviors. Infants with greater excitability will likely attend to novel stimuli, while the more inhibited will tend to avoid new events. On the other hand, the inhibited are more likely to attend longer to familiar stimuli than the uninhibited, who tend to be more distracted. In addition, when positive affect is interrupted, the inhibited will more likely be shamed, whereas the uninhibited will tend to be frustrated or angry. Ultimately, these predispositions will either be reinforced or extinguished as the forces of social learning take over.

During the neonatal stage, social interactions are most evident by the mother-infant relationship. Attunement (connecting) and misattunement (not connecting) speaks to the early affective interchange that clearly shapes behaviors related to separation and attachment, a dimension that underlies most interpersonal relationships. The dynamics of separation and attachment are studied in neonates by observing such factors as the length of eye contact, the frequency and duration of smiling or crying, and the amount of proactive or passive behaviors. These inscripts represent actions used to measure the degrees of variance between attachment and separation.

In terms of approach-avoid behaviors, the now classical studies by Mary Ainsworth (1962) in the 1950's with toddlers, is considered the landmark series of studies in this area. Toddlers were observed with their mothers in a room filled with toys. The ability to separate was measured by their reactions to their mother when she came into the room, then left the room only to later return again. Separation was measured by the toddler's ability to distance (separate) from their mother and engage in play activates, and to seek proximity (attachment) with their mother when she returned. In *secure attachments* the toddler's comfort zone for closeness with the mother, and the exploration of the toy-filled environment, was by far the greatest. In *insecurely avoidant attachments* there were relatively fewer mother-toddler interactions; in this dynamic, the child failed to show distress at separation, and in fact maintained the greatest degree of separation and the least degree of attachment. In *resistant and ambivalent relationships,* the mother was overanxious, with the child being wary of any separation as evidenced by minimal, if any, exploratory behaviors. Unfortunately, these toddlers gained little comfort from being close to their mother, and instead showed anxiety and distress. The most damaging script is the *disorganized/disoriented relationship,* in which a mother's behavior is duplicitous and unpredictable, leading the child to display both disorganized and disoriented behaviors ranging from startle to fear to shame to distress to anger.

These behavioral scripts were interestingly, and to a statistically significant level, found to persist into adulthood (unless there were specific interventions, such as psychotherapy). This demonstrates the all-encompassing role that early attunement or misattunement play in determining the ability to be both intimate and independent. At this level, social learning takes place through affective associations, and is learned through modeling and conditioning. This takes place at both implicit and explicit levels.

Explicit learning is cognitively based at both the late-secondary level (orbitofrontal cortex) and at the higher complex level (pre-frontal cortex). When maintained at semantic and declarative (conscious) levels, behavior is activated and directed through explicit self-instructional thinking. This type of thinking encompasses such executive functions as decision-making, problem solving, and judgment.

Affect is largely cognified at these higher levels of cognition; however, since affect underlies memory, the explicitly learned information will still need to become associated with affect in order to be retained. If there is too little affect during declarative learning, then one will need to use some strategies to induce affect, such as through vocal intonations, hand gestures and other means to activate and amplify affect.[41] It is also necessary for one to practice and review the learned information with vigor and intent, thereby integrating the explicitly learned information with the lower levels of the brain; this process takes place through the hippocampus-amygdala circuit that will transform short-term memory into long-term memory. What is happening is that declarative learning is being transformed into procedural memory.

When affects get activated and amplified frequently and intensely, neural processing becomes more implicit and more procedurally based. When positive affect becomes associated with new learning, it will be integrated into positive scripts. When negative affect becomes associated with this information, this information will either fail to become fully consolidated into memory, and thus remain dissociated, or it will instead be integrated into a negative and maladaptive script. As we shall later see, negative affects and negative scripts cannot integrate into the self-system.

Most behaviors are learned through implicit means; in other words, unlike the conscious effort entailed in explicit instructional learning, implicit learning takes place at the unconscious level. There are two fundamental associational processes in implicit learning, modeling through mirror neurons, and reinforcement through behavioral conditioning.

Modeling is a genetically inherent tendency toward imitation, and is thus the first mode of social learning. It is an apparent example of the analog principle whereby two people duplicate the actions of one another. It entails the process of affect attunement, which takes place at primary levels, and thus gets stored as implicit memory. How these mirror neurons resonate is, as Allen Schore (2002) points out, similar to the physics phenomenon known as *sympathetic vibrations* as seen when two pendulums, swinging together, will move toward a state of consonance and synchronization. This takes place at molecular levels similar to the protein synthesis process in mirror neurons. We shall see, in Chapter 6, that attunement takes place when each person experiences the same affect; at the brain level this means *mirroring* and *mutualizing* the profile of neural firings. Like the gravitational pull between two objects, imitation is a very basic mode in relationships. When observing two people interacting, you will find variations between degrees of imitation and mutualization versus incongruency and misattunement.

Imitation is, therefore, one of the earliest vehicles for social behavioral learning. Modeling looks at learned behavior as developing from the social reinforcement gained from approval. As discussed earlier, issues of separation and attachment can be observed in the attunement-misattunement dance between the mother and her infant. It is during attunement

---

[41] There are a number of strategies discussed in Chapter 6 and in the Appendix.

that imitation and bonding takes place, and it does so through such mutualized activities as reciprocal cooing, smiling and stroking; mutualized attunement follows the prescripts to maximize positive affects and minimize negative affects.

Modeling can therefore be seen as an associational learning process that takes place implicitly through mirror neurons. For mirrored behaviors to become learned behaviors that become stored and consolidated into long-term memory, depends on conditional social reinforcement. Conditional reinforcement links a stimulus to a response, for which there are two primary methods, *classical conditioning* (from Ivan Pavlov) and *instrumental conditioning* (from B.F. Skinner).

Classical conditioning deals directly with the autonomic nervous system and is mediated by lower pre-limbic areas of the brain (such as the reticular activating system and the cerebellum). Many of you are familiar with the Pavlovian experiment demonstrating that, when a bell-ring becomes associated with food, that bell-ring will then come to elicit the salivation response that is naturally elicited by food. Learning takes place when the two stimuli are associated together in time and space. Many phobias are learned through classical conditioning; for example, if while walking through a park and you see a snake, the park itself can come to elicit the same fear you had when seeing the snake.

Instrumental, or operant conditioning, is mediated by the amygdala and hippocampus, parts of the limbic system that operate at a higher level than structures activated in classical conditioning. Unlike classical conditioning, which focuses on the pairing of stimuli in time and space, instrumental conditioning focuses on the behavioral response and its consequential reinforcer. There are three types of reinforcement: *positive* reward reduces negative behavior and increases positive behavior; *negative* reinforcement is the absence or withholding of reward that will diminish positive or negative behavior; and *punishment,* which increases negative behavior and decreases positive behavior.

There are several important reinforcement principles. First, behavior that is reinforced will be learned, while that which is not will extinguish. Second, negative behavior tends to gain attention over positive behavior; pain trumps pleasure, since it is more essential and necessary for survival. Third, behavior is best learned through constant reinforcement, and maintained (consolidated) through intermittent reinforcement. Fourth, immediate reinforcement is more effective than delayed reinforcement. Finally, both positive and negative reinforcement have a higher success rate than punishment; punishment will activate greater levels of negative emotion than negative reinforcement, while reward activates positive emotion. Thus, positive reinforcement is the most potent, negative reinforcement the next, and punishment the least effective, especially since negative affect interferes with learning.

We have looked at three basic processes involved in behavioral learning. The earliest and most basic is modeling, followed by classical conditioning, and finally by instrumental conditioning, the latter operating at a higher level of brain functioning. Learning also takes place at the higher pre-frontal levels through declarative learning. Declarative or instructional learning takes place with more complex cognitive development that allows *executive* processing (in the prefrontal cortex) to inculcate the behavioral instructions. Behavioral learning is thus both bottom-up and top-down. This has helped fuel the great debate as to whether behavior is determined from our genes and from our past (bottom-up), or whether we have the capacity for top-down free will.

Conclusion: Self-Will and Behavior

I will close this chapter with a brief discussion of self-will and behavior. We will take this up at far greater length in Part II, since wellbeing is largely based on this issue. The question of determinism and free will goes back to the earliest philosophers. There has always been the question as to why we do what we do. Is it because God or the Devil "made me do it?" Does nature and external circumstances play the major role? Is our behavior determined by our temperament, by past learning and future anticipation? Is it due to our genetics, our mental or physical health, our parents, social networks and friends? These arguments may seem fanciful in the abstract, but has real life implications. If agents outside our self are determining our behavior, then we are not truly responsible for our actions. It also challenges the whole idea that we have the inner capacity to change.

I submit that we do have degrees of free will. In fact, free will is a basic precept of existentialism, which emphasizes the existence of the individual person as a free and responsible agent determining his or her own development through acts of the will. Paradoxically, if we don't believe this, then we don't have it, whereas if we do, then we do have it. In other words, each of us has the power of will that comes with recognizing that our self is the agent of our behavior. One may say that even if true, is not our behavior actually determined by our brain and mind? Yet, we have already seen how plastic and changeable the brain is, and as to the mind, the question becomes who's in charge of our thoughts and feelings?

I propose that free will represents an evolutionary change from the deterministic and reactive-based functioning that characterizes most animals. It was with the advent of the self that the self-as-agent was put in charge of our functioning. As noted earlier, unlike most animals, we humans have the ability to modify nature to best "fit" our needs; thus, events do not determine our behavior; instead our *self* does. An argument I use to support the idea of free will is that nobody can make you do something; ultimately it is you who makes the decision. Even if someone threatens your life, you can still refuse to do what they demand. You may argue that your decision was not really a choice because you were threatened; yet even with this dire consequence, you did not have to comply. True, in most cases it would really be stupid to resist, yet we know that some choices are really stupid.

Will is the capacity to make choices, while free will is the power of self-direction. The former implies that all decisions, conscious or unconscious, are part of the person, while the latter suggests that each person has the capacity for consciousness and volition. The concept of will is thus quite important when we talk of behavioral motivation.

We have already discussed the critical role of affect in motivation; yet, what transforms affect into action? We know that affect is activated by specific profiles of neural firings; what activates these neural profiles is the sensory-motor activity of the body and brain that analogically replicates external stimuli. However, we do not necessarily need external stimuli to activate a given neural profile. We can activate it bodily "as though" there is an external stimulus. Cognition can also activate affect by thinking, as behavior can be activated and motivated by *doing*.

The idea that doing is what motivates behavior may sound like an oxymoron, just as believing that there is free will makes it so. Although somewhat controversial, there is considerable neuroscience evidence that motivation does come from doing, and when we assume that the unconscious is part of the self, then it is our unconscious self that also makes decisions. As to the latter, this is why it is so critical to make the unconscious conscious, so that we are able to utilize higher cortical levels for decision-making.

In regard to motivation and doing, we have already seen how behavior shapes our brain and mind. William James, the 19th century *father* of American psychology, first became aware that doing motivates behavior. Having trouble getting out of bed each morning, he began to ponder what would motivate him to do so. After a period of time he just began getting out of bed, rather than thinking about getting out of bed, and concluded that it was the act of getting out of bed that motivated him to get out of bed. Many of us have had similar experiences. We procrastinate about exercising each day only to find that once we get started we feel motivated. This may occur because we are maximizing the interest-excitation that comes with movement, as well as the triggering of dopamine and various endorphins. In addition, there are the laws of inertia which state that an object in motion will stay in motion, while an object that is stationary will remain stationary; in other words, like-behavior begets more like-behavior.

Chapter 5: The Script System

In the past four chapters, we have focused on the major components that make up a scene.[42] We have seen how these components are analogically linked together by their affect to form a scene. When families of scenes interconnect, we have the formation of a script. Scripts form to better regulate affects than does the simple inscript. Scripts do this by organizing and managing families of scenes by way of *mini-scripts*. Without scenes being organized and managed, chaos would reign supreme and development would consequently be stunted. Mini-scripts coassemble to form *subscripts*, which in turn join together to make up a script. Thus, the formation and structure of scripts is hierarchical. Scripts give us the relatively predictable and consistent reactions to events; as such they could be thought of as making up our personality.[43]

Some scripts work directly on affect regulation, others do so at more oblique and complex levels. This applies not only to scenes in the present, but also to those stored from the past and those projected into the future. A script is thus the past, present, and future, a narrative that has already been written yet is constantly being re-written; or as Tomkins so eloquently puts it, "the world we perceive is a dream we learned from a script we have not written;" (Vol 3, p.13) in other words any set of scenes is indeterminate until the future, which either magnifies or minimizes our experiences. We could say that our experience of the present is based on our scripted memories from the past and our expectations about the future, all of which are fused into a script. Scripts tell us *the where we are coming from and where we are going* that helps determine how we live our life; scripts are not fixed, but are constantly changing.

As remembering changes our memory (during recall and reconsolidation), so too will the activation of a script automatically modify that script from what it was. Each script is at any moment, an approximation of that script a moment ago, and of that script that will immediately follow; put another way, each script is an approximation, rather than an exact duplicate, of one another that varies along a continuum between degrees of similarity and degrees of difference. In the analogical system, the focus is on similarity, yet since change is continual, divergence takes place as levels of change increase. When there is sufficient change, both among the interconnected components that make up an individual scene and the arranged order of co-assembled sets of scenes, then the script itself becomes different.

Although change is built into the very fabric of scripts, the degree of change varies among scripts. Some scripts are very fluid and constantly in flux, their component parts loosely connected, while others are relatively fixed so that scenes are tightly bound together. Too little or too much entanglement, and commensurately too little or too much variation, diminishes the efficacy and adaptability of a script. When scenes are rigidly assembled and fixed in constant reiterations, we are stuck in too much sameness; yet, when scenes are too disconnected and disparate, then there is chaos as one is caught in a sea of constant flux. These poles are often the conditions we find in mental disorders; the first represented by depression, the second by mania; some vacillate from one state to the other, from order to

---

[42] A scene not only exists in the present, but may also be from the past or anticipated future.

[43] According to Tomkins, affects make up his motivational theory, while scripts make up his personality theory.

disorder, from rigidity to chaos as we see in bipolar disorders. Most of us, however, are somewhere in-between these two states of being.

The degree of internal connectivity, that is the degree to which scenes and scripts are co-assembled, depends on three significant factors: inborn temperament, experiential learning and the present context. The inhibited personality tends toward sameness, the uninhibited toward change; connectivity requires similarity, yet relies on its ability to adapt to changing circumstances. Learned experiences are what scripts are made of and are thus critical in determining interscript development. Finally, there is the context in which scripts are activated and magnified that will influence the formation of more complex scripts

Temperament, experience, knowledge and context also help determine which scenes and which scripts get activated. For example, scenes with the greatest affect charge will be the most salient and urgent. Thus, a distress scene can change to an anger scene if anger-rage becomes more intense than distress-anguish. This is what we usually see in wife abuse: a husband who believes he is constantly "nagged," and whose script is to avoid such scenes, may over time react instead with rage and attack. We can also see this change if a child, whose script has been to enthusiastically approach dogs, may instead turn to fearful avoidance if attacked.

This means that scripts have the property of modularity. Modularity refers to the "property of any system that permits its subsystems degrees of freedom of combination and recombination." (Tomkins, 4, p.55) An individual scene is ordered in a relatively invariant linear sequence, so that changing a scene to a better scene requires the minimization of negative affect and the maximization of positive affect through modifications in cognition, emotion, and behavior. For scripts, however, the ordering of scenes is variable, so that change takes place by changing the order in which scenes are arranged. Rescripting works at both levels, first through amplifying or inhibiting the components that make up a scene, and then by reordering the assembly of scenes that make up a script. For example, a passive-aggressive script consists of both shaming scenes and angry scenes. When shame is greater than anger, we have a **shame**-anger script in which passivity will be dominant; if, however, the situation changes, so that it becomes more enraging than embarrassing, then the ordering of scenes will change to a shame-**anger** script. This shift in dominance is often the case when one is criticized and reacts first with one affect, and then with the other.

Scripts develop and grow through experiential learning, which when co-assembled with knowledge and understanding, become critical factors in shaping the formation of scripts; this in turn allows for greater complexity, and thus greater adaptability. The ability to organize and arrange sets of scenes and scripts, and to develop rules for managing these scenes and scripts, provide a higher and more effective level of affect-regulation. Unfortunately, many simpler and less complex scripts tend to be insufficient and therefore relatively ineffective in their management of scenes; this in turn limits their success in the regulation of affect and emotion.

There are a number of factors contributing to these limitations. Scripts operate as a regulatory system that essentially weighs both the costs and benefits necessary for adaptation. Remember that the prescriptive goals that guide scripts cannot be completely fulfilled, since positive affects cannot always be maximized, nor can negative affects always be minimized, nor can affects always be expressed. To cope best, in very difficult situations, requires one to compromise the benefits gained from positive affect by allowing the costs incurred by negative affect; for example, a socially anxious person may be willing to suffer through the anxiety of an interview in order to get a job. In fact, the process of learning very often operates in a cost-benefit context that entails the endurance of distress for the reward of knowledge.

Scripts are incomplete because they are always changing and thus do not have all the information necessary to optimally adapt to changing situations. This lack of completeness will lead to inaccuracies that speak to the insufficiencies of scripts as optimal affect regulators. Scripts also tend to be (indirectly) self-validating and thus self-sustaining; for example, the passive-aggressive script will validate and maintain the shame and anger that comprises it.

That scripts are insufficient regulators of affect-scenes certainly sounds disheartening. Are we doomed to a life of constant sorrow and suffering? Not necessarily. First, scripts do vary as to the degree of imperfection so that there is a continuum from least to most negative. And there is room for optimism, since a class of scripts called *affluence scripts* can develop. Moreover, optimizing scripts are governed by higher ratios of positive to negative affect. Optimism, equanimity, altruism, fulfillment, happiness, love and success are examples of affluence scripts. These scripts enhance the self and represent self-agency scripts that are essential for the integrated state of the self, and ultimately for the attainment of wellbeing.

The Formation and Structure of Scripts

The emergence of scripts, like any developmental system, is a bottom-up process based on increasing levels of complexity. As discussed earlier, scripts are analogs of scenes that are formed from affect. Although scripts are highly magnified analogs of affect, they retain many of the properties of their underlying affect. This provides scripts with an inside track for regulating affect.

Some basic similarities between affects and scripts, which will subsequently become clearer, are as follows. Just as affects compete for urgency and salience, so do scripts Just as affects amplify their activators, so scripts will make a good scene better or a bad scene worse. Just as affects coassemble or fuse with each other, so can scripts coassemble through their capacity for modularity, whereby sets of subscripts can form into a more complex *interscript* script; for example, a shame-script can connect an anger-script with a disgust-script. An affect is analogically based on the pattern analysis of its activating stimulus, while a script is based on the analogically patterned assembly of its subscripts, each of which resembles each other as based on their patterns of coassembled families of scenes (Diagrams 5.1 and 5.2). And finally, just as affect-amplification can enhance the magnification of a script, so the magnification of a script can amplify its embedded affects.

As the basic unit of the brain is the neuron, the basic unit of a script is the scene. As neurons interconnect with other neurons to form neural networks, scenes coassemble with other scenes to form networks or families of scenes. As networks of neurons coalesce to form the anatomical structures of the brain, networks of coassembled scenes come to form the mini-scripts and subscripts that make up script. Like the brain, scripts act as the overseer and governor of functioning. As it develops and evolves bottom-up, it functions top-down. As scenes are directly affect based, scripts are cognitively based rules that govern, at prefrontal and complex levels, how we interpret, evaluate, predict, and control events.

The formation and structure of scripts is bottom-up and hierarchical, and reflects the dynamics of self-organizing complexity (by way of the analog principle). Complexity is an emerging process that proceeds from a relatively simple organized system to a relatively complex organized system. It is relative because what was once complex becomes simpler in relationship to an even higher-ordered complex script.

Scripts develop from simple inscripted scenes to a complex general script. A scene is essentially a specific *event→response* action sequence. Scenes vary from simple inscripted scenes, to learned complex scenes. At birth, and soon thereafter, the scene is inscripted. Although inscripts are innate and universally fixed for each infant, the affect scene itself will be different for each infant as based on his/her parenting experiences and inborn temperament. One newborn may have relatively high affect sensitivity and inscripted reactivity levels as compared to another infant. In addition, scenes are activated in a given context, which is never exactly the same, not only among different people but for the same person as well. Thus, from birth (if not in utero) each scene will be experienced differently.

In a matter of several weeks to a few months, these scenes begin to change as the newborn begins to retain and store new experiences into implicit, primary memory. Now a history, albeit short, is developing; so too is the ability to anticipate what might happen. Adding to the complexity of these scenes is the nature of the relationship between infant and mother, as exemplified by the Ainsworth studies. A scene with a distressed mother, whose tension level is high and prolonged, will provide a very different experience for an infant than one whose distressed mother has less tension and is able to calm herself down more quickly.

Not only is each infant exposed to a mother with differing intensities and durations of distress, but to a mother whose response to stress may differ as well; thus, each mother has a different affect-regulation script that impacts greatly on the scene the infant is experiencing. A distressed mother, who experiences prolonged distress, may become angrier or more lethargic than the mother whose script is to engage with the infant and thus relieve the distress that newborn is experiencing. We must also include the impact of the infant on the mother; the uninhibited and highly sensitized newborn will influence the stress level of the distressed mother differently than will the relatively calm baby.

We can add many other factors that will further compound the experiences of a given scene. In this respect, a scene takes on meaning within the multi-dimensional context in which it is happening. Contextualizing a scene significantly transforms the relatively simple inscripted affect-scene into ever-increasing levels of complex-scenes. Increasingly, complex-scenes require increasingly complex-scripts to manage and regulate their affects. As cognition, emotion and behavior increase in complexity, so too does the evolving scene.

Scripts are essential in managing the coherency necessary for adapting to changing environments. As the component scenes that make up a script become more complex, their efficacy toward adaptation increases. Scripts evolve from their inscripted protoscripts; for example, the shame inscript is to hide in order to reduce the shame, while the enjoyment script is to maintain contact with its source so as to increase the enjoyment. Thus, positive inscripts increase their positive affects, while negative inscripts decrease their negative affects.

Soon after birth these inscripts develop into learned *affect-scripts* which function to directly manage and control scenes. As scenes coassemble, they become more complex as they change from the automatic shame-and-hide script to a slightly more complex shame-and-avoid, or shame-and-escape, script. To avoid or escape will be more successful at reducing shame than just closing one's eyes or covering up one's eyes and turning away. If these affect-scripts fail to reduce shame sufficiently, the shame script may become a shame-anger script characterized by a shame-and-attack sequence. Now we move beyond the simple affect script, which uses detachment strategies for hiding, escaping or avoiding, to a more complex strategy that combines one affect script with another affect script. Now begins the development of ever-emerging complex scripts.

The formation and structure of a script is hierarchical. As earlier outlined, a *script* is made up of *subscripts* that are made up of *mini-scripts* that in turn are made up of *scenes*. A child with a fear script has likely experienced many fear-terror scenes that form into fearful mini-scripts and subscripts that come to make up a fear script.

The self represents an overarching general script. As you will note in Diagram 5-1 below, script formation is hierarchical. The basic unit consists of individual scenes, which then coalesce into families of scenes that are bound together by their common affect. When families of scenes combine, as based not only on their affect, but also by the similarity of their rules and organizational structure, they form a subscript. As subscripts co-assemble to form scripts, scripts co-assemble to form the general script we call the self.

Scripts are relatively consistent and predictable patterns of thoughts, feelings and behavior. Since these functions are bound together by their affect, they represent a structure that is definable; however, this hierarchical structure is not fixed, but is always changing; for example, the structure of an office building will change when there are changes in its foundation.

Diagram 5-1 The Self
Robert Kayton

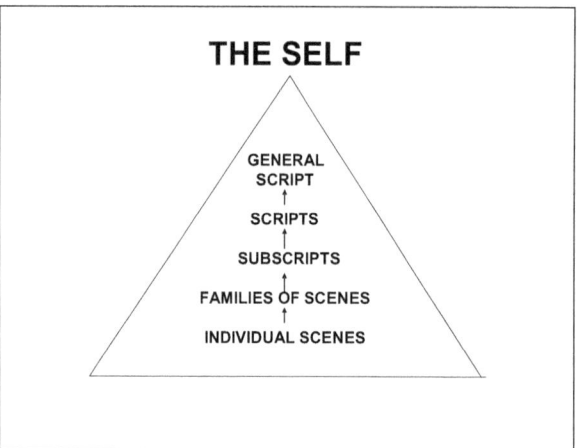

This applies to the structure of a script as well, which will change when the underlying coassembly of scenes changes. This bottom-up process of ongoing change also applies to changes in which simpler scripts become more complex scripts; thus, when subscripts change, the overall general script will change as well; as a consequence, scripts get re-structured when subscripts get re-ordered.

Often a given script will act more like a subscript in a given context, while a subscript may instead function as a script in another context. Scripts can be seen in a modular framework, whereby moving one part in relation to another, will change the composition of the whole. For example, in Table 5-1, you will notice that there are three co-assembled scripts: shame, fear and anger.

These scripts differ in their constellation of subscripts, which is based on scripts that are the most salient and urgent (viz. that which has the greatest affect charge). This in turn depends on the many factors in which the event is contextualized.

Table 5-1 Reordering of Scripts

Reordering of Scripts

Situation A	Situation B	Situation C
Shame Script	Fear Script	Anger Script
Fear Subscript / Anger Subscript	Shame Subscript / Anger Subscript	Shame Subscript / Anger Subscript

For example, a shame script may become activated at a public event (A), in which fear or anger may instead act as subscripts; if the situation is private, shame may act as a subscript to the more dominant scripts of fear or anger. In situation (B) the context may be more threatening, say the potential loss of one's job, or more enraging if one feels they are being treated unfairly (C).

To continue the earlier example in the development of the distress-anguish affect script for the developing infant, let us follow the development of a depression script from a highly distressed mother, as illustrated in Diagram 5-2 on the next page. If this mother has a distress-anger script, she will display this on her face and through her bodily gestures. The infant, through mirror neurons, will internally replicate and experience her distress-anger. If frequent, intense, and prolonged, the distress-anger affect will become embodied in the muscle and skin tissue of the baby's body.

Diagram 5-2 Development of a Depressive Script

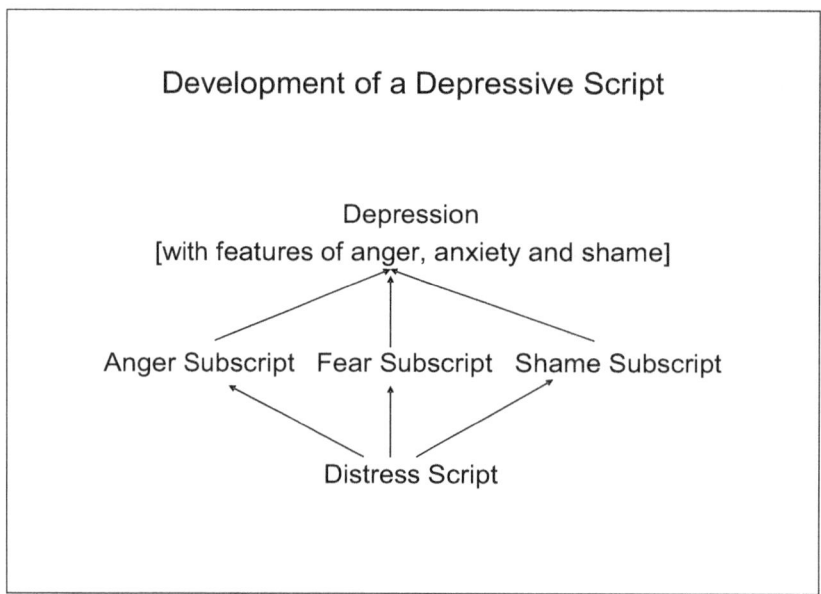

Soon, the infant will feel tense when mother simply enters the baby's room, or just hears her. Now these encoded and embodied visceral reactions have been learned and stored in the muscles and tissues of the body. We now have the beginnings of a distress script, one in which embodied cognitions lead to the primary emotions and behaviors culminating in a depression script.

When these reactions occur in anticipation of mother coming, we now have an anxiety script in which neural firings are increasing in their density and rate leading to a state of hyper-alertness. As visual and auditory memory develop, the young child can picture what may happen, and think about this happening in words and thoughts.

We now have greater complexity as these distressing, fearful and angry scenes begin to form schemas, images and preconceptions about the world of the angry mother. New affect scenes and subscripts, such as those involving attack-back anger, or hiding from mother as shame expressions are displayed. Like the nexus of neurons that form structures that magnify basic mental functions, so scripts will magnify its component subscripts and scenes from which they are embedded. Mental disorders can develop through the magnification of these affect-based scenes and scripts.

Types of Complex Scripts

There are many ways to classify scripts. At the basic level, we refer to positive and negative affect-scripts. Then we have co-assembled affect-scripts, such as shame-anger or distress-fear scripts, the named order indicating which script is more basic or dominant. At higher levels of complex scripts are those that regulate affect indirectly through various cost-benefit strategies. The most complex scripts are highly cognified and are made up of the fusion of multiple complex scripts; these are the self-scripts.

Some of you may be familiar with such pop-scripts as the child-parent-adult scripts, the dance-away lover script, the love-addiction script, the macho-man script, the imposter script, the commitment script (based on intimacy anxiety), impression management script, or the type-A script. In many respects, these labels encapsulate and type a person's personality style and provide a great deal of information about how that individual operates in life.

Ideoaffective Cost-benefit Scripts

Cost-benefit scripts are those characterized by maximizing payoff strategies in order to regulate affect. With the exception of the optimizing affluence scripts, all other cost-benefit scripts tend toward greater degrees of negative–to-positive ratios. Many of these cost-benefit scripts are mostly defensive scripts, based on inhibiting negative affect, often at the expense of activating or amplifying positive affect. These negative, defensive scripts act as subscripts to those scripts we classify as the mental disorders.

In traditional affect-script theory, there are five negative cost-benefit scripts: damage-repair, limitation-remediation scripts, contamination scripts, antitoxic scripts, and nuclear scripts.[44] The script that has the greatest relevance for emotional rescripting is the damage-repair script. It is the least negative and most likely script to be transformed into a positive affluence-script. It is also the most ubiquitous script, given its function as a social governor of interpersonal conflicts. The purpose of a damage-repair script is to repair the damage incurred by shame.

A very recognizable complex damage-repair script is represented by a sequence of shame-anger-guilt-rapprochement. In this familiar interpersonal dynamic, one person feels shamed by another, and consequently becomes angry as a defense. Then the shamed person attacks and shames the "shamer." Soon guilt (shame + fear) sets in when one of the players feels he went too far and may have irreparably threatened the relationship. He may then engage in a rapprochement-script to repair the damage. Mutual shaming underlies power struggles in which shame dominates the person who feels less powerful; in order to gain more power, one then shames and thus de-powers the other person.

The damage done in a damage-repair script can also be enacted internally through one's own inner dialogues. Many of these internal narratives consist of the self-as-protagonist, and the *other*-as-antagonist. In these musings, one seeks self-reparation by replaying the event as a victory rather than as a defeat, such as imagining oneself cleverly getting the upper hand over a sarcastic and critical boss.

Ideological Scripts

Cost-benefit scripts are technically called *ideoaffective scripts* because they are largely based on affects and emotions. At a more cognified level are *ideological scripts*.[45] These scripts are

---

[44] In brief, the most negative script is the *nuclear script*, which combines negative affects into a script that some describe as like a "metastasized cancer," or a "black hole." The *antitoxic script* is based exclusively on eliminating fear or anger through whatever means there is available and no matter the cost: this script makes up the addictive scripts. In a *contamination script* one tries to de-contaminate disgust scenes by bifurcating them into good *(uncontaminated)* or bad (contaminated). Obsessive-compulsive disorders are a good example of a contamination script. In the *limitation-remediation script* the goal is to limit negative distress scenes in the hope of transforming and remediating them into more positive affect scenes. These scripts attempt the optimizing strategy of *affluence scripts*, but fail to do so because negative affects get absorbed in this script as its cost. This script is emblematic of depression.

more highly organized complex scripts than are cost-benefit scripts. They relate to one's ideology, ones relatively coherent set of fundamental beliefs about the world and how to live in it. There are two basic bimodal ideologies, the *normative* and *humanistic*, which correspond in politics to conservative or liberal, right-leaning or left-leaning. There are, however, exceptions such as left-leaning conservatives and far-left liberals

An important postulate in humanistic ideology is that an individual person is the ultimate measure of value and worth, while for the normative worth is independent of the self and is instead determined by objective norms. In humanistic ideology people are inherently good, while for the normative the individual is inherently bad and must do some penitence to become good. For the humanist, the means used to attain a goal is valued, while the normative values the end result. The humanist values affect while the normative devalues affect. Humanists value play, novelty, risk, familiarity, freedom from fear, and allows anger and protest to be a right. Normatives value work and the norm, and use aggression, fear, shame, distress and contempt as punishment for norm violations. Humanists adhere to imagination, wish, and the maximizing of positive affect, while normatives adhere to discipline and authority. Humanists strive to minimize conflicts and differences, and to promote plurality in order to enhance positive affect and minimize negative affects. Normatives promote order, hierarchy and conformity so as to maximize "normal" behavior, and is indifferent to conflict unless serving the purpose of maintaining the norm. Humanists are tolerant and work toward ameliorating weaknesses, and tend to be nurturing and forgiving; normatives tend to be intolerant, punish weakness, and focus on toughness and perfection.

Normative thinking is mediated by the amygdala, while humanistic thinking takes place at the higher-level anterior cingulate-gyrus. Normative thinking is bimodal, all-or-none and is relatively concrete and fixed, while humanistic thinking is multi-faceted, abstract, diverse and adaptable. Normative thinking is parallel two-track thinking whereby ideas are bifurcated into either/or, black-or-white; this allows for contradictory thinking to take place that is conflict-free; for example, judging someone as bad means discounting what they do that is good, since that would conflict with bad-**or**-good thinking. Humanistic thinking considers ambiguity and processes information as good-**and**-bad, right-**and**-wrong.

These ideological scripts are relatively stable and fixed as compared to the more fluid ideoaffective, cost-benefit emotional scripts. As such they become part of complex self-scripts that come to form our personality and character. An example of self-scripts can be found in Eric Berne's identification of the Child, Parent and Adult roles in his landmark book *Games people play,* (1969), We shall discuss the self and its self-scripts in greater detail in Part 2, *The Integrated Self.*

Ideological scripts are overarching schemas that appear to operate at higher cognitive levels. However, there is accumulating evidence that these beliefs are also mediated at the lower levels of the brain. During political debates, neural imaging shows that the part of the brain most associated with reasoning, the dorsal lateral prefrontal cortex, was quiescent, while areas that deal with emotion (orbitofrontal cortex), conflict resolution (anterior cingulate gyrus), moral judgment (posterior cingulate gyrus) and reward and pleasure (striatum), were more active.

[ff] Taken from Tomkins Polarity Scale. George Lakoff (*Moral politics*, 2002), a cognitive neuroscientist and linguist, developed a cognitive formulation and child-rearing model that is very similar to Tomkins, yet was independently developed.

There are many factors leading to the development of one or the other ideological script. One proposal is that ideology evolved from our hunting-gathering society. Normative scripts are rooted in the hunters, whose society was stratified, exploitative, competitive, authoritarian, and oppressive. They were dominant, alpha members. On the other hand, humanists may have developed from the gatherers who were more egalitarian, communal, cooperative, and oppressed. They were submissive beta types.[46]

Recently, it has been postulated that ideology may be genetically inherited as a predisposition toward one or the other pole, although its fruition depends on a combination of childhood and later-life experiences, as well political, social and cultural influences. This tells us that environmental and genetic factors co-evolved, as based on their interconnection. Tomkins speaks of the *nature-nurture accord*, namely that nature gets actualized or modified by experience dependent learning (epigenetics), such as modeling, instruction and parental rewards or punishments.

Defensive Scripts[47]

Many of you are familiar with, or at least aware of, Freudian defense mechanisms. These defenses operate as scripts, and in particular, as cost-benefits scripts; for example, the benefit of *intellectualization* is that one will not have to experience negative emotions, while the cost may be an inability to develop intimate and emotionally-fulfilling relationships. When a defensive-script comes to characterize a person's personality, then that cost-benefit script has become a defensive self-script (see Chapter 7). As a defensive self-script, rather than a cost-benefit script, intellectualization is, for example, relatively fixed and generalized to the point that characterizes the way a person functions and is thereby considered a personality style; and as a personality style, intellectualization now comes to describe a person who is labeled as cerebral and intellectual, introverted and reserved.

These defensive scripts form to regulate negative affect, but unfortunately end up creating more negative affect. Many defense mechanisms are adaptive in the short-term, or were adaptive at one time or another; they become maladaptive when used regardless of the situation or circumstances.

Denial is used to disavow the presence of negative affect [*Pollyannaish denial* is to make the negative positive, while *counterphobic denial* is to do the opposite of what is feared]; *repression* acts to detach negative cognition from its associated negative affect; *isolation* and *intellectualization,* to detach the affect charge associated with a cognition by cognifying that affect; *projection* is to attribute ones feelings and thoughts (in terms of wishes or fears) onto another person; *sublimation,* is the channeling of ones charged affect into socially acceptable behaviors; *overcompensation,* acts to diminish negative affect by exaggerating opposing thoughts and behaviors; *negation* acts to disown ownership of a negative act or belief; I call negation a "confessional disclaimer" because one denies their intent even though the issue was never brought up by the other person; an example of

---

[46] Some anthropologists now argue that hunters may actually have been more egalitarian than were the gatherers.

[47] Like the changes made in the DSM, changes in the definition of defense mechanisms will change as well. The protocol that I was trained under (DSM II) dates to the 1960's and so my definitions will reflect how defenses were then generally defined.

negation is when a person states, "I don't mean to be critical of you but…" In addition to the unsolicited denial of criticism, is the use of a "yes-but" statement.

Defensive scripts can be adaptive for certain scenes, when employed in a judiciously selective way. In trauma, for example, repression or denial can initially be a healthy response; in fact, in trauma denial is the initial reaction and is based on the surprise-startle inscript that is quickly replaced with fear-terror. In trauma, one is suddenly inundated with stimuli and affect, which is so overwhelming that higher cortical functioning is truncated; thus, one may best adapt initially to the trauma by using simple denial. Denial can also prevent the consolidation of the traumatizing scene into long-term memory.

There are many other incidences where denial is adaptive, one being when one has to wait for the results of an academic or medical test; in these circumstances, worry unnecessarily prolongs the activation of negative affect and therefore promotes greater negative memories. If denial (or any defensive script) is dominant too long, a price will be paid when attention needs to be placed on the denied scene or subscript. For example, when a person is working in a chronically stressful job and yet maintains that it is tolerable (because of the reward it may lead to in the future), he or she may end up suffering from such problems as chronic fatigue syndrome, or act out this frustration with others that can both damage close relationships and sabotage work opportunities.

In situations that require complex executive functioning, such defenses as isolation and intellectualization may be very adaptive. Overcompensation, like counterphobic denial, can also be adaptive in some performance situations; it can aid survival in dangerous situations for which anger and attack behavior is more needed than fear and escape. Projection may help anticipate adaptively, although one needs to also be aware that one's assumptions are personalized projections so that alternative assumptions should be considered as well. In negation one admits to knowing what their intension was, albeit by denying its existence. Sublimation is different than other defensive scripts, since by definition it channels affects "into socially acceptable behavior;" it is a positive script.

Most often, however, defensive scripts become negative and maladaptive, and therefore will likely interfere with both one's functioning and one's sense of wellbeing; the integration of the self will be thwarted by the dissociative and disintegrative nature of negative scripts. When defensive scripts lose their efficacy, yet are still maintained, they will worsen because of their inefficiency (needing more energy to maintain itself), and develop into a fixed and negative (defensive) self-script that ultimately could develop into a pathological self-script, namely a mental disorder.

Often these defensive self-scripts evolve from defensive subscripts. For example, *reaction formation* is a script in which one not only *does* the opposite, as in counterphobic denial, but also *becomes the opposite* by incorporating oppositional behavior into the self; as such, a reaction formation script can evolve from defensive subscripts like counterphobic denial or overcompensation. Other examples include some of the personality disorders such as Obsessive-Compulsive Personality Disorder or Paranoid Personality Disorder, whereby *isolation* of affect and *projection* become fixed into the person's character structure.

Diagnostic Scripts

Mental health disorders can be thought of as maladaptive scripts. Rather than following the prescripts to amplify positive affect and inhibit negative affect, as well as to magnify positive scripts and minimize negative scripts, they instead do the opposite by increasing negative affect-scripts and decreasing positive affect-scripts. The treatment strategies for each will be mentioned in this section; a full discussion of each will be discussed in the next chapter on function-focused rescripting.

Depressive disorders are based on distress-anguish scripts, which dampens both enjoyment-joy as evidenced by the absence of pleasure in anhedonia, and interest-excitement as seen in the indifference of apathy. When parasympathetic inhibition dominates, the depressed condition is that of a *vegetative state*; when sympathetic excitation dominates, one may then be in a *manic state*; and when each state is of equal strength, one may then succumb to the tension of an *agitated state*. The treatment is to (a) reduce the distress while increasing enjoyment and interest; (b) develop realistic beliefs and expectations; and (c) engage in assertive pro-active behaviors. Bipolar Disorders are combinations of distress and excitement; the goal is to inhibit negative scripts and excite positive scripts, except for mania in which we work to diminish interest-excitement.

Anxiety Disorders are primarily based on scripts derived from fear-terror. The different types of anxiety disorders vary according to their source. Panic Disorders are characterized by startle, followed by terror, whose source are the symptoms themselves, such as the rapid heartbeat, difficulty in breathing, and profuse sweating. Panic differs from anxiety in that the former is primary and subcortical and is essentially a startle-terror "affective" biological disorder, without anticipatory fears; when anticipation enters the picture, a panic attack becomes more of an anxiety attack, triggered not only by biological affective sensations, but by cognition as well. For pure panic attacks, behavioral strategies work best; when cognition enters the picture, then a combination of cognitive-behavioral techniques is recommended.

Post-Traumatic Stress Disorder (PTSD) is also a startle-terror script that clearly supports the idea that an affect or script will amplify or magnify its activator- i.e. PTSD will reactivate and even intensify the original traumatic scene. Like panic disorders, PTSD is largely amygdaloidal and is thus more responsive to behavioral approaches, especially exposure-desensitization. PTSD also represents a dissociated condition whereby the traumatic scene becomes detached from the scenes and scripts that make up its self-script.

Specific Phobias are fears related to specific objects, places or things. Social phobias are scripts often characterized by the anticipatory fear of being shamed. Both are cognitively processed so that the symptoms are emotional and based on anticipatory cognitions. Obsessive-Compulsive Disorder (OCD) is based on the combination of fear-terror scripts with disgust/dissmell scripts. These may include *contamination-scripts*, when cleanliness or dirty thoughts need to be controlled. The behavioral approach of exposure/response prevention is the principal technique used. Generalized anxiety disorders are scripts of anticipation; the worrying characteristic of this disorder entails fear, although there may also be distress scripts evident.

Chapter 6: Function-Focused Rescripting[48]

Function-Focused Rescripting is a structured, strategic, top-down approach whose primary purpose is to expeditiously regulate affect, first through body-focused rescripting, then through the restructuring of negative cognitions and emotions, and finally to the modification of negative behaviors. By changing these components, we change a given scene, and by changing the scene(s), we change the script. Our principle and targeted goal is to modify the affect charge, since by doing so, the very nature of a scene changes. All things being equal, this change can then reverberate throughout the hierarchy of script formation and thereby alter the very structure of higher-ordered complex scripts. As negative scenes begin to dissipate, not only will the negative affect-scripts diminish, but higher ordered cost-benefit defensive scripts will lessen as well. Taking this even further, we can assume that higher-level self-scripts will become more positive and thus more amenable to integration.

Paradoxically, as we work top-down we set the stage for bottom-up emergence. As simple affect-scripts evolve into higher-ordered complex self-scripts, we are speaking of changing multiple affect scenes and scripts. As we continuously minimize negative affect-scenes, essentially by inhibiting the negative affect associated with given events, we are changing the fundamental components that make up a script and therefore promoting bottom-up emergence. By reordering and changing scenes that make up the foundation of scripts, we ultimately change the evolving hierarchy of scripts through the dynamics of *self-organizing complexity*.

Self-organizing complexity is a theory covering the dynamics of almost everything, from the universe, to evolution, and to the development and evolution of the self. Its application toward understanding the emergence and integration of the rescripted self is to understand how integration takes place through the activity inherent in self-organizing complexity. We will examine this theory in Section B on integrating the emergent self through bottom-up rescripting; top-down rescripting is the basis for new learning and for the development of the functioning self, while bottom-up rescripting is the basis for integrating the emerging self.

To function competently in life means that a person is successful in his or her personal relationships, career, and personal wellness, especially health and play. Some people do well in one or two areas of life, others in none, yet still others in all three; however, just because someone functions well in all three areas, does not mean that that person feels a sense of wellbeing; although to function well is a necessary means for developing wellbeing and happiness, it is nonetheless insufficient; it is the integration of the self that is both the necessary and sufficient factors for wellbeing.

Successful functioning requires that affects be successfully regulated, thus allowing higher and more complex levels of the mind and brain to exert greater executive control over lower levels. Optimal functioning also necessitates good communication between these different centers. Our goal, in terms of affect-regulation, is to excite positive affect, inhibit negative affect, and express both negative and positive affect in adaptive ways. The balancing of excitation and inhibition underlies the process of affect-regulation. Rescripting is my method for changing the negative to the positive, the dysfunctional to the functional, and the maladaptive to the adaptive.

---

[48] I would recommend the reader examine the workbooks listed in the references. These present many excellent self-help techniques.

How is this achieved? It is generally considered that the natural progression in evolutionary development is toward adaptive functioning, unless otherwise interfered with by genetic deficiencies, or experiences and events that interfere with optimal learning.[49] Some call this Eros,[50] life's *energy force*, namely that intrinsic to life is the urge to live, and the better one lives the more likely one will continue to live; without this dynamism, life would cease to be. Devolution is the opposite of evolution and is characterized by the many problems in living that interfere with the genetically programmed tendency toward progression. These factors may be physical or psychosocial, and if the latter, it is learned and thus can then be unlearned. Unlearning entails what we call desensitization, or extinction, while learning involves encoding, storing, and consolidating new coping strategies into long-term memory.

Affect-regulation, as the underlying dynamic in functioning, can best be understood along the excitation-inhibition polarity. This simple rule of thumb follows the dictum to do the opposite of the affective urge, and prescribes that when affects are excited to an unhealthy level we use inhibitory techniques, whereas when affects are overly inhibited, we use excitatory techniques; the goal is the "excitation-inhibition balance." When we look at such excitatory affects as fear-terror, surprise-startle and interest-excitement, relaxation is used to inhibit the degree of arousal. With the inhibitory affects of shame-humiliation and enjoyment-joy, we then use excitatory techniques. For affects that are both inhibitory and excitatory, such as distress-anguish and anger-rage, we will use a combination of relaxation and excitation techniques to break the antagonistic bind, especially when agitation dominates; when a vegetative state is dominant, excitation approaches are most efficacious. Relaxation and inhibition are *the* interventions of choice for anger-rage.

There is a major exception to this rule of regulating affect through combinations of inhibition and excitation. The alternative mode to improve functioning is to excite negative affect until it habituates. This is called *affect-tolerance training*. Habituation is how the brain and mind desensitize when overly sensitized. We all know the advice to face our fears, meaning that we need to emotionally experience an affect, rather than inhibit it through denial and avoidance. The technique of choice in tolerance training is called *exposure/response prevention*, in which a person subjects himself or herself to the negative event until the negative affect subsides. In most cases of fear, this is the strategy of choice, although its efficacy with other affects is more tenuous. We shall discuss this further in the coming chapters.

When such coping skills are learned, encoded and stored, our next goal is to consolidate them into long-term memory. Now the focus shifts from learning to practicing, and practicing, and more practicing. Practice is the basis for storing and consolidating information, and ultimately for integrating these proactive skills into the core structures of the brain and mind. We will now look at rescripting the four primary components of a scene, namely affects, cognition, emotion and behavior.

---

[49] This is reflected in psychotherapy, where we search for historical and situational factors that lead to disturbances in functioning.

[50] Freud believed that opposed to Eros was Thanatos, the anti-life forces. In affect-rescripting terms this means that we all have both positive scripts and negative scripts and that life is a battle between Life or Death.

Rescripting Affects

Affects consist of patterns of bodily sensations and reactions that are activated by neurological patterns in the brain. When working on affect-focused rescripting, we are working directly on the body, not the mind or behavior. In particular, our focus will be on the Autonomic Nervous System, which is responsible for most of our physical symptoms, as well as bodily expressions that give us the felt-feel of our affects. For example, in fear-terror, there is sympathetic-arousal that increases heart rate, body temperature, and muscle constriction. When this is displayed in the face and body, we feel its discomfort, if not the pain experienced with fear-terror.

In Chapter 1 we reviewed some of the major features of affects. For example, affect is the basis for motivation; thus, reducing negative affect will reduce negative motivation, while increasing positive affect will increase positive motivation. Affects connect an event to our reactions; reducing negative affect reduces this connection, while increasing positive affect will increase positive reactions. Affect expression gives us the feel of an affect; by lessening negative expressions we lessen these negative feelings, while increasing positive expressions will increase positive feelings. Affects communicate information about oneself to oneself and to others.

Affects are also necessary for consciousness; in this respect when we inhibit awareness of negative affect we feel better; however we must not do so at the expense of higher and more complex cognition, which may depend on our awareness and experience of a negative affect in order to change a negative affect-script into one that serves adaptation; for example, if disgust or fear is activated by a loved one, but is denied or rationalized away, then one is deprived of the information that comes with those feelings that may become very costly in the future.

There are several principles related to the interactions between and among affects that are important in using affect-focused rescripting techniques. For example, the activation and amplification of one affect can reciprocally inhibit, activate or amplify other affects. In addition, the speed, magnitude or aggregate amount of change in one affect will proportionally modify and influence the degree of change in other affects. Thus, we can work on affect-regulation by regulating reciprocal affects. For example, to calm anger-rage we can activate enjoyment-joy, or to inhibit fear-terror we can activate interest-excitement.

I used this excitation-inhibition regulatory principle with a patient of mine. She was very worried about being too dependent on marijuana. She understood that once started she could not stop because, "I could not tolerate the feeling of 'coming down';" thus the need for more. I pointed out that this was usually the case. I suggested that she up-the-down by becoming more active, just as she needed to down-the-up by slowing down when too high.

Another principle is that the reduction of any negative affect is rewarding and will likely activate a positive affect. This speaks to the need to work toward minimizing negative affect, since doing so will likely activate positive affect. On the other side of that coin, the interruption and reduction of any positive affect is punishing and will probably activate a negative affect; shame, for example, is based on the interference of positive affect. Our goal therefore is to not only activate positive affect, but to maintain its activation as long as possible.

Another important maxim is that the ratio between or among affects is more significant than the level of any singular affect. We saw this in our example of risk taking: when fear is proportionately greater than excitement, we find less risk taking than when excitement is greater than fear. This tells us that we can influence our decisions by regulating these affects toward one or the other behavior. Although we typically think of risk-taking as bad, we should remember that not taking risks can also lead to adverse consequences; to avoid a job interview because of anxiety means one does not get that job; thus, whether to take a chance or not depends on the context and situation.

Another affect principle states that when two or more affects compete for amplification that which is most salient, urgent and intense will win out. In the risk-taking example, saliency can be dealt with at the emotional level, while urgency focuses more on regulating these two corresponding affects such as fear-terror vs. interest-excitement. Intensity relates to the rate and density of neural firings that is modified by increasing or decreasing the neural firings of one-or-another affect.

Finally, there are several maxims related to affect energy dynamics. For example: the amplification of an affect expends energy metabolically; the longer the affect duration the greater the energy cost; affect profile gradients expend energy according to their steepness and direction. The expenditure of energy will dissipate an affect, while conservation will maintain an affect; since fear-terror is metabolically very high, it will tend to lose its energy relatively quickly, while distress-anguish and anger-rage are more energy efficient and thus its duration will be longer.

What we call psychiatric symptoms is most often related to unregulated affect (although personality disorders entail the over-regulation of affects). The overall treatment strategy is to use relaxation and inhibition techniques with sympathetic arousal affects of increasing neural firings, and to use excitatory and arousal techniques when parasympathetic inhibition dominates. In addition, the feel of an affect is encoded in its expression; therefore, we work to change the expression of negative affects and enhance the expression of positive affects.

In addition to decreasing negative affect and increasing positive affect, another important strategy is to increase our ability to tolerate negative affect; increasing the tolerance level for negative affect will help expand our comfort zone. Another fundamental strategy is to do the opposite of the urge;[51] basically this is a behavioral exposure technique that will then act as a correction factor. The paradoxical maxim to do the opposite should, of course, be flexible and utilized appropriately so as to maximize optimal functioning.

Before we discuss the various affect-focused techniques, it is important to consider that psychotropic medications represent a chemical treatment for optimizing affect-regulation. That is what medication management is all about, namely to give an upper when one is way down, and to give a calmer when too far up; this strategy follows the excitation-inhibition principle.

Table 6-1 on the next page lists seven affect-focused techniques that can be used to control and manage one's affects.

---

[51] First proposed by Viktor Frankl in his existential therapy approach he called *logotherapy*.

Table 6-1 Affect-Focused Rescripting Techniques

Affect-Focused Rescripting Techniques

1. Affect Recognition Training
2. Systematic Body Focusing
3. Muscle Relaxation Training
4. Autogenic Relaxation
5. Affect Expression Modification
6. Distraction

1. Affect Recognition Training

It is important to first recognize, characterize, and quantify your affect. For example, people often mistake distress, or even excitement, as anxiety. It is important to identify which affect you are experiencing, attend to their qualitative differences, and quantify the intensity of that affect, such as using a SUDS scale (Subjective Units of Disturbance Scale) of 1-7 (or 1-10) so as to rate the intensity of your emotion.

It is recommended that you frequently and regularly practice identifying the affect being experienced, and then rate its intensity level on the SUDS scale. This will not only enhance your awareness of that affect, but also help identify whether its intensity is increasing or decreasing. Conscious awareness is, of course, the necessary and essential element for intervention and regulation.

The "Affect Recognition Worksheet" [Appendix 1] can be used a guide. It should be filled out at least three times a day and whenever you become aware of an affect or emotion. Remember, the focus is on your body and not what is in your head. Hopefully you will get into the habit of checking your affective and emotional levels so as to increase your awareness of what your body is telling you. We know, for example, that people who are unaware of their bodily sensations and feelings run the risk, not only of making poor judgments, but the risk of such diseases as hypertension.

2. Interoceptive Body Focusing[52]

Body focusing not only enhances affect recognition, but is also used as a method for affect-regulation. The goal is to focus inwardly on a specific set of interoceptive bodily sensations, namely the affect itself, and hold onto this focus. You can place yourself in situations that activate such negative emotions as fear or shame, (*in-vivo exposure*), or activate these sensations in artificial settings (*in-vitro exposure*), such as in your home, by imaging a negative event, or by engaging in some activity that will trigger these negative sensations. Because you do not have to go out and face the real situation, it offers an intervening, and consequently less threatening, desensitization opportunity; ultimately, however, you will need to face the real situation.

---

[52] There has been a plethora of studies using fMRI's which demonstrates that when you focus your attention on a body part, or for that matter an image, the corresponding area in the brain will be activated.

In-vitro desensitization is most often used with panic disorders whereby sympathetic symptoms of panic are directly induced, the goal being habituation-extinction and/or the increased tolerance for these excitatory symptoms. For example, you could accelerate your heart rate by running up-and-down a staircase or simply jog while standing stationary; dizziness can be activated by spinning around on a swivel chair; labored breathing, by breathing hard through a straw. By so doing you are "getting used to" and habituating to these symptoms, thereby gaining greater affect tolerance; it is important to focus on these sensations as they are occurring so as to truly desensitize rather than avoid attending to them; it is of course imperative that you be medically fit to safely engage in this activity.

As discussed earlier your brain has a relatively good map of your body [see Appendix 17], which can improve your ability to identify an affect, especially since affects are composed of patterns of physical sensations. As you focus your attention on these body parts and their sensations, they will intensify because its affect is amplifying as you concentrate on them. As you continue to focus on these symptoms they will begin to habituate as their neural firings begin decreasing; this diminishment of firings will innately activate enjoyment-joy.

If you believe you can no longer stand the intensity of these sensations, you can instead modulate its intensity by refocusing your attention away from your body and begin using the relaxation and calming techniques we will discuss next; you should continue this until the affect subsides to a tolerable level; in this situation, it is best to determine the highest level you can tolerate. The goal is to then extend this tolerance level training to a greater intensity level, or increase its duration. This approach is called *graduated desensitization,* since increasing your tolerance level is done step-by-step; for example, if your highest tolerable SUDS level is 7, you continue exposure to say a level of 8, and so forth, until you could stand a 10; I am not suggesting that you will come to enjoy the sensations, but better tolerate them. Actually, what is taking place is that the scale itself will begin to recalibrate, so that what was once a 10 becomes a 5 or 6. [See Graduated Desensitization Worksheet in Appendix 2]

The basic principle underlying affect-focusing tolerance techniques is that the higher the amplification of an affect, the greater and steeper will be its diminution. This is partly due to the greater energy cost expended as an affect continues to increase in intensity. In addition, there is a reciprocal interaction between competing affects; for example, the greater the degree of fear-terror, the greater will be the amount of enjoyment-joy that follows as one habituates and relaxes.

There is another body focusing technique that adds a cognitive component to it that is called *systematic body focusing*. As you maintain your focus on your affective sensations, you are to then hold this attention until an image comes to mind; do not force yourself to find an image, just let it come to you. By attending to your affective sensations, an analogical image, that is a mental representation of that affect, is often brought into consciousness as the sensations are cognified. This will provide you with valuable information about what thoughts and beliefs are associated with your affect, and give you the added opportunity to utilize cognitive and emotional strategies as well. By so doing you will have far more tools to work with. Thus, body focusing helps make the implicit explicit, thereby providing higher-level cognition to better regulate affects.

3. Muscle Relaxation Training:

Diaphragmatic Breathing (DB) and Progressive Muscle Relaxation (PMR) are two of the most commonly employed muscle relaxation methods. They are most useful for the steady and level affects of distress-anguish and anger-rage, as well as the increasing levels of fear-terror and interest-excitement. For both DB and PMR, you begin by first tightening your muscles, then holding onto this tension for a few seconds, followed by a rapid and complete release of this tension. In the first step, there is an increasing rate of sympathetic arousal; as you maintain this tension, there will be an increase in both the affect density and the rate of firing, so that when you completely release this tension, there is a corresponding decrease in its rate and density, leading to the affect enjoyment-joy. Remember that the greater the amount of change in one affect will proportionally modify the amount of change in its reciprocal affect, so that the greater the tension and faster its release, the greater will be the amount of enjoyment-joy

In general, relaxation is counter-indicated for the vegetative state of depression (distress-anguish), and is best done during the sympathetic dominant state of agitation. In addition, relaxation is also useful in fear-terror, anger-rage, and interest-excitement [For instructions on Diaphragmatic Breathing and Progressive Muscle Relaxation see Appendices 3 & 4]

4. Autogenic Relaxation

In autogenic relaxation, you begin by focusing on your body, or on a pleasant image, as you describe the relaxing "felt-feel" of your body in calming self-talk. For example, while focusing on your jaw, you might say *my jaw is loosening up,"* and when your focus on your stomach say, *"my stomach is warm and soothing*. Obviously, this induces the *enjoyment-joy* affect. [A full worksheet on autogenic relaxation is presented in Appendix 5]

5. Affect Expression Modification:[53]

This approach focuses on either intensifying or inhibiting an affective experience through body sculpting, posturing, or facial and voice changes. This affect modification approach is based on the principle of reciprocal-affect-inhibition, whereby activating one affect will inhibit another. It also reflects the analog principle: affects of increasing rates of neural firings will be characterized by increasing rates of motor activity; while the affect with decreasing levels of neural firings (enjoyment-joy) will be characterized by decreasing levels of activity; finally, affects with steady rates and densities of neural firings will be characterized by pressured and tense neuromuscular experiences. Thus, by assuming the musculature of anger-rage, you can reciprocally inhibit shame-humiliation or fear-terror. By talking slowly, softly, and rhythmically you can induce enjoyment-joy, or by talking quickly, intensely and loudly you can activate interest-excitement. In a well-known study by psychologist Paul Ekman (2003), it was demonstrated that practicing a "genuine" smile (which is as much expressed by the gleam in one's eyes, as by the upturned mouth) will activate enjoyment-joy and decrease depression. This fits the theory that expressions not only reflect affect, but simultaneously gives us the "felt-feel" of that affect. Thus, you can change your mind and change your feelings by changing your physical expressions. (We will later discuss this as the "as-if" approach)

---

[53] This approach essentially follows the integrative technique to do the "opposite of the urge."

Some specific examples of counter-expressions for the major affects are as follows: In fear-terror, work to change your stiff and tense posture and musculature to one that is relaxed or engaged; your voice should be lowered and the energy level less frenetic. In distress-anguish you will want to employ the affect displays associated with enjoyment-joy, unless there is a great deal of agitation, then it is often best to implement the expressions of interest-excitement. Anger-rage is best countered by enjoyment-joy expressions, while shame-humiliation is best reduced by interest-excitement or anger-rage. Disgust/dissmell is best dealt with by leaning toward the aversive source, by relaxing and smiling, by altering the curled lips found in the sneer, and by speaking in a modulated voice. Such simple counter-expressions can have surprisingly fast and effective corrective qualities.

6. Distraction

Distraction involves the re-focusing of your attention, both affectively and cognitively. We will discuss the latter under cognitive refocusing later, so here we will just look at the former. Many of us affectively re-focus naturally, as when we tighten our biceps in preparation of an injection by a dentist, or by scratching the surrounding skin tissue to ease an itch. Thus, when you recognize the bodily locus of an affect, you can then shift your attention to a part of the body that feels pleasant, and just maintain that focus. To help locate and concentrate on a part of your body you can just touch it and then maintain the felt-feel experience of that touch when you withdraw your finger. For those of you who can do this well, you might then try to mentally transfer and replace the negative sensation with the transposed pleasant sensation. This is a well-known hypnosis technique used for pain control.

Rescripting Cognition

Both topographically and developmentally, the structure of cognition exists at the primary, secondary and complex levels. When primary or *early secondary* thinking dominates, our thinking will be more irrational. In the development of cognition, these earlier levels were age appropriate; a four-year-old needed some degree of unrealistic thinking, such as fantasy, in order to soothe and regulate his or her affect. In addition, reality at this age is very different than for an adult. The child is relatively helpless, vulnerable, and dependent and must actively adapt to his world. His world is rigidly and concretely seen as black-or-white, which will be experienced this way until abstract thinking emerges at about eight years of age; in addition, with negative affect triggered, so will negative cognition be more pronounced. In addition, distress, frustration, fear and anger are more likely to get a parent's attention than positive affect, and thus be reinforced.

Affects not only shape our thoughts, but also supply the fuel that makes our beliefs seem more valid and powerful; some call these cognitions *hot.* Since early secondary cognition is still highly affect laden, so too are the fundamental schemas from which a child's beliefs, expectations and perceptual styles develop. This is an essential point when working to change beliefs, namely to also work with the underlying affect. Remember, although an affect will trigger cognition, cognition in turn will amplify its triggering affect; the emotional component is as much cognitive as it is affective. The more intense the emotional feel, the greater the affect (and consequently the validity of cognition), whereas the more complex the emotion, the more it is cognified.

Schemas are the basic cognified blueprint that shapes our developing beliefs, expectations and styles of thinking. They analogically evolved from the innate affects and got shaped by early experience-dependent learning. Consequently, schemas co-evolved with the development of primary cognition, which then came to dominate early secondary thinking.

A schema is defined as "an outlook or assumption that an individual has of their self, others, or the world, that endures despite objective reality." (APA Dictionary) Although encoded in both preverbal and embodied (affect-laden) images, we can identify seven primary schematic extrapolations, as listed in Table 6-2 on the next page.

Table 6-2 Primary Affective Schemas
Robert Kayton

Primary Affective Schemas

- Distress-Anguish: *Too much pressure*
- Anger-Rage: *Attack to protect myself; The World is Unfair*
- Fear-Terror: *Future is threatening*
- Shame-Humiliation: *Self is bad, incompetent, inferior*
- Disgust/Dissmell: *I/another is loathsome, obnoxious*
- Interest-Excitement: *This is challenging or creative*
- Enjoyment-Joy: *This is pleasant, comforting, satisfying, funny*

As you look at this list, try and identify if one or several of these schemas represent ways in which you find yourself frequently thinking; this will tell you which affect tends to dominate. Since these are direct cognifications of affect, you can apply some of the cognitive techniques we will be discussing to augment the affect-focused techniques already covered.

These primary schemas get transformed into secondary cognition, which makes up the core beliefs we have about our self, about others, and about the world we live in. Since these core beliefs develop early in life, when brain development is still largely dominated by lower level processing, reality is perceived in self-referential, concrete, and affect-charged styles of perception. Cognitive theory describes these assumptions and expectations as irrational, and their cognitive style as largely defensive and distorted. Not only is such thinking unrealistic, but there is a notable absence in critical thinking. In critical thinking, judgment, problem-solving, and decision-making are logical and evidence-based. When these early secondary modes of thinking come to dominate an adult's perception of the world, they become highly maladaptive. Cognitive-focused rescripting works to minimize these negative cognitions, and replace them with realistic thoughts that are both positive and adaptive. [See "Defensive Beliefs" in Appendix 6]

In addition to these negative beliefs and expectations, there are a number of maladaptive styles of thinking. These are presented in the "Maladaptive Styles of Thinking" questionnaire in Appendix 7.[54] These often characterize a thinking style that distorts reality through the filter of cognitive dissonance, a.k.a. compliance bias.

---

[54] Taken from Aaron Beck and outlined by his protégé, David Burns. Many consider Beck and Albert Ellis to be the founders of cognitive therapy.

Absolutistic thinking is a rigid, fixed, bi-modal, and compulsively driven mode of thinking. Many of the *general beliefs* we hold also fit into this category. For example, to be loved and accepted unconditionally or to be perfect and in control at all times, are absolutistic beliefs that illustrate an invariant thinking style. There are three types of absolutistic thinking: *imperative thinking* consists of the rules and exhortations contained in commands using such words as "*should*," "*must*," "*have to*," "*ought*," words that personify the unrealistic expectations someone has of herself or of others; *certaintistic thinking* relates to beliefs that are expressed as indisputable and irrefutable, with no room for alternative possibilities; these beliefs can be identified by the use of such words as "can't," "never," "always," "forever;" finally there is *dichotomous thinking*, which is characterized by polarized, either-or thinking, such as good or bad, right or wrong, for which there are no degrees of freedom and instead there is just one *or* the other.

The next category is *exaggerated thinking* in which issues are blown out of proportion. Among the categories of exaggerated thinking are: *catastrophizing*, which is predicting the worse possible outcome, a thinking style often found in anxiety; then there is *awfulizing*, that is taking the absolute worst possible perspective, a style most often found in depressive thinking; finally, there is *overgeneralizing*, of making blanket assumptions based on a singular event, e.g. "she did X... therefore all women do X." This is the thinking we find when we stereotype others.

The next category is *constricted thinking*. This style of thinking is the opposite of exaggeration because, rather than inflating an issue, it is instead significantly diminished in proportion to the whole. There are two types: *selective perception* in which the focus is only on one of many features, such as a minor error in an otherwise superb performance; the other is *minimization* in which there is discounting, negation or oversimplification of information so that things appear insignificant, e.g. "it was nothing."

Misattribution relates to falsely attributing the cause of some event. There are three types of misattribution: *personalization* takes place when someone takes what another person says or does, in a self-referential way as a statement about one's own character; *internalization* is a bit different and refers to taking and incorporating responsibility for some negative event; the agent is not the other person, but the self. Finally, there is *externalization* in which responsibility is blamed on others. Misattributions are among the leading causes of interpersonal conflicts.

The final category, *arbitrary inference,* relates to conclusions based on either illogical reasoning or inadequate data. There are several types that fit this classification: *magical* or *superstitious* thinking, as seen when we knock on wood after saying something, as though this act will protect us;[55] *emotional reasoning* is by definition an oxymoron, since reasoning is a function of cognition, and not of feelings;[56] *mind reading* is similar to misattributions since a person believes he or she knows what another person's motives or thinking are;[57] The final two forms of arbitrary inference include *fortune telling* and *labeling*; the former, akin to magical thinking, refers to the belief that one can know the future, while *labeling* is to brand

---

[55] Worrying is particularly subject to magical thinking, as we shall soon see.

[56] This does not mean that we ignore our emotions since they do send us important information that should be considered when we act; however, emotions are not rational and therefore our reasoning must rely on objective evidence.

[57] Neuroscientists sometimes publish articles on the "neuroscience of mind reading;" Unfortunately this gives readers the false impression that we could read another person's mind. Wrong! What they are actually referring to is the ability to effectively empathize with others. It more properly should be "the neuroscience of emotional attunement."

someone with an all-inclusive, and often pejorative descriptor, such as you're lazy, stupid, or a liar.

Cognitive therapy works to challenge, reframe and modify these irrational beliefs, expectations and styles of thinking. It is important to remember that these modes of thinking take place implicitly, are protective and defensive in nature, and were viable and adaptive during earlier stages of cognitive development; The idea that maladaptive thinking continues into adulthood, when no longer efficacious, speaks to its resiliency in terms of reinforcement. These modes of cognition are reflective of cost-benefit scripts whereby the gains from dysfunction are greater than its costs.

As an example, let's look at the tenacity and degree of superstitious thinking found among chronic worriers. Such thinking serves two primary purposes, to prepare and prevent, e.g. "when I worry I will be better able to handle the situation and it will lessen the likelihood it will be as bad as I fear." In truth, worrying lessens one's ability to deal effectively with a given situation, given the effects of increased anxiety on cognition and behavior; its reasoning is faulty and maladaptive since worrying is neither objective nor constructive and is mediated more by the amygdala than by higher cortical levels. We know that the superstitious belief that worrying will prevent something bad from happening is clearly irrational. One's adherence to this myth is evident when one tries not to worry; there will likely be an increase in anxiety that is fueled by the heightened fear that because one is not worrying something bad will likely happen. Since fears will tend to amplify if unchecked, worries can easily catastrophize. When the worst doesn't happen, then the chronic worrier will probably attribute this to the power of worrying, rather than because it simply was unlikely to happen in the first place. There is a cautionary tale attributed to Winston Churchill, who asked a dying friend what his greatest regret was; purportedly his friend said, "worrying about so many things that never happened."

We could easily assume that when beliefs are stored early in life and in deeper areas of the brain, they are more resilient and less easily modified. Many of our fundamental beliefs are developed when our orbitofrontal, prefrontal and left-hemispheric cortices were in their infancy of development. Our evolving schemas are thus based on lower-limbic and right-hemisphere activity, and thus are not available for rational and realistic re-appraisal. These primary and early-secondary beliefs, which are laid down in early childhood, come to have their entire history neuropsychologically interconnected with many other systems. Time has allowed layers of dense neural networks to form and develop synaptic connections that become integrated throughout the brain. To change these fundamental networks and the plethora of reinforced experiences makes these core beliefs highly resistant to change.

These primary and secondary beliefs are strongly entrenched and are far more affectively imbued than are beliefs and expectations processed at higher complex levels. However, we do learn from experiences, and as our brain matures, so does our mind. This allows us to establish constructive counter-beliefs.[58] Unfortunately, adopting a counter-belief does not necessarily eliminate the targeted maladaptive belief, since both can exist at the same time, albeit at different levels of consciousness. For both unrealistic and realistic beliefs to be manifest at the conscious level at the same time would add to dissonance and chaos; some order will likely be established through defensive scripts that will make one belief implicit and the other explicit. Most often, however, the boundary between the conscious and

---

[58] The more frequently and immediately one practices using the counter belief, the more likely it will replace the maladaptive belief.

subconscious is relatively permeable so that contradictory beliefs, at an implicit level, can manifest themselves explicitly as symptoms.[59]

Whether it is a rational belief or an irrational belief, that which becomes dominant will depend both on how well scripts regulate affect, as well as the context in which an event occurs. We have all experienced periods in life when we interpret a given event differently than we did in the past. We may no longer fear going to the dentist as much as we did before, or find ourselves fearful at meeting a colleague when we never did before; what makes for these changes in affect are changes in context. When negative affect is low and positive affect high, our higher more complex executive thinking will dominate; when negative affect is high and positive affect low, lower level cognition will prevail.

Affect trumps cognition; therefore, to establish more realistic and adaptable thinking, we need to better regulate our affects. This applies not just to negative affects, but to positive affects as well. Remember that too much *interest-excitement* can lead to irrational activities, such as over-spending or gambling, or that too much *enjoyment-joy* can lead to inactivity or drugs. Thus affect-regulation helps not only to balance and control affects, but to help modify thinking. Affect and cognition are married for life.

Cognitive Rescripting Techniques

Cognitive rescripting identifies and targets maladaptive and distorted beliefs, expectations, and cognitive styles that interfere with our functioning and wellbeing. We should not forget that these beliefs are constructed by schemas based on affect, not reality. When these schemas are negative, they are defensive and based on protecting one from negative affect.

We shall now examine a number of cognitive strategies and techniques that you can use to modify and restructure your thinking. Like affect recognition, you must first identify your negative beliefs, expectations, and styles of thinking. You can use the questionnaires on general defensive beliefs and maladaptive styles of thinking found in Appendix 6 and in Appendix 7.

Once these maladaptive cognitions are identified, you are then to restructure them as positive and adaptive cognitions. Like affect-focused rescripting, it is imperative that you practice using cognitive restructuring techniques over-and-over, again-and-again. Most often we underestimate how much, and how long it will take to notice a difference; therefore, it may be best to overestimate your expectations, which could then act as a corrective factor to any unrealistic wishes. Remember, many maladaptive beliefs were consolidated in early childhood, and so it will take a considerable amount of time to change them. The more you practice and put effort into these approaches, the more likely your thinking will change. Although the learning curve will be steep, it is steepest in the beginning; when established as a habit pattern, it will no longer take effort.

In addition, it is equally important to practice these techniques by putting a great deal of affect into the positive belief, and as little, if any, into the negative belief. The validity of cognition is proportional to the amount of affect that is imbued in that belief. The goal is to reduce or eliminate the negative affect-charge in negative beliefs, and amplify the positive affect-charge in positive beliefs. Table 6-3 on the next page lists some of the cognitive techniques used in cognitive rescripting therapy.

---

[59] This is the psychoanalytic definition of symptoms, namely that symptoms are expressions of internal conflicts.

Cognitive rescripting therapy is essentially Cognitive-Behavioral Therapy (CBT) that is integrated with affect-rescripting therapy. CBT runs the gamut from a highly structured approach, which we will be discussing in this chapter, to a relatively unstructured approach called *cognitive talking therapy*. As is apparent, the latter is done within the context of the therapeutic dialogue between the patient and therapist. I often used a combination of both the formalized approach and the narrative approach, depending on the patient and the circumstances. Some people prefer either one or the other. Most people are open to both. When this is the case I usually began using structured techniques (partly for teaching), and then move into the dialogical interchange; many times, we would go back and forth as when affect dysregulation brings on symptoms it is then best to use structured techniques. Using both approaches promotes top-down learning that is function-focused, while talking therapy promotes the bottom-up consolidation of this learning that is essential to the integration of the self and ultimately the attainment of wellbeing.

Table 6-3 Cognitive Rescripting Techniques

Cognitive Rescripting Techniques

1. **Refocusing: Thought-Stopping; Mindfulness**
2. **Internal self-talk: Self-Statements; Self-Instruction Training**
3. **Reframing: Re-Labeling; Disputation; Counter-Thinking:**
4. **Logical Analysis**
5. **Interpretation and Insight**
6. **Narrative Metaphors and Stories**
7. **Fantasy**

1. Refocusing

Thought-Stopping: This approach can be used for many modes of thinking, from *ruminating* about the past, *obsessing* about the present, or *worrying* about the future. In thought-stopping there are two steps, the first is to intervene powerfully by interrupting your negative thinking, and then refocus attention, quickly and intensely onto something completely different. Because the negative affect associated with these thoughts is bound together like glue, you will need to forcefully disrupt your negative thinking and immediately refocus your attention to something very different; you will need to refocus with sufficient intensity that it will jolt your attention away from those powerful negative thoughts. Intervention needs to be sharp and sudden, such as loudly saying "stop it" to yourself, pinching yourself, or snapping a rubber band placed around your wrist; The intensity and strength of your intervention will then activate surprise-startle and therefore empty your mind for a millisecond; this brief pause will allow you to refocus your attention. When refocusing, it is best to focus on a totally different set of thoughts or images. To maintain this refocused attention will probably entail a lot of effort; at first you will likely find that your thoughts will spring back to your negative thinking; however, with practice, it will get easier and easier to maintain the new focus of attention. Many people will reach a point where they can just turn off a negative thought in an eye blink, unless the affect is recent and highly charged. As an added benefit, over time thinking in general will become less negative.

During the daytime, it is best to refocus on something that is interesting and involves such features as novelty, curiosity, creativity and problem solving. These themes are more likely to hold your attention. When trying to fall asleep, however, you will not want to trigger excitation but instead induce inhibition; therefore, it is best to refocus on images and thoughts that are pleasant and comforting, such as *lounging in a hammock on a beautiful day while listening to the gurgle of a softly running brook*. The added benefit in doing so is that both sleep and enjoyment-joy entail the same neurochemical, acetylcholine.

Other thought-stopping techniques rely more on visualization than vocalization, and are graduated image-altering approaches. For example: *picture the disturbing event or scene and then imagine slowly dimming the lights, or drawing a curtain over the image, or seeing the image disappear as it telescopes away, or change the channel as if seeing it on a television set.* When the imagined scene is gone, focus on new positive images that enter your imagined field of vision by turning up the lights, opening the curtain, or having the image enlarged

Mindfulness: The goal in mindfulness training is to be in the immediate present, rather than the past or future. Mindfulness is sometimes referred to as the American mode of meditation; however, rather than emptying the mind as is done in meditation, the goal is to fill the mind with the moment. The value of being in the *now* is intrinsic, since most of our psychological problems involve regrets about the past or worries about the future. There has been a good deal of research showing that mindfulness not only soothes the mind and soul, but also benefits our physical health. [See Appendix 8, "The Practice of Mindfulness"]

2. Internal self-talk

Self-Statements: Internal self-talk entails repeating a series of positive self-statements in order to encode them into memory. There are two major kinds of self-talk, one focuses on self-affirmations to enhance self-esteem, the other on coping self-statements to enhance self-efficacy. The following are examples of some affirmations: *I love and accept myself the way I am; I deserve the good things in life as much as anyone else; I am open to discovering new meaning in my life; It's never too late to change; I respect and believe in myself apart from others' opinions; The greatest success is living well; I'm a unique and capable person just as I am.* Each statement is to be repeated many times. [See Appendix 9, "Affirmational Self-Statements"]

Self-Instruction Training: Self-instruction training is a step-by-step approach you can use to monitor, manage and organize your thoughts and behaviors. In addition, it is used for problem-solving, decision-making, and time-management. One well-known self-instruction technique is called Stress Inoculation (Meichenbaum, 1985) which is geared to handle a specific situation that is coming up, such as taking an examination or giving a talk. There are four phases in which coping self-statements are developed to handle each phase. The first phase is to prepare for the situation: *I can develop a plan to deal with it, just think about what I can do about it,* or *remember to stick to the issues and not take it personally*. The second is to confront and handle the stressor: *I can convince myself to do it, one step at a time, don't think about my stress, just focus on what I have to do*. The third stage is to cope with feelings if overwhelmed; *when stress comes just pause and relax, stress is normal and will begin to* *subside.* The final phase is to evaluate your coping strategy: *I handled it pretty well, I made it out to be much worse than it really was, it did not work but with practice will work in the future.* [See Appendix 10 "Anxiety Inoculation"]

3. Reframing

In many respects reframing can be said to be the principle goal in cognitive rescripting. Essentially, it involves putting a positive and more realistic perspective to an event than was the viewpoint initially held. As discussed earlier, cognitive dissonance is a major defensive process that distorts events in order to confirm one's core beliefs; when an event is dissonant and incompatible with your beliefs, you will implicitly minimize that which does not fit your belief, and magnify that which does. It is basically a defense against negative affect. Reframing helps reduce the dissonance.

Re-Labeling: As discussed earlier, labeling is a maladaptive cognitive style since it globalizes and marks a behavior as good or bad. Re-labeling is a basic approach to reframing. For example, one who changes her mind a lot could be labeled either as wishy-washy or as flexible; someone who expresses his opinion can be labeled as egotistical, or as honest and assertive. Or a non-traditionalist can be labeled a troublemaker or an independent thinker. [See Appendix 11 "Re-labeling Worksheets"]

Disputation: This approach is based on challenging your maladaptive thoughts and styles of thinking to better reframe a given thought. Among the challenging queries are: *What is the evidence for my thought? Is this always true? Even if true, what is the worst thing that can happen? How likely is it that it will happen? What can I do if it does happen?* [See Appendix 12 "Disputation Exercise"]

Counter-Thinking: Although similar to disputation, countering does not involve challenging questions. Instead, one simply presents a different and more adaptive thought to counter the negative thought one has. For example, change "I feel powerless and helpless" to "I am powerful and in control of myself, or "I feel like a victim of outside circumstances" to "I am in control of how I deal with events." [See Appendix 13 "Counter-Thinking"] Like all reframes, it is essential to say the negative belief in a slow, monotonic, and monosyllabic way; this will help lessen the negative affect. For each positive counter-belief you need to be passionate, such as exaggerating your facial, vocal and bodily movements; this will help bind and condition positive affect to each positive statement.

4. Logical Analysis

Logical analysis uses such reasoning approaches as probability thinking, problem solving, evaluating the evidence or facts behind the irrational belief, and consequential thinking via a cost-benefit analysis. However, it utilizes a more dispassionate and reasoned approach. It is clearly a top-down process using complex, pre-frontal executive thinking.

The goal in logical analysis is to appeal to rational, higher-order reasoning so as to assess the validity of one's thinking. Often we reason by feelings, which by definition is irrational. If this is what you do, then convert your belief from a feeling statement ("I feel she does not like me") to a declarative statement ("she actually never said she did not like me"). Logic is not subjective, but objective. To attain this state, you should first detach emotionally, and then use a scientific and logical assessment. To help in this analysis you could imagine yourself presenting a scientific study for peer review, or imagine being in a court of law presenting evidence to the judge and jury. It is important to understand how hypotheses are formed, such as discerning meaningful patterns, using inductive reasoning, and recognizing cause-and-effect relationships.

5. Interpretation and Insight

There are a number of cognitive approaches that focus on the meanings associated with thoughts and ideas. These approaches are the backbone of talking therapies, which involves the exchange of ideas. The underlying hypothesis is that our thoughts and ideas carry meaning beyond just the literal content of what is being expressed. We assume that our verbiage consists of symbolic analogs connecting the conscious and unconscious, past and present, self and others. By understanding these connections, we gain insight into ourselves that can help lead to change.

Insight is a reframe, an understanding of some event or experience that is meaningful. This means that insight, like any epiphany, is accompanied by a charged emotional reaction that captures one's attention. Insights, unfortunately, have a way of waning off with time. This means that you should continue thinking and feeling the insight in order to solidify and consolidate this experience into a changed perspective. An insight means little if it does not get stored and integrated into the mind, a process that entails both procedural and declarative learning.

6. Narrative Metaphors and Stories

A more inclusive cognitive approach involves your internal narratives. These inner dialogues not only identify dialogical scripts, but helps shape these scripts. In addition, unlike an inner monologue, there is an interchange between two characters, which by default means that there is a self that is interacting with another imagined person or self-representation. Most often these stories have a plot with a beginning and end. A common theme, for example, is the shame-based damage-repair script: in this internalized script, one feels hurt or invalidated by a specific person, perhaps a friend, and then engages in an inner dialogue whereby revenge is enacted by successfully shaming the shamer. Since these internal stories are fictions, you can change them to fictions that are more helpful and adaptive. [See Appendix 14, "Narrative Rescripting"]

7. Fantasy and Visualization

We have thus far focused on words and syntax. Fantasy and visualization are also important cognitive tools. Many cognitive techniques utilize visualization as a means to inhibit or activate different affects. Most notable are placid calming scenes or a "safe" place to go when anxious and fearful. Others entail actively asserting yourself, or figuring out a great theorem. These images activate positive affects.

Another fantasy approach uses the damage-repair script mentioned earlier to de-cathect (emotionally disengage) from an actual scene that is deeply troubling and humiliating. It involves picturing yourself rescripting the scene by directing anger-rage against that person, and then calming yourself down by using a relaxation technique. For example, if belittled by an acquaintance at a public gathering you could re-imagine that scene, but this time powerfully attack that person verbally and/or physically. Since this is fantasy, and no one really gets hurt; you can imagine whatever you want to as long as it diminishes shame through aggressive or assertive actions; this is an example of *reciprocal-affect-inhibition*. You should then calm down and relax since anger-rage is toxic; you should practice this rescript-relax exercise until the negative feelings are neutralized and extinguished.

The Daily Log

The Daily Log is a well-known worksheet designed to help identify and understand your reactions to events on a daily basis. There are five columns: Affect/Emotion, Date of event, Event, Interpretation of Event, and Thoughts about the event. [See Appendix 15, "Daily Log Worksheet"]

Rescripting Emotions

Emotion is the biological, and cognition the thinking part, of the mind. Emotions can be thought of as the affective component of the mind that gets triggered by cognition. From this linear perspective, the cause-effect sequence is: event → affect → cognition → emotion → behavior. However, emotion is also called an *ideoaffective complex*; this means that from a nonlinear perspective, emotions are combinations of affect and cognition. In this respect, an emotion is a feeling; when cognified it is a feeling about a feeling, and when sensory it is the "felt-feel" experience. For example, when I would ask patients how they felt about an event, I could get an answer reflecting their cognitive appraisal, such as "I feel like I really need to get that project done," to "I feel scared that I will fail," to "I feel shaky even thinking about it." When one tends toward the former, then there is a need to balance this propensity to intellectualize and cognify emotions, while if too affective, then some cognifying will be beneficial. As affect-regulation is fundamental to our functioning, so too is emotional-regulation.

Emotional Rescripting Strategies and Techniques

The obvious goal in emotional regulation is to decrease negative emotions and increase positive emotions. Since emotions are combinations of affect and cognition, focusing on both is necessary to attain this objective. In general, when affect dominates an emotion, it is best to first work toward reducing the affective charge; if instead, the emotion is highly cognified, it is then usually best to begin by using cognitive reframing techniques. Regardless of which modality dominates, ultimately there will be a need to deal with both affect and cognition.

Highly cognified emotions, in which there is little affect charge, will ultimately require the activation and amplification of affect. Since the strategy is to begin at the cognitive level, you will likely do best by focusing on your body while also concentrating on your thoughts and beliefs as you identify the affect that was activated. For example, if your thoughts are that "all is hopeless," then you need to recognize that you are likely depressed and that, therefore, your affect is distress-anguish. Knowing that the locus for this affect is in the diaphragm,[60] you can focus on these sensations. By doing so the affect will amplify and thus give meaning to the depressing thoughts. This will then give you the opportunity to

---

[60] As earlier discussed the locus of all affects is in the body, and especially in the face and skin tissues. In general, though, there are specific foci that characterize each affect. In the ascending affects it is in one's breathing, in enjoyment-joy and shame-humiliation it is in the face, in anger the jaw and biceps, while in disgust it is taste and in dissmell smell.

intervene, first by the affect-focused approach of relaxation, and then the cognitive strategy of reframing. It is important to associate these feelings and thoughts to an identifiable event. A number of questions should be reviewed, such as whether similar events elicited this same emotion, to query about the meaning this specific situation holds for you, what core belief underlies your interpretation, and finally, what expectations and cognitive style was evident.

The next step is to challenge and reframe your cognitive response to that event. It is important to be passionate about, and dedicated to, finding a very different, if not opposite, perspective of that event. Attune to your body to note whether there are any changes in affect, while continuing to reframe and challenge these beliefs. The final step is to practice this procedure, over-and-over again until the negative emotion not only decreases in intensity, but also begins to feel less-and-less negative. Continue to practice this process until the negative affect is either neutralized, or becomes transformed into positive emotions.

We have already reviewed both affect-focused and cognitive-focused techniques. It is important to keep in mind that behavior, which is the final rescripting area of functioning, is the expressive part of emotion; remember, when we remove the letter *e* from the word emotion, we have the word *motion*. Although behavior is triggered by emotion, it also has a feedback effect on emotion as well; thus, when behavior acts as an emotional release, it can either reduce the intensity of that emotion, or amplify it through the neural process of secondary self-amplification.

Rescripting Negative Emotions

Our goal in rescripting negative emotions is to minimize both negative affect and negative cognition. It is important to remember that each affect will impact other affects; therefore, reducing negative affect can activate positive affect, while increasing positive affect can minimize negative affect. For example, reducing fear-terror will activate either interest-excitement or enjoyment-joy while increasing enjoyment-joy will decrease fear-terror. We can also use cognitive strategies, such as reducing disappointments by setting realistic expectations, reduce anger by challenging the fairness fallacy, or increase happiness by focusing on what to do in order to engage in more fulfilling activities.

Anxiety is the emotional equivalent to fear-terror. Some near synonyms for anxiety are nervous, scared, worried, concerned or apprehensive. At the cognitive level, one is likely expecting something bad to happen. It is often best to first intervene affectively, using relaxation and calming approaches; this is especially indicated when fear-terror is acute and intense, for otherwise the cognitive interventions cannot work because the amygdala will rule; when calmer, you could then decatastrophize. A fundamental rule, whether interpersonal or intrapersonal, is to avoid rationalizations like "it will be okay," or "I tried my best." Instead, it is best to first empathize with the anxiety and then, when calmer, you could cognitively review the situation better. I often tell the story of what I learned from one of my daughters, who while crying profusely about an event would then cry even more intensely when I tried to verbally reassure her; it wasn't until I hugged her and attuned to her emotional state that she finally calmed down enough to become open to reassurances and meaningful discussions about the incident.

Stress, depression, despair, sadness, boredom, despair, loneliness, unhappiness, and agitation are derivatives of distress-anguish. The cognitive theme in distress relates to feeling pressured, especially when there seems to be too much to do in too little time, leading one to feel overwhelmed. On the other hand, one may feel there is too much time and too little to do; this may lead to feeling bored. For depression, thoughts are about hopelessness, of feeling trapped and stuck in a sea of sameness where nothing will change. For disgust one feels repulsed, contemptuous, and resentful. Disappointment is about unrealized expectations and feelings of being deceived. Shame elicits feelings of rejection, insignificance, and hurt, which can then elicit the shame-anger response.

In anger one is mad, indignant, or furious. The cognitive belief in anger is based on the belief that one is being treated unfairly. Most people believe there is a universal truth as to what is fair and what is not fair. Unfortunately, this could not be further from the truth. Fairness is in the eyes of the beholder, and follows what could be described as the reverse golden rule; instead of *do unto others as you would like others to do unto you,* the fairness fallacy instead says, *others should do unto me as I would do unto them.* This is an unrealistic expectation that identifies this belief as the *fairness fallacy.* Often one feels disappointed, which then provides the platform for shame-anger.

Rescripting Positive Emotions

Rescripting positive emotions entails amplifying positive affects, such as through body focusing techniques, and strengthening positive thinking through reframing and other such strategies. However, we do know that not all positive emotions are healthy, as we've observed in the excitement of mania and the joy of drugs.

Freud postulated that pleasure is the absence of pain.[61] This dictum fits our postulate that the reduction of a negative affect will trigger a positive affect; thus, the inhibition of fear-terror can activate excitement, while the inhibition of anger-rage can activate enjoyment-joy. However, we also know that blocking negative emotions will not necessarily elicit positive feelings. In addition, the absence of a negative emotion does not eliminate other negative emotions. Nevertheless, our goal is to enhance "feeling good."

Rescripting Behavior

Behavior makes up the fourth and final component of a scene. As discussed earlier, behavior evolved from inscripts, which constituted the first and most basic mode of affect-regulation. The idea that behavior is derived from inborn fixed action patterns (FOP) that change through experience-dependent learning is an important fact for understanding the strategies used in behavioral modification. Knowing that action patterns are tied to inscripts provides us with critical information about its underlying emotion, and therefore it's underlying affect and belief. For example, we know that moving against or away from another person is based on negative affect, while moving towards a person is usually based on positive affects; however, because behavior is learned,[62] it will therefore follow the rules inherent in behavioral learning theory.

From a behavioral point of view, learning is viewed as "a more or less permanent change in behavior resulting from personal experience with an environment." (APA dictionary) Behavior is learned while actions are not. Since the brain, and especially the motor cortex, mediates behavior, learning will impact the brain and change its structure. Keep in mind that learning is a neurological process involving synaptogenesis (development of new neural

---

[61] In actuality, pleasure is the emotion based on enjoyment-joy. In addition masochistic acts combines pleasure *with* pain.

[62] When an action is modified by experience-dependent learning, it then becomes a behavior.

connections), neurogenesis (growth of new neurons), and pruning (loss of unnecessary neurons and their synaptic connections). These processes lead to the state of *having been learned*. This having been learned state is how memory develops and represents the structural changes that accompany memory consolidation. Neuroaffects, when combined with cognition and emotion, make up the mind. Behavior is the expression (or suppression) of these mental processes, at least at the linear cause-effect level.

Learned behavior is the behavior that, when triggered by emotion, connects behavior to its activating stimulus event (i.e. S-R). Behavioral learning can be procedural, that is learning through doing, or declarative through instruction; the former is implicit, the latter explicit. Implicit learning is bottom-up and is based on neuromuscular activity. Learned information is stored in procedural memory that becomes consolidated in the body and in the pre-limbic and lower limbic areas of the brain. Its behavior is implicitly expressed through primary emotions.

Declarative learning is top-down and takes place at secondary and complex levels [in the orbitofrontal-prefrontal areas]. The integration of this learned information is both top-down and bottom-up and will over time, become processed and activated implicitly as habits. This is evident in learning to dance or play a sport. It may begin with instructional and declarative learning, but when coupled with hands-on procedural learning, it comes to be processed at more implicit levels. We therefore see that although declarative memory is initially processed at higher centers, further practice and procedural-use will lead these memories to become stored, processed and then integrated at the lower-levels of the brain and the mind. What once required active and calculated consciousness, now becomes more automatized; these behaviors become habits and are nearly as automatic as a reflex or instinct.

Unlike fixed and rigid inscripts, behaviors can change through social learning that then leads to more varied and diverse behaviors. In fact, when there is a given event, we can better predict affective and mental processes than we can behavior. Too many factors are involved with behavior, such as past learning, one's ability to regulate affect, the many ethnic, religious, cultural, family and social factors, as well the immediate circumstances.

Early social experiences lay down the foundation for all later behaviors. It begins with the social interactions between mother and infant. Attunement and its counterpart misattunement, that is connecting or not connecting with others, speaks to the early affective interchange that shapes behavior related to separation or attachment. This separation-attachment dimension helps underlie interpersonal relationships; it also helps explain why shame is considered the *master emotion* governing relationships, since shame mediates intimacy.

Behavioral Rescripting Strategies and Techniques
The primary goal in behavioral rescripting is to learn assertive and prosocial behaviors. Behavioral learning takes place either through top-down instructional-learning or bottom-up associational and experiential learning. Most behaviors are learned through implicit means. Unlike the conscious effort entailed in explicit instructional-learning, implicit experiential-learning takes place at the unconscious level. The two fundamental associational processes in implicit learning are modeling and reinforcement. Behavioral reinforcement includes classical (Pavlovian) and instrumental (Skinnerian) methods and their offshoots, such as exposure-response prevention, paradoxical intention, and reciprocal inhibition.

Table 6-4 Behavioral Rescripting Techniques

```
Behavioral Rescripting Techniques

A. Modeling
B. Conditional Reinforcement
   Classical Conditioning
   Instrumental Conditioning
C. Specific Conditional Reinforcement Techniques
   1. Exposure Desensitization
   2. Paradoxical Intention
   3. Reciprocal Inhibition
   4. Experiential Learning
D. Instructional Learning
```

Modeling

As stated earlier, "modeling is a genetically inherent tendency toward imitation," which takes place through mirror neurons in the brain. It entails the process of affect attunement, which takes place at a primary level through these mirror neurons. Attunement is essential for bonding and empathy and is the basis for intimacy. Imitation is likely the earliest mode of social behavioral learning

Mirror neurons make up the neurology of empathy. These neurons simulate the same patterns of neural firings as is occurring in the other person, thus triggering similar affective experiences. This *mutualization of affect* underlies empathy, namely the capacity to experience another's affective and emotional state.

Given that one who is empathic knows and feels another person's emotions, there is a higher likelihood that one can better deduce what another person is thinking. If I feel your pain, then I feel your distress-anguish and are probably thinking such distressing thoughts as "this situation is unbearable." If, on the other hand I can feel your joy, then it is a more likely I can assume you are thinking about how wonderful that event was.

As you can see, modeling applies equally to both negative and positive behaviors. Thus, you will want to reduce negative modeling and increase positive modeling. You could, for example, purposely imitate or counter your own posture or actions in relationship to another person. You can also visualize the actions of an admirable (or disliked) person in a given situation, such as meeting an important client or an attractive man or woman and emulate (or not) their behavior. It is critical that you experience the affective sensations of these action patterns. Try to then reproduce that behavior in real situations. We shall review this mode in Section 2, when we discuss the "as if" and "do the opposite" techniques.

When relating to a person you would like to get closer to, attunement can elicit the mutualization of affect with that person, which is what we mean when we say there is "good chemistry" between people, each feeling validated by the other. To further enhance closeness, attend to the other person's posture, verbiage, vocalization, tempo, and the sensory modality that person uses when communicating. To better attune you may judiciously adopt the other persons verbiage: for example, does she say, "I *feel* that you...," or "I *see* that you

…," or "I *hear* that you …;" not only will this help in bonding, but will help you better understand how that person processes information (e.g. visual, auditory or proprioceptive). Of course, we can do the opposite of what that person is doing when we want to disown these behaviors and feelings.

Conditioned Reinforcement
Conditioned reinforcement entails learning that links a stimulus to a response. As discussed earlier, the two primary types of conditioning are classical conditioning and instrumental conditioning. Classical conditioning takes place when two stimuli are associated together in time and space, while instrumental conditioning focuses on the response and its reinforcer. We also learned that positive reinforcement is the most potent, negative reinforcement the next, and punishment the least, since negative affect interferes with learning. In addition, we know that reinforced behavior will extinguish if not reinforced; that negative behavior gains more attention than positive behavior; that behavior is best learned through constant reinforcement and maintained through intermittent reinforcement; and that immediate reinforcement is the most effective.

Reinforcement Strategies and Techniques
By manipulating the reinforcer, one can strengthen or weaken the behavior. Just as behaviors can be learned through conditioning, they can also be unlearned and deconditioned. In essence, this means eliminating or changing the reinforcer. This is more difficult in classical conditioning since learning is consolidated at lower levels of the brain. Nevertheless, let us now consider some specific behavioral strategies related to classical and/or instrumental conditioning.

1. Exposure Desensitization
This approach helps develop greater affect tolerance. This can be done gradually, or all at once. Exposure means facing the event that triggers a negative emotion. The more frequent the exposure, the more likely the behavior will change. *Exposure/response prevention* follows the strategy of doing the "opposite of the urge;" if you feel anxious at parties and usually leave early, then stay at that party; it is likely that the level of anxiety will begin to decrease after a while.

2. Paradoxical Intention
Paradoxical intention also entails the tactic to do the opposite from what the inscript or learned behavior calls for. If the behavior is to avoid or escape, then move toward it; if to move toward, such as in addictions, it is then to avoid; if to attack, then retreat; if it to race and go faster, slow down; if it is to vegetate, get active. These decisions, of course, need to be judicious since many situations may require that you follow the urge.

3. Reciprocal Inhibition
Reciprocal inhibition is a form of classical conditioning, whereby activating a desired behavior will inhibit an undesirable behavior. This follows the principle of reciprocal-affect-inhibition. For example, a shy or angry person who says hello to others is more likely to inhibit avoidant or attack behaviors from others.

4. Experiential learning
Experiential learning is more naturalistic, and uses exposure modification. Engaging in a sporting activity will be exciting, while being in a nurturing environment will be relaxing. These two affects are critical for positive learning and memory consolidation. All of us can benefit from maximizing our time in environments that naturally induce positive experiences.

Instructional-Declarative Learning
Instructional learning takes place with more advanced and complex cognitive development that allows *executive* processing in the prefrontal cortex to inculcate behavioral instructions. Instructional learning is the traditional academic mode of teaching. Instructional training involves a number of specific steps to reach a certain goal. Among the psychological problems in which instructional training is used to treat include stress and anger management, impulsivity, social skills training, assertiveness, communication training, problem solving, and compliance training.

Instructional Principles and Strategies
Teaching through declarative learning requires a number of principles. One is that constructive behaviors are best learned when interest-excitement is dominant, and stored when enjoyment-joy is maximized; interest requires novelty, while enjoyment requires constancy. This means that information is best presented in unique ways to enhance learning. This requires being succinct, relating information to your personal experiences, and laying out the positive consequences such learning will entail. Learning is best achieved when using *variant repetition*, which is to vary the ways you practice these new behaviors.

Of critical importance in instructional learning is motivation, and what is essential to motivation is both affect and willpower. *Will* is exemplified when we make choices, and carry out these choices in self-directed behaviors. Our ability to make choices highlights the principal that all decisions, conscious or unconscious, are part of one's self, so that willpower encompasses self-agency.

The concept of *will* is quite important when we talk of behavioral motivation. We have already discussed the critical role of emotion in motivation; affect is the fuel that energizes us to act, while cognition is what directs our behavior. However, when all is said and done, behavior is the ultimate arbiter of motivation. This means that motivation comes from doing, as exemplified in the Nike slogan "just *do* it." The idea that motivation comes from doing means that rather than waiting until you are motivated to do something, you should begin to take action even if not motivated, since action is what underlies motivation. This fits with the laws of inertia that says that once action, or inaction, is initiated, the behavior will continue until something intervenes; in other words, inaction leads to further inaction, while doing leads to more doing.

Many people question whether behavior defines the self. Behavior reflects scripts, which are an essential part of the self, but not representative of the whole self. Yet, we must accept ownership for our behavior, even if our behavior is mediated implicitly. Regardless of our awareness and intent, each of us is responsible for what we do. A person does what he or she does, and their entire self will live with the consequences.

On the other hand, we need not attack our whole self, but instead address our attention to the behavior itself. When we get a disease, some will certainly personalize it to the whole self, but most often we treat the diseased part of our self as a dysfunctional system. This is how we can best deal with our behavior. By taking responsibility without (whole) self-judgment, willpower is enhanced. Importantly, we learn and integrate when our assessment of our self is free of negative beliefs and emotions.

Part II: The Emergent Self: Integrative Rescripting and Wellbeing

In our discussion on the evolution of the neuroaffective system, we saw how nature gave us the necessary and essential tools for knowing and coping with life. We also saw that our biologically based inscripted action patterns were extremely limited in their ability to deal with the complex world we live in. In fact, these automatic mechanisms did not even meet the essential requirements necessary to safely survive in the world: it was our parents who provided the essential vehicle for survival during the early months of life.

It was through the cognification of affects, and the subsequent development of scripts, that the journey toward independent functioning began in earnest. Now the mind becomes the principal arbitrator that deals with the world. There are two primary tasks of the mind, namely to successfully regulate affects in order to allow for the development of higher mental processes, and the ever-increasing role in directing how we function in the world. These higher and more complex processes came to be known, collectively, as the *self*.

There is a growing chorus of neuroscientists who attribute affect-regulation to the origin of the self, as literally reflected in the title of Allan Shore's (1994) book, *Affect regulation and the origin of the self: the neurobiology of emotional development*.[63] In other words, when affects are successfully managed, then higher and more complex neural, mental, and behavioral systems can organize with greater degrees of cohesion and coherency. As these systems become more integrated as a whole, they come to form a more integrated self.

The more integrated the self, the greater will be one's capacity to competently function in the world. Scenes and events will be handled with greater efficacy as one's affects, cognitions, emotions and behaviors are unified rather than divided. Given these developments, our focus will shift from affect-regulation to the organization and regulation of the self, namely *self-regulation*. In rescripting terms, we are referring to the re-ordering of self-scripts through the general mega-script we call the self.[64] When the self is well-integrated and successfully regulating affects, its principle function moves to the re-ordering of its self-scripts into a more complex organized system that, as an integrated whole, will lead to a state of emotional wellbeing.

Functioning effectively gives us the means to secure our life and liberty. Concretely it means that we have the skills and strategies to do well in our relationships and in our career. We have already discussed how successful functioning is an essential condition for wellbeing and happiness. Success brings us a sense of pride, respect and perhaps prosperity. We now know that there is another, less tangible level of success that has less to do with the practicalities of life; this is what we call self-fulfillment. This is the *being* in wellbeing, the sense of oneness within, of inner peace and self-acceptance, of knowing who one is, of having self-integrity; this is the person we say who has it *all-together*.

To be all-together means to be integrated within. As functioning relates to the pursuit of happiness, integration relates to the emergence of wellbeing. The well-integrated self provides the cohesion, coherence, harmony and synchronicity that helps bring about feelings of contentment and equanimity. As you may notice, the word *wellbeing* is a melding of *well* and *being*, which highlights its truly integrated nature.

---

[63] Lewis (1971) specifically says that "it is through the inhibition of shame that gives birth to the self."
[64] This is akin to Freud's executive ego.

As we shift our attention from the structural-functional self to the emergent-integrated self, we turn from left-brain, top-down thinking to right-brain bottom-up thinking. In practical terms, we move from a specific and focused linear approach to a holistic, nonlinear complexity-approach; this necessitates changing the language and style to best fit the process. We shall describe emergent integration in broader strokes whose language is more lyrical and less prosaic, given that integrative rescripting has a somewhat mystical and transcendent quality to it as compared to the evidence-based science of function-focused rescripting.

Chapter 7: The Self and its Self-Scripts

The *self* has been the subject of inquiry since human beings first evolved self-awareness. Since then, poets and philosophers have written and pondered the nature of the self. If we just look at the last few centuries it is likely that there are enough volumes on the self to fill many libraries. We shall therefore skip the usual review of the literature and instead get right down to understanding the self within the rubric of rescripting. Since nothing is new, yet nothing is the same, this section, like that on the functioning self, will also be a re-working of self-theory into the affect-rescripting model of the self. Our postulate is that wellbeing comes about when the self is well integrated. This, therefore, requires an understanding of what our self is, how it operates, how it develops, and how it emerges into an integrated whole.

To be or not to be, that is the question

Most claim that the existence of the self is in itself, self-evident; in other words, it is evident to the self. Descartes' answer was *cogito ergo sum*, "I think therefore I am." We could add a plethora of other self-evident truths. The most revered is immortalized in the words of Thomas Jefferson that "all men are created equal, and are endowed by their Creator with certain inalienable rights that among these are life, liberty and the pursuit of happiness [i.e. wellbeing]." Other self-evident truths include *sentio ergo sum* "I feel, perceive, and experience; therefore, I am;" *ergo ego sum*, "I do, therefore I am." Then we have Bishop George Berkeley's French quotation, e*sse est percipi*, "to be is to be perceived." Adding another in German, we have *ich bin meine Autobiographie*, "I am my autobiography." To complete this rather pedantic exercise, I will add one other maxim, and do so in Spanish so as not to offend our Latin cousins: *contexto lo es todo*, "context is everything." Why I place context alongside other so-called "truths," is to emphasize the importance of how our situation, environment, and a host of other factors influence our ability to function.[65]

Our thoughts, feelings, behavior and self-scripts are contingent on the present context. Although self-scripts are fixed as a trait, they are also (state) dependent on the context as well. Although a triggering event may seem to be the cause of one's response, in truth it is the self that is responsible for one's response; in other words, the situation impacts the self, and as such, this impacted self acts as the agent of one's response.

Shakespeare, however, presents an interesting dichotomy. In essence, we know and experience our self because we can distinguish our self from our non-self. As you read these passages there is automatically an intuitive sense that it is you who is reading this, for if not, you would not be able to know. And if you are instead thinking of something else as you are reading these words, you still have an implicit sense of being, although you are being elsewhere than with these words; in short, you know who you are and who you are not. When you move your hands or make a statement, you know that you are the agent of these actions. When you think, you attribute your thoughts to yourself. When you feel blue or happy, you know those feelings belong to yourself. This awareness of self is especially evident when you realize you are not being yourself, as if you are disconnected from your self; this is illustrated when you say, "that's not like me," or "I wasn't myself today" or "I'm

---

[65] In fact, contextualizing the self was a major part of William James' theory on the self. [*The Principles of Psychology* (1890), Chapter X, The Consciousness of Self."]

besides myself." These statements reflect a knowing of self since you could not be aware of feeling different unless you are *aware* of your self.

The knowing-self is a self-referential self-state, reflected in the "I." The *I* not only reflects the knowing-self, but also the self as agent; *I* is Freud's Ego. Then we have the self-state identified as the "me." The *Me* is the object, not only grammatically, but of the *I* as subject. Finally there is "myself." *Myself* is the self both as object and subject that integrates the *I* and *Me*.

Although we may not always be consciously aware of our self, there is nevertheless an implicit awareness of self; thus, the self is omnipresent. Some say that non-self is the state that comes with death, while others identify non-self with various physical or mental disorders. These ideas present a number of interesting questions: Is there self when someone is comatose? Does a person, who is suffering severe neurological damage to parts of their cortex or limbic system, have self? Does a person going through a psychotic episode, or someone suffering from a dissociate disorder such as multiple personality disorder, have a self that is cohesive? We shall address non-self in the final chapter, *Disorders of the Self*.

That Shakespeare posits his challenge as an interrogative suggests that he may have considered that we have a choice in determining the existence of our self. Some say that our self comes into existence only when we become consciously aware of it, while others believe that implicit self-awareness does not necessarily require consciousness, at least at an explicit level. Put differently, the self exists both consciously and unconsciously. These states, however, are not individuated states of being but permeable states of being. We know that we forget and then remember, and then forget again, as our attention shifts from one state to another state, and then back again. Often, we assume that each state is in contact with the other state, although what is going on at one moment may seem quite different from its previous state. Hopefully this and other existential and epistemological challenges will become clearer in this chapter.

Since the self is evident at the conscious level, how do we know it exists at the unconscious level? If consciousness depends on the activation of an affect, how do we know that our body is sending out sensory-motor impulses? We know because we have an interoceptive experience of these internal sensations. We are continually getting proprioceptive information from our bodies, whether we are aware of it or not. This is inherent in our movements and their accompanying sensory-motor changes, as well as in the affective changes that accompany changes in posture and facial expressions. We also know of the existence of self because others may draw attention to our affective expressions, as when someone points out that we look happy, or sad, or nervous.

We also know that there is an unconscious self through neuroscience research studies. (Antonio Damasio, 2010) In neuroscience studies using fMRI on subjects working on a given task, we could see the orbitofrontal cortex light up alongside activity in the upper brain stem, even though the subject reports being unaware of anything going on internally. When given specific cues, these same subjects can then identify what sensations they were having at the time they reported not being aware. Damassio was also one of the many neuroscientists who identified the parietal lobe as being home to the self.

Our self is not only revealed through these internal sensations, but by our ability to see and touch our external body. When we recognize that our body belongs to our self, we begin to form a body image that helps make up our physical-self; this body image is tangible and concrete, unlike the abstractness of a mental-image. Prior to this, our self operated implicitly through our sensing-self; now we have a knowing-self. By default, when we know and see our bodily self, we have gained a cognitive awareness that allows us to know that we think, perceive, feel and act.

The implicit "knowing" self takes place at the subliminal preconscious level. This implicit level of being is not a scripted state in itself, but relates to degrees of awareness and non-awareness. Nevertheless, these distinctions are very important, especially in terms of the emergence of the self. As Freud so often emphasized, making the unconscious conscious gives rise to those insights necessary for the ego/self to grow. We shall emphasize the significance of increasing awareness as a fundamental feature for greater functioning and greater wellbeing. In essence, by making the implicit explicit, we are integrating those parts of the self that are cut off from the self-aware self.

Given that there is a self, I will define the self [66] as a *general mega-script that encompasses the totality of all self-scripts.* This definition looks at the self as a part-whole configuration, one in which the whole is greater than the sum of its parts. However, when we look at the self as a totality, we are not dealing with a linear model whereby the whole is greater than the sum of its parts; instead, the integrated self follows the laws of nonlinear dynamics whereby the whole is exponentially greater and far more complex than the total sum of its parts.

The Composition of the Self

There are many ways to categorize the parts that make up the self. In the rescripting model, self-scripts make up the composition of the self, as seen in Table 7-1 on the next page. As you will notice the self is divided into two major categories, the structural or functional self, and the emergent or integrated self. The functional self is made up of its four basic self-scripts based on functioning, each of which evolved into a self-script; thus, there is the affective/bodily self-script, the cognitive self-script, the emotional self-script, and the behavioral/doing self-script. Together, the organization of these self-scripts provide order and stability to its structure; hence, the *structural self*. The functional/structural self is primary to that of the evolving emergent/integrated self.

The emergent self is also called the integrated self since its self-scripts are merged into a cohesive and coherent whole (which in turn evolves into emotional wellbeing). Instead of structure, the emergent-integrated self entails extensionality and dimension in both time and space, and thus follows the course of nonlinear dynamics. The emergent self consists of two major self-scripts, the social *self/other self-script* (Allan Schore, 1994), and the personal *autobiographical self-script*. Since the emergent self evolves through integration, it is also identified as the integrated self; thus we have the emergent/integrated self.

---

[66] It is important to recognize that the Self is not a thing, but a dynamic construct, much like Freud's Id, Ego and Superego; the Self seems like a thing because there is composition and definition to it; in truth, it is a metaphor for executive mental functions.

Table 7-1 Composition of the Self
Robert Kayton

Composition of the Self

The Structural Self
- Affective Self-Scripts
- Cognitive Self-Scripts
- Emotional Self-Scripts
- Behavioral Self-Scripts

The Emergent [spacial-temporal] Self
- Selfother Self-Scripts
- Autobiographical Self-Scripts

The Functional (Structural) Self

The functional self is essentially an affect-regulating mega-script that manages and organizes its primary components, namely the affective physical-self, the cognitive-self, the emotional-self, and the behavioral-self. Like affect-regulating scripts, one component may be dominant, as when pain (and its affective component distress-anguish) activates the affective physical-self, or when test-taking (and its affective state of fear and shame) elicits both the cognitive-self and the emotional self; as usual, context plays a critical role in determining which component is dominant.

Affect-scripts and their derivative self-scripts provide us with our basic sensing-self that comes through the interoceptive experiences associated with an affect. This is the earliest form of self and is likely the precursor to all other self-states.[67] Often these affective scripts operate implicitly. As discussed earlier, our self is not only revealed to us through these internal affective sensations, but also by our ability to see and touch our external body. Beginning at around 18 months a child recognizes that her body belongs to herself, giving her a known, tangible and objective self. By default, when we know and see our bodily self, we have gained a cognitive awareness that allows us to know what we think and perceive, and how we feel. It is also the beginning of our developing self-identity.

The cognitive-self is revealed through our schemas, beliefs, ideology, social discourses and internal narratives. When we listen to our self thinking and talking, we gain a greater understanding of who and what we are.[68] This is an example of the knowing self. The cognitive-self appears as a steady state of being, yet we know that, at the same time, it is also a dynamic state of becoming. Thus, our self is always changing, whether it is top-down through our explicit self, or bottom-up through our implicit self.

Emotional self-scripts represent the *limbic feeling self*. It is the structural component of the self that actually integrates the affective, cognitive and behavioral modalities. When we

---

[67] A self-state refers to a relatively stable configuration of self-scripts that exists at a particular time, as in a *state of mind*.

[68] This self-knowledge can be used to modify our cognitive-self by modifying our beliefs.

ask a person how she feels, we can identify whether the affective or cognitive emotional state is most amplified; this was earlier illustrated when one person says she feels tense and enraged, which directly addresses her feeling state, while another says she feels unfairly treated, which is actually a feeling about her feeling state.

The behavioral-doing self can be thought of as the major self-script involved in self-agency, and entails the bodily-self in motion. We are continually getting sensory-motor information from our bodies, whether we are aware of it or not. This is inherent in our movements: as we move about we feel our muscles contracting, our tissues and breathing changing, as well as our experience of a constantly changing environment. Our behavior is also that part of the self that is objectively observable to others.

The Emergent (Integrated) Self

The integrated-emergent self entails dimensionality, both in time and space. These two dimensions are represented by the *autobiographical-self* that is extended in time, and the *selfother-self* that is extended in space. Dimensionality also exists topographically as when we refer to the conscious-self, preconscious/subconscious-self, and the unconscious-self.

The autobiographical self is the temporal self, and consists of all the stored emotional memories and scripts accumulated during one's lifetime. It is our personal story, our saga and our legend. Although our history seems fixed in our mind, it is constantly being rewritten whenever we recall a memory. As discussed earlier, simply remembering an event or scene from our past will change that memory from what it was, to what it now becomes; in this regard, the act of recalling an event will automatically change the memory of that event. This is largely because remembering occurs in a different context than before, and so will be experienced in a slightly different way than it was originally. When that memory re-consolidates into the memory centers of the brain, it is stored in that modified state. Neurochemically the molecular structure itself has changed through changes in its protein synthesis. Thus, we speak of a *living past*.

Where there is memory, there is anticipation. Armed with experiences and knowledge gained from the past increases our ability to better predict what might happen in the future, and how to better deal with that event should it happen. This gives us a significant, evolutionary advantage and is likely the primary purpose for memory and remembering. If we do not learn and store what we learned from the past, then we will likely repeat that event in the same way in the future; then the past truly becomes prologue.

Selfother self-scripts make up our interpersonal self, the self-in-relationship to others. As referenced earlier, George Berkeley stated that for the self to exist it must be perceived by others; we exist because we know that others perceive us. It is when we internalize others into the personal space of our inner self that our selfother-self comes to be. This perception is attained when others respond to our affect expressions that call into being our sense of self. In the words of Francis Broucek, our sense of self emerges in the *contextual embrace of other selves*. The role that seeing and being seen by others play in the development of the self, now comes together in the form of the selfother-self. It evolves from what Alan Shore calls the *selfmother-self*, and comes into being at the age when we become aware of our body.

The Functions and Properties of the Self

Self-scripts regulate affect-scripts, while affect-scripts regulate affects. Affect-regulation controls affects by balancing the degrees of excitation and inhibition, whereas self-regulation reorganizes scripts by balancing the degrees of convergence with corresponding degrees of divergence. It is the self that manages and organizes these self-scripts into a cohesive, harmonious and coherent whole. This means maximizing positive scripts and minimizing negative scripts; doing so automatically changes the self. Through self-regulation and management, order is established, which then allows for the emergence of a higher and more complex reorganization of scripts. Although self-regulation manages scripts, it does not necessarily mean that there will be a homeostatic equilibrium that balances opposing systems. Instead, self-regulation manages scripts so as to yield optimal benefits. Self-regulation can vary from being overly tight through too much convergence, to overly loose through too much divergence. If too tight and rigid, adaptive change is compromised, whereas if too loose and irregular, we get chaos and *dis*order.

Self-regulation is top-down, while self-integration is bottom-up. Self-integration largely depends on self-regulation. When optimal top-down regulation reigns, we gain an inner sense of cohesiveness and coherency, and thus an integrated state of being. These conditions provide us with a clearer sense of the self-as-agent, with the attendant power of will (willpower). Self-agency and willpower (together with wisdom, as we shall soon discuss) are the necessary and essential elements for attaining emotional wellbeing. The emergent process, set in motion through self-regulation, leads to the integration of the self through self-organizing complexity, and follows the laws of nonlinear dynamics.

Self-organizing complexity is a bottom-up process that is a naturally occurring process in evolution. Just as cells form naturally into colonies of multi-cellular organisms, which in turn evolve into more complex organisms, so do families of scenes form affect-scripts, which form into more complex scripts that we call self-scripts, and ultimately to the mega-script we call the self. This was illustrated on page 71 in the hierarchical diagram of the self.

Affect-regulation is linear and understood in cause-effect terms: thus, affect activates cognition, which triggers emotion, which leads to behavior. On a practical basis, identifying the cause of some reaction gives us the opportunity to deal with the causative factor, and thus change the reaction. Knowing that smoking causes cancer, that treating other people badly will lead them to react negatively, or that failing to study an assignment will likely reduce one's performance. A major point in Part I was to emphasize that by understanding the underlying cause-effect relationship, we can improve our ability to function well.

The linear cause-and-effect model is retrospectively deterministic and prospectively predictable; thus, when we look back on an event, it seems that it was predetermined. This is often what we do with historical and autobiographical analysis, namely to identify the self-evidentiary facts that by fiat, led to the outcome. In addition, we assume that if we know all the factors that cause a certain outcome, then we have the blueprint for accurate predictions. This is what economists and meteorologist do. We learn by examining the successes and failures from the past in order to make better predications about the future. This will help us use these skills and strategies to better live life successfully.

Yet, there is also ample evidence that events are often unpredictable and that history is often based on chance occurrences. Yet we cling to this linear way of thinking largely because our brains are structured this way. It is our default means of processing data, since it was more adaptive in a stimulus-response world where survival depended on identifying a situation and reacting appropriately.

In self-regulation, we instead analyze data in nonlinear, part-whole terms. It is a systems approach that takes-into-account feedback, as well as *feedforward*.[69] For example, it holds that there are two or more dimensions and modalities to analyze phenomenon, rather than the one-dimensional stimulus-response sequence inherent in linearity. We have the trees and the forest, sameness and change, part and whole.

Self-regulation is the necessary process that allows scripts to organize into a coherent and cohesive whole. Together with extensionality and modularity, cohesion and coherency make up the essential properties of the integrated self. By definition, cohesion is what defines integration. Cohesion of the self is like the glue that binds parts together into one completed configuration. This provides for greater stability and strength. Coherence is characterized when the cohesion of its parts fit together in a congruent and harmonious way; put another way, the parts go well together and are compatible so that there is a synergistic logic to their formation and structure. This is partly why we regulate scripts in order to minimize or eliminate negative scripts, thereby allowing positive scripts to cohere. As stated earlier, negative scripts impede integration, while positive scripts promote integration; since integration is healthy, then only positive scripts can successfully bind together into one unified whole.

Extensionality is what gives the self its multi-dimensional nature. It extends spatially, as between the internal and external world, the conscious and unconscious, the body and mind, the self and selfother-self, as well as temporally, as with the past, present and anticipated future. Extensionality is what helps give the self a sense of consistency and continuity by enlarging and tying together spatial and temporal dimensions.

What some call the "extended self" relates to the incorporation of one's environment into the self. Our bodily sense of self goes beyond the corporeal-self to include the immediate space surrounding our skin, whether it be the air we breathe or the clothing we wear. It can also take the form whereby objects, such as one's possessions, become a part of one's self; a house or car can be a metaphor for one's self so that other's comments, whether positive or negative, get personalized. I recall a friend who talked about his car as though it was his best friend and named it as he would a pet. Sports players and the "home team" also display this extension of self as they become a part of one's family.

The self also has the property of modularity. This is a given since the self is a script, albeit a mega-script. Without modularity, self-scripts would not have the flexibility to be re-ordered into a new organized structure. This property is also necessary for integration to take place, as evidenced by the fact that a modular system is by definition an integrated system. It epitomizes the dictum that *the whole is [exponentially] greater than the sum of its parts*.

The Formation of the Self: Development and Emergence

As already discussed, the formation of the self develops through a combination of linear development and nonlinear emergence. In the former, development proceeds gradually as a linear progression from one stage to another. Like the sweep of an analog clock, in which the hands move in synchrony with the pace and movement of time itself, we can observe how

---

[69] Feedback is reactive; information is fed back to the self. Feedforward is progressive; information is provided to the self about the future, about what might happen.

development moves from one state to another. Each changed state absorbs the components of its earlier states; temporally, these states merge together into an emergent state of being.

Nonlinearity is more inexplicable because we cannot observe change. It is like a digital clock, whereby all we see is one time, and then the next time, as 1:05 suddenly becomes 1:06. Unlike the continuity of linear change, nonlinear change is discrete. Rather than showing continuity from one state to another, each state is completely new and different. Diagram 7-1 on the next page illustrates the differences between linear and nonlinear change. As you will notice, the first box depicts linear and contiguous changes from A through D, while in the second box each stage emerges as discrete and different from the stage that preceded it.

Diagram 7-1
Linear vs. Nonlinear Changes in Time
Robert Kayton

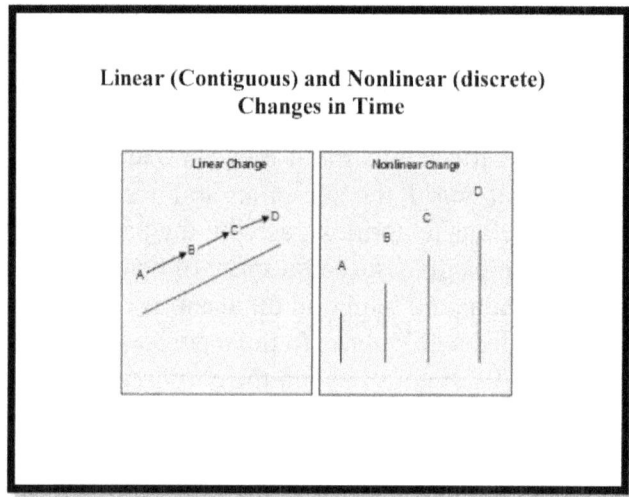

We shall first examine the linear process in the development of the self, and then the process of emergence through the nonlinear model.

Stages of Self Development

The origin of the self is rooted in our affects, and begins when these affects are regulated through scripts. As we have said, the self is conceptualized as a megascript that incorporates all other scripts, from the simple affect-scripts to the more complex self-scripts.

Let us begin at the beginning, before the birth of the self, to a state identified by the eminent neurologist and neuroscientist Antonio Damasio (2010) as the *protoself*. The protoself begins its development before birth. Although some believe that the self begins very early in fetal life, it is more aptly the protoself that begins to form, and that takes place late in fetal development. It is at this inscripted level that affect-induced action patterns are evident. We know that the fetus reacts with distress-anguish when hungry, and with enjoyment-joy when satiated. Given all the kicking that is going on in the mother's belly, we could also assume that there is also interest-excitement, as noted when a new sound is introduced. It is possible that even anger-rage, fear-terror or shame-humiliation exist at some level, while it is likely that disgust and dissmell exist in their pre-affective drive state.[70]

It is at birth, however, that the core (physical) self begins in earnest as the neonate begins her relationship with the external world. The environment the baby is born into is filled with new and different stimuli. These stimuli will activate a far greater range of neural firings than while in the womb, which in turn will activate and amplify a greater set of affective reactions. It is through affect-regulation, especially the inhibition of affect, that order gets established, which then allows for a more complex organizational structure that will come to form the template for the developing self.

Regulation coordinates similar systems and balances opposing systems. How this process takes place varies among scripts. Some regulation scripts manage both affects and scripts in a constant and steady way, so that there is relatively little fluctuation between the amplification of positive affects to the amplification of negative affects, as well as the magnification of positive scripts to the magnification of negative scripts. Other regulation scripts allow for a looser and less organized system that allows for greater swings between positive affects and negative affects, as well as between positive scripts and negative scripts.

At both the protoself-stage and the neonatal-stage, affect-regulation is governed through innately inscripted action patterns. When we observe a newborn, we see a very fluid stream of facial and bodily movements that are in constant flux. There is little filter between the neurological patterns of neural firings and the (analogical) bodily expression of these patterns. It is through these inscripted regulatory patterns, together with parental intervention as external regulators, that order gets established. Inscripts are precognitive protoscripts that regulate affects automatically without a self as governor; this is what we call *autoregulation*. When there is distress, the infant cries and flails about, which helps reduce that distress until he or she is fed, or their diaper is changed.

Affect-scripts likely begin between 3 to 6 months after birth. This is when memory, cognition, and self-agency all make their appearance in the life of the infant. Affects now become stored in the muscles and tissues of the body, and become the remembered *sense of self*. This sense-of-self is based on the infant's embodied images of his or her sensing and experiencing affective-self. At this point the self is interoceptive and represents the core of ones being. This sensing-self underlies the physical-self that is emerging during the first half-year of life, as the prototypic cognitive-self begins its emergence as well. We can say that the body, the mind and the self coevolve, and thus are forever linked. It is with the development of memory that begins the journey toward the autobiographical self.

At this early stage, self-agency gets its start and so, therefore, does the doing-self. This is evidenced by what Tomkins calls *autosimulation* which takes place when the baby learns to suck his or her thumb as a self-induced strategy to reduce distress. Autosimulation instigates critical components that define the integrated self, namely the wisdom gained from past experiences and the self-agency and willpower to carry out appropriate actions in both the now and in the future.

Autosimulated affect-scripts soon transform into more complex scripts as the baby begins using her thumb, and then using external objects outside her body, such as a pacifier. This begins the process of identifying objects that belong to her body and those that do not.

[70] Animals also have a protoself, since they too have inscripted action patterns, affects, and affect-scripts.Many scientists now agree that some mammals and birds also have a higher-level complex self, because they have been shown to have self-awareness.

Certainly, the act of sucking her thumb produces different sensations than sucking a pacifier; in the latter, sensations are experienced solely in the mouth, while in the former the locus of internal sensations is felt both in the mouth and in the thumb. Through the intrinsic integration of these two body parts, and the differentiation between the thumb and the external affect-regulating pacifier, these experiences coalesce to form a new unified sensation. As we climb the complexity ladder by adding new factors, such as multiple body parts or objects, the template for one's body image is forged.

The importance of affect-scripts in the developing self is also evident, given that these scripts now take the place of the autoregulating inscripts. We shall soon see that the maturing self comes to act as its own governor, not only in regulating one's own affects, but also in managing and organizing one's own scripts. Taking ownership is essential to optimal self-regulation, and is the basis for self-agency and willpower.

At the primary stage of development affects are experienced, not just in terms of inscripted action patterns, but also as affect-regulated scripts. For example, when fear-terror or interest-excitement get activated, and then amplified, there will be the excitatory rush of adrenalin; if this excitation is inhibited, there may then follow either the positive experience associated with enjoyment-joy or the negative experiences related to distress-anguish, anger-rage, or shame-humiliation. As you can see, the sensing and experiencing self is already evolving into states of greater complexity.

Thus, at around three months old the infant begins to develop both a physical sensing-image of self, and a cognitive mental-image of self. Between six and nine months these self-images expand into a core *feeling-image* of the self that operates implicitly at the physical level. The cognitive unconscious is also developing, and is pre-eminent in establishing the central foundation from which the *thinking-self* evolves. At this age, children engage in *protocommunciation,* a term described by Dore (Schore, 2003, p.480) reflecting, "…vocalizations accompanied by affectively salient tones, gestures, and facial expressions that signal internal affective states." Audio-visual linkage, that is the integration of visual images and semantic words, has not yet developed; thus, there is still a strong reliance on the reciprocal attuning and misattuning of the vocal (though not yet semantic) interchange between mother and child.

At about two or three years old, the child develops *object permanence* (or *object constancy*),[71] namely the ability of a child to understand that objects exist even when they cannot directly be sensed. This capacity was first reported by Jean Piaget while studying infants' reactions while playing peek-a-boo with their mothers. In this game, the mother hides her face with her hands and then abruptly moves her hands away to reveal her face. The one-year-old usually laughs with glee, suggesting that when mother was hiding her face with her hands the child literally did not know her mother's face was still there, so that when it reappeared, it was a surprise-excitement-joy reaction.

As the child matures, so does her perceptual–motor skills mature, so that she now has the capacity to explore; in the peek-a-boo example, she can now physically pull her mother's fingers apart, thus displaying self-agency; this activity becomes more urgent and frustrating as she begins to suspect that it is mother's face behind those fingers; after a period of time the game is no longer fun. She has desensitized to it, and in its stead is an awareness of object permanence. Now, when mommy leaves the room, she still exists to the child and will

---

[71] *Object permanence* was Piaget's label, while *object constancy* came from Freud.

reappear again;[72] "out of sight" no longer means "out of mind," since now an image of her mother is retained in memory.

Between eight and nine months old, another notable change takes place in the developing self. The child now begins to shy away from strangers. Although labeled *stranger anxiety*, the avoidant behaviors may relate not just to fear, but also to shame or distress. Nevertheless, this represents the development of the capacity to differentiate between those who are familiar and those who are unfamiliar. Only those who are familiar, such as parents and significant others, will be responded to positively, while those who are unfamiliar are experienced as a threat. This presents a clear advance in the development of the selfother self.

In addition, the child is now becoming more mobile, and begins to explore his environment. There will be an increase in interest-excitement as the child discovers new things, and the enjoyment-joy that comes with manipulating them. The experiencing-self is now greatly expanding, as is also the knowing-self. Clearly wisdom, self-agency and willpower are increasing as well.

Between nine months and twenty-four months of age, critical brain-mind changes take place that helps set the foundation for the later, self-evolving integrative processes. As Allan Shore points out, before two years old the self-image is actually a fused *selfmother* image. At two years, an image of self-as-distinct-from-mother begins to emerge. This change leads to the disorganization of the infant's primary selfmother system, which is displayed by the chaos we see during the so-called "terrible-twos" (which, interestingly, is often more evident at age three). This chaotic disorganization, however, will ultimately lead to a higher and more complex form of organization.

From an affect-script perspective, the emergence of the self as different from the mother takes place partly because shame-humiliation becomes the most, if not one of the most salient and urgent affects at this age. Shame, which later becomes cognified as rejection from others, is now activated because the self is now separating from the security of a fused selfmother dyadic image. Metaphorically, this is expressed when Adam and Eve were thrown out of the Garden of Eden and became aware of their selves; and what they first did with this self-recognition was to cover up their nakedness. (Broucek, 1991)

Shame is the primary affect associated with self-awareness. We can say that as affect-regulation is the origin of the self, shame gives birth to the aware, knowing-self. It is when the physical representation of one's physical body, which has external outlines and dimension, that one's body-image truly emerges. This comes about at around eighteen months when the child is now able to identify herself as different from others. At this age, the left hemisphere begins a growth spurt over the already developed right hemisphere, as the hippocampus also begins its development. Accompanying these neurological changes are mental changes that allow the child to be more capable at identifying herself as different from others; as stated, this is an age characterized by shame-anger scripts. In addition, it is also the time when the self becomes separate and different from others, which will automatically trigger shame. Being separate and different are key themes among shame-scripts, and is the precursor for social scripts dealing with separation and intimacy.

It is through the integration of the interior and exterior parts of our body that allows us to label the physical-self. Self is now formulated, not only as an implicit sense-of-self, but also as an explicit and observable self. Now, interoceptive bodily experiences are integrating with the exteroceptive identification of one's physical body.

---

[72] This is also when trust or basic mistrust begins.

From these basic beginnings, there develops a more complex, symbolic and semantic schema of the self that comes to fit a multi-dimensional person. Along with the physical-self, there begins to evolve the conscious aware-self, the doing-self, and the thinking-self. In addition, the seeds from which the autobiographical-self and the selfother-self begins to grow are planted at this time as well. This is accompanied by significant neurological changes that are accompanied by changes in affective and cognitive functioning. Cognitively, semantic language begins in earnest. Not only is interpersonal communication more verbal, there is a dialogical-self that is evident in the internal self-talk we call thinking

Finally, when the child sees and experiences himself as different from her mother, he will introject this maternal image into herself so that it becomes a part of his self. The merger of the self with the perceived mother, now becomes a part of the *selfother-self*. This internalization helps bridge the loss that comes with differentiation, so that now fusion can take place within the self. It is likely that internalization is based on mirror neurons that help integrate the parental image into the inner core of the self. Since empathy and bonding take place through mirror neurons, so the binding of mother with the self maintains this bond internally. As such, the birth of the self, as both object and subject, takes place when the "other" is internalized to form the selfother-self.

Thus, by the age two or three, the core self is established and primed to emerge into higher levels of complexity. At about eight years-of-age, other significant changes take place in the brain, such as the closure of the corpus callosum that ushers in the capacity for both abstract thinking and the communication between the hemispheres. Now the self takes on a broader and more complex image. In adolescence, cognitive abilities allow for greater coherency in one's life story, and therefore greater self-knowledge and understanding. By young adulthood, autobiographical memories become further modified as one's personal narrative grows; this is coupled with a greater understanding of emotional nuances as one's self-differentiation continues to evolve.

In adulthood, the self consists of the many beliefs and expectations that have developed over time. Neural circuits in regions of the prefrontal cortex mediate cognition and emotion that impacts on self-reflection. We assume, therefore, that by adulthood the self is fully developed as a construct. However, this does not mean that one's self is integrated as a whole. Integrative emergence takes place largely through the dynamics of self-organizing complexity.

The self represents an overarching general script whose formation is hierarchical. The basic units of a script are scenes, which coalesce into families of scenes that then develop into affect-scripts, then cost-benefit scripts, and finally complex self-scripts. Looking at this hierarchy in terms of levels of complexity, we see that complex scripts consist of simpler subscripts that are based on their levels of complex organization. We earlier noted that a script hierarchy could be seen, not just in terms of complexity, but also in terms of their relational prominence. In this respect, we look at the hierarchy between a script and its subscripts, which boils down to which script is most salient, intense and urgent within a given context.

This hierarchical structure evolves bottom-up and, as earlier stated, is based on the principle of self-organizing complexity. Bottom-up activity reflects not just the process of developmental evolution or of increasing levels of complexity, but as a dynamical system based on changing information. Thus, although the evolved hierarchy is bottom-up, the flow of information is both bottom-up and top-down.

We will look at the nonlinear integrated model of the self in the next chapter. Suffice it to say that the self is organized vertically, either from the most dominant and complex script to the least dominant and complex script. Given what we believe about the evolutionary-based triune brain, earlier structures and systems are incorporated into later structures and systems; yet the fundamental default program always subsists at the primary level.

Chapter 8: Integration and the Emergent Self

> Integration might be the principle underlying health at all levels of our experience, from the microcosm of our inner world to our interpersonal relationships and life in our communities.
> —Daniel Siegel

Let us now turn from the macro-level of linear, stage-based development to the micro-level of nonlinear emergence. Linearity refers to the relationship between variables in which changes in one variable are associated with, and are directly proportional to, changes in another variable. When we add two to three, we get five in a linear model. In nonlinearity, the change is exponentially different, so that increases are instead to the second, third or of a greater power. This is exemplified when we say that increases in affects are amplified (linear), while increases in scripts are magnified (nonlinear).

Rather than the stage-based model of self-development, we instead look at the emerging self as based on self-organizing complexity. This will take us away from the realm of the observable and familiar, to one that we cannot observe and thus, appears mysterious. Like the analog-digital clock model, change is discrete rather than sequential. What once was, no longer is. Change takes place in distinct segments in which each change is new and different from that which preceded it. When scripts change enough so that it is more different than similar to what it was, it is a new and different script. As small changes accumulate, there comes a point where there is a *just noticeable difference.*[73] Change is continually taking place at the molecular level; what we notice is not this microcosmic changing process, but the changed overall structure that is new and different. This nonlinear change is what self-organizing complexity is about.

In many respects complexity theory is chaos theory, but more so. It is more comprehensive and therefore more applicable to the study of psychosocial systems. Complexity theory proposes that out of randomness emerges order. While complexity theory is strikingly similar to chaos theory, complexity theorists maintain that chaos, by itself, does not account for the coherence of self-organizing complex systems. Rather, complex systems reside at what is called the *edge of chaos*. This edge of chaos does not refer to being on the brink of chaos, but is actually a dynamic state that is in-between chaos and order; in other words, the dynamics of complexity exist as we are moving toward chaos.

A complex system is one in which numerous and independent elements continuously interact, and spontaneously organize and reorganize themselves into more and more elaborate structures. Its large number of interconnected components, when acting in concert, act as a dynamic process that produces coordinated patterns of behavior not available to any one component of the system in isolation from all other components. These component states are adaptive, allowing the system to adjust to new and different situations. There is a built in automatic self-organizing process in which order in the system forms spontaneously.

Complexity is progressive so that over time, the system becomes larger and more sophisticated, producing amazing novelty, some say *near-perpetual* novelty. As with chaos, states of self-organizing complex systems cannot be divided, but are merged into the complexity of the whole system.

---

[73] This is known as a JND in Experimental Psychology

In addition, there is the phenomenon called *time irreversibility*, namely that once a state has morphed into another state, it cannot return to its previous state. This is not only because the newly formed whole is greater and therefore different, or that its molecular or neuronal structure has changed, but also because we cannot replicate the same context that existed in the earlier state. These ideas question our understanding of such traditional concepts as regression and transference; in other words, when we regress to an earlier stage of behavior, or transfer our feelings from past scripts onto the present situation, they are not identical either to the original script or its succeeding reiterations. We are not living in the past, but bringing forth our latest rendition of the past, and all of this is taking place in the context of the now and anticipated future.

The hidden order that is inherent in the evolution of complex systems is part of the laws of nature we do not yet understand. Complexity theory attempts to explain how millions of independent agents can unintentionally demonstrate patterned behaviors and properties that, while present in the overall system, are not present in any individual components of that system. This is beautifully illustrated when we see a flock of birds flying in a harmonious formation, as if a single unit moving here and moving there. This synchrony can also be seen in synchronized swimming; however, unlike being orchestrated top-down as in synchronized swimming, the pattern of flying flocks of birds is taking place spontaneously. In fact, if we look at an individual bird in the flock, it might appear that its flight is completely random, yet when we look at the whole, there is order and symmetry. Complexity theory attempts to discover how these many disparate elements work together to shape the system as a whole, as well as to its outcome. In addition, we would like to know how each component changes over time so that we may better harness its future trajectory.

Thus, from a multitude of independent components, each interacting with each other, emerge an infinite variety of forms that allows for the spontaneous self-organization that takes place in a system. These components are not an organized fixed structure, but are instead a complex adaptive system that is constantly revising and rearranging itself automatically; thus, all emergent states evolve from the interactions of many different components, and not from some overseer or governor. There is no master controller of the system; instead coherence is emerging automatically. Although the self will act as a governor that regulates and organizes scripts top-down, its emergence is taking place spontaneously from the bottom-up. As we shall see, this interconnection between top-down organizing and bottom-up reorganizing, is a critical dynamic underlying the integration of the self. Thus, emergence reflects a "universal capacity of organisms to act as the originators of their own development." [Ingold, 1990]

Complex systems are unpredictable and therefore defy the ability to foresee or calculate the outcome of any given change in the system. Because a system depends on so many intricate interactions, the number of possible reactions to any given change is infinite. Minor events can have enormous consequences because of the chain of reactions they may incite.[74] Conversely, major changes may have an almost insignificant effect on the system as a whole.

---

[74] This is illustrated by the so-called *butterfly effect,* which postulates that a minor event can cause extraordinarily large effects. The term itself was coined by Edward Lorenz, and is derived from the metaphorical example of the details of a tornado (exact time of formation, exact path taken) being influenced by minor perturbations such as the flapping of the wings of a distant butterfly several weeks earlier.

Because of this, strong control of any complex system may be impossible. While it may have order, no one thing absolutely governs a complex system.

When we speak of self-generating bottom-up organization, this does not take away from the need of top-down strategizing. It is unlikely that our civilization would spontaneously emerge without some direction from its inhabitance. The dance between top-down regulation and bottom-up emergence is apparent in many systems. In the American political system, we have the division between states-rights [bottom-up] and a strong Federal government [top-down]; between free market capitalism [bottom-up] and the federal regulation of our financial systems [top-down]. Capitalism assumes that less top-down regulation impedes bottom-up self-organizing dynamics, and thus is a threat to change. The argument is that a free market allows for creativity and new opportunities, while too much order from the top will lead to stagnation. Those who adhere to greater government regulation take a top-down perspective and fear that the absence of adequate controls can lead to chaos, as in an economic depression. Yet, many believe that an optimal balance between just enough order and just enough spontaneity will lead to the greatest advantage and benefit.

In a self-system we speak of self-regulation, whereby the self acts to govern itself. At the basic level this means that more complex self-scripts, especially of the cognitive-self and the emergent-self, will best regulate the affect-self and the physical-self. This illustrates the integrative and interactional nature of self-scripts, and the importance of self-regulation.

As Daniel Siegel (1999) explains, "a complex system is said to regulate its own emergence…self-organization emerges from the interactions among the basic elements that comprise the system…[and is]…quite open to influences outside of ourselves—from people we meet, experiences we have in the world, books we read…[the] triangle of well-being, the system of mind, brain, and relationships, might be more fully understood in these terms, and we might apply the principles of complexity and integration to creating health across each of these three aspects of our lives."

Siegel's quote eloquently brings together self-organizing emergence, complexity *and* integration. Integration is the primary process from which the self evolves into a higher and more complex being, and this takes place through the dynamics of self-organizing complexity. It is important to keep in mind this very promising and hopeful process. When we feel as though we are regressing and falling apart, it likely means that some event set off a state of disequilibrium that will likely, over time, lead to greater levels of integration. This is how wisdom evolves. We could, of course intervene in this chaotic state, and either inhibit or accelerate this naturally unfolding process. For example, taking drugs can inhibit integration, while putting in the effort to handle and then move beyond the chaos can help enhance the integrative and emergent processes.

The integrated-self is, therefore, an emergent system. The integrated-self consists of the totality of all self-scripts, whose interactions must somehow be processed to ensure a coherent, accurate, and rapid representation of the world as our experiences change. Through the property of modularity, the self-system has the capacity to continually reorganize itself through self-organizing emergence. The self-system's nonlinearity and potential for chaos poses formidable problems from which its components and functions must be bound together to produce an unbroken, fluid stream of experience, and the way this is done is referred to as *binding*. Binding occurs through the synchrony of its component parts that produces a unitary, coherent and holistic representation of the world. In many respects binding is like the process we earlier discussed whereby neurons that fire together (synchronize), get wired (bound) together."

This principle of binding is significant for understanding the process of integration. The integration of the self takes place as self-scripts become activated at the same or proximate time, allowing positive scripts[75] to get expressed both cohesively and coherently. First of all, for integration to take place, this interactivity is occurring at the same approximate moment. We know that time is critical in associative learning, so that when scripts become activated at different times there is little opportunity for them to bind together. Temporal integration is important at another level, and that is because it is the basis underlying the emergence of the autobiographical-self; it is only when these past and future scripts merge into the present that they become integrated as a whole.

The APA dictionary (2003) defines the integrated self as *a personality in which the constituent traits, behavioral patterns, motives, and so forth are used effectively and with minimal effort or without conflict. Those with integrated personalities are thought essentially to know themselves, and to enjoy and live life fully.* The dictionary also goes on to say that the integrated personality is the same as the well-integrated self.

As you may have noted, the integrated-self is relatively conflict free. The integrated-self, although a product of optimizing self-regulation (and consequently optimizing affect-regulation), is also what maintains these optimal states. The integrated-self is far more capable of meeting our prescribed needs, especially by maximizing positive scripts and minimizing negative scripts. The more integrated the self is, the greater the degree of emotional wellbeing.

We look at the integrative process in terms of a part-whole relationship whereby different self-scripts bind together, leading to the coherency of the self as a whole. At one level this could mean that self-scripts are so intimately connected together that they display harmony and synchrony, while still maintaining their individuality; at another level, these self-scripts synthesize so tightly and coherently that they lose their individuality as they merge into the self as a whole. Both perspectives are valid. When we look at a woven carpet, we can see both the interconnected individual threads or the rug as whole, or when listening to a symphony we can hear both the harmony of many discrete sounds, or the blending of all into the sound of one.

Some may argue that the state of oneness is a higher state than the state of many, while others say that both states reflect a natural, ongoing flow from one state to the other and then back again. Integration reflects cycles of increasing levels of complexity that is identifiable by alternating states between divergence and convergence that ultimately leads to a state of emergence (and so forth, and so on).

Diagram 8-1 on the next page illustrates the self, not as a hierarchical structure, but as a part-whole integrated system. As you will notice, the upper spokes of the pentagonal represent functional self-scripts. The bodily physical-self is at the apex indicating its essential prominence, while mental (cognitive and emotional) and behavioral self-scripts reside at its sides. Below are the two components of emergent self-scripts, the autobiographical-self and the selfother-self. Each self-script is connected to all other self-scripts, which together make up the whole. In nonlinear terms, each self-script is interacting with all other self-scripts at the same time, while it is also impacting on the whole self, again at the same time. The whole self is not the sum of its parts, but is far greater than the sum of its parts. To examine the interaction of just two self-script is not sufficient, since it excludes the impact of all other

---

[75] Remember that negative scripts impede integration and instead serves to promote disintegration.

self-scripts. This does not mean that relating two self-scripts is of little value; it just means that the data does not consider the whole, and will thus be distorted.

Diagram 8-1
The Integrative Self
Robert Kayton

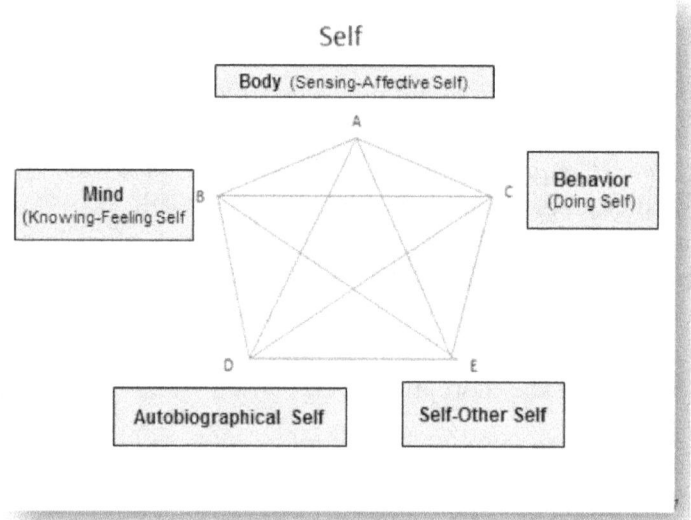

To summarize, the process by which self-scripts integrate into higher levels of complexity can be seen, at the mega-level, as perpetually ongoing cycles from states of relative chaos and disequilibrium to states of relative order and equilibrium. In the chaotic state, disintegration takes place, which then allows for the emergence of a more organized complex state. This is the natural order of life. At the more basic script level, we see this dynamic in terms of similarities and differences, of convergence and divergence whereby a script changes when differences outweigh similarities.

From a topographical perspective, the integrative process takes place through both top-down organization and bottom-up emergence. These processes are going on instantaneously as a coevolving, synchronized system. As the mental cortical-self is regulating and organizing scripts top-down, the bodily limbic-self is regulating and reorganizing the cortical-self bottom-up, each operating as partners in an ongoing dance. For example, crossing a street is largely an implicit bottom-up activity. However, when one peripherally sees a car approaching, then conscious top-down processing will take over. Thus, there is a coordinated interaction between higher and lower levels of the mind. In this example, bottom-up processing was dominant until danger was perceived, then top-down processing took over. In this respect, they function as an integrated self-system.

When the self-system is instead poorly integrated, then there may be either too much bottom-up activity or too much top-down activity, without an interactive equilibrium to help balance these systems. Ultimately, however, we strive toward an optimum level of top-down and bottom-up synchronization so as to better inform our self as to what is going on emotionally, and what is going on cognitively; when well regulated, the self-as-organizer can function more effectively. In this regard we refer to spontaneous and automatic self-regulation since the self-system is regulating itself. This is what self-organizing complexity is all about and how this leads to the well-integrated self and its subsequent state of emotional wellbeing. The more one integrates, the more one is self-integrating.

Our conscious-self as subject, that is the pronoun "I," has the power to govern top-down regulation and organizational functioning. By utilizing our wisdom, agency and willpower we have the power to also indirectly control our own emergence; by using our accumulated wisdom wisely, we can exert our agency and willpower to indirectly determine our ultimate bottom-up emergence. In other words, as "I" am organizing and regulating scripts top-down, "I" am automatically changing bottom-up; "I" organizes "me" in integrating "myself."

Thus, (my)self can be thought of as the "I" and the "me." "Any action that can be planned, initiated, carried out from beginning to end and remembered as a personally written script will be subsumed under the umbrella of 'me'." (Nathanason,2008) The "I" likely develops later, beginning with self-awareness at age two. As you may recall, Tomkins and Nathanson pointed out that the first act of the self is autosimulation, the infant's purposeful act of thumb sucking. We could also say that when the infant begins to modify inscripts, it is also an act of the self-agency; not that the infant contemplates this, since it is an implicit action, yet it is purposeful and intentionally directed by the infant.

The Emergent Self

In this section, we will discuss the temporal and spatial aspects of the emergent self, namely the autobiographical self and the selfother self. Unlike the structural based functional self, the emergent self represents the dynamic system of integration. Since Einstein, we know that time and space are interlocked, and that time is a variable of space, thus making the spatial dimension more primary than the temporal dimension; in other words, time is relative to space. Since the autobiographical self is mostly temporal, and the selfother self is mostly spatial, we can thereby assume that the selfother self is primary to the autobiographical self; thus, the autobiographical self is relative to the selfother self as evidenced when we think of our past, or envision the future, it will most often be expressed in terms of selfother scenes.

The Autobiographical Self

> We are what we were, and become where we go. By rescripting the past, we change who we are and by doing and living our future now, we become that future now.

Time is a peculiar phenomenon. On the one hand, there is *real* time that is objectively measured by such mechanisms as todays atomic clocks. Objective time is precise, fixed and linear. Yet, our experience of time is subjective and based on our perception of time, which is variable and nonlinear.

Since time variability is based on perceived time, rather than on real time, there develops *temporal illusions*. An illusion is a mistaken sensory perception. Among the kinds of temporal illusions people have are as follows:[76] people tend to recall recent events as occurring further back in time than they actually did, and distant events as occurring more recently than they actually did; shorter intervals tend to be overestimated while longer intervals tend to be under-estimated; time intervals associated with many changes may be

---

[76] Wikipedia

perceived as longer than intervals with fewer changes; the perceived temporal length of a given task may shorten with greater motivation; the perceived temporal length of a given task may stretch when broken up or interrupted; auditory stimuli may appear to last longer than visual stimuli; time durations may appear longer with greater stimulus intensity (e.g., auditory loudness or pitch).

Distortions in time are related to a number of factors, among which are context, affects, space, and age. Recent studies show that time is partly a function of one's culture. Some societies have no conception of time, such as the Piraha of the Amazon who live only in the present. Nomads base time on the seasons of the year. Those who live in rural areas also base time on the seasons and move at a more leisurely pace than do urbanites. Americans live at a far greater pace than those in Latin countries. Some religions date the beginning of time to about 5500 years ago, while scientists date time to the big-bang, some 4-5 billion years.

We all have experienced periods when time itself seems to drag on, while at other times it seems to go by too fast. Some of these differences are based on affects: when engaged in an activity where interest-excitement is activated, time seems to fly by, while when having to sit through a boring lecture, which activates distress-anguish, time seems interminable; when lying on a beach, time seems to stop; in surprise-startle time seems frozen, and yet it is paradoxically experienced as forever. In other words there seems to be a direct correlation between affect gradients and the perception of time. For affects with increasing gradients time seems to go by faster, while for the non-gradient affects, time seems slower. The excitatory, increasing gradient affects are experienced more in the now than either the non-gradient affects or decreasing affect of enjoyment-joy. Enjoyment-joy is inhibitory, as evidenced by the downward-angle of decreasing rates and densities of neural firings. It also appears that the non-excitatory affects extend more in time, given the reduced energy costs as compared to the increasing rates and densities of the excitatory affects.

In physics, there is an inverse correlation between speed and time in which time seems to slow down when an object speeds up, and conversely, time speeds up as an object moves more slowly. The *spatialization of time,* that is the findings that time is relative to space, was one of Einstein's great discoveries. The experience of time, as relative to space, is exemplified by our conceptualization of time in spatial terms. Thus, to progress in time is to move *forward*, while to regress in time is to move *back*ward; to look at the future is to look *ahead* while to go *back* in time is to look at the past. Time "flies" or it "crawls." When scheduled, time is infinite or it is finite. The past is depicted to the left, and the future to the right in western cultures, but is often the opposite in other cultures. We gesture backwards when speaking of the past and forward when speaking of the future. Spatial-visual imagery certainly affords a more stable image than does the *fluid flow of time*; this relatively fixed spatial image provides a far better model for conceptualizing time, and thus for communicating about it to oneself and to others.

Time also seems to speed up with aging, which often causes people to increasingly underestimate a given interval of time. This fact can likely be attributed to a variety of changes in the aging brain, such as the lowering of dopaminergic levels. When the elderly look back in time, it seems that time has lost its dimensionality, as though time has flattened or leveled out so that it is difficult to remember whether an incident occurred two years-ago or five years-ago, unless there are specific markers that help anchor an incident to a given time frame. In a non-controlled survey of seniors, I found that a majority of them experienced their feeling-self as they did two-to-three decades earlier, yet acknowledged that this did not apply to their physical-self and behavioral-self.[77]

By convention time is cast in three dimensions, past, present and future. Even this division can be controversial. What is the present? Does it not end the moment it begins and thus becomes a part of the past? Unlike the one-dimensionality of the present, that is the *specious present* (William James), the past can be divided into the distant or recent past. And what about the future? How do we know it exists? Dimensionality is imaginative as we look to the near future and the distant future. Nevertheless, our autobiographical self is based on the integration of the past with the present and future, all melded together as one.

Blinder (2007) points out that "one's self is both a story and a locus of being." (p. 277) He believes that "the concept of autobiographical self emerges...as a function of the child's representational capacities." He further points out that "personal autobiographical memory is functionally and structurally related to the use of cultural myths and social narratives." This comes about through interactions with parents, teachers, relatives and peers. "Parent-child conversations are a medium through which children can begin to understand the meaning of past experience." (p. 278) He also points to the lack of specific memories before age three.

With greater socialization opportunities, and furthering autonomy, there is an even greater push toward increasingly higher-level cortical structures, especially the orbitofrontal and prefrontal cortices. By age eight, the two cerebral hemispheres get connected via the corpus callosum, allowing a greater interchange between the implicit right hemisphere's sense of self and the explicit left hemisphere's conceptualization of the self.

The autobiographical self is the temporal-self that consists of all the stored emotional memories and scripts that have accumulated during a lifetime. Although one's history seems fixed in our mind, it is constantly being rewritten whenever we recall a memory. As discussed earlier, simply remembering an event or scene from our past will change that memory from what it was, to what it becomes; thus, the act of recalling an event will automatically change the memory of that event. This is largely because remembering occurs in a different context than before, and so will be experienced in a slightly different way than it was originally. When that memory reconsolidates, there are changes in its molecular structure, leading to what now becomes a revised memory.

Our past reflects the story of our self, or better said, the many stories that make up our life. A story has a plot with a beginning, middle and end; it is a script that is made up of many scenes and events. For each of us, these scripts help define us as a person. They explain our character, temperament and make-up. Although there are many commonalities among different people, each of us has a unique and individualized story. When we are first getting to know someone, we rely not only on our immediate experience with that person, but also on his or her life story. Many of our questions will be about a person's origins and childhood, how they got to be where they are now.

Although the past seems known to us (though different when remembered), the future seems indefinite to us. This can evoke fear or excitement, depending on one's expectations. When we anticipate good things we are excited, and when we predict bad things we are fearful. We all have a need to try and make the unknown known, so we try filling in the blanks. Some people look at what is possible, which opens up so many imagined outcomes that it can become a fertile field for unrealistic expectations, good and bad. Often what is

---

[77] In another non-controlled study, I found a relatively high, though not-significant correlation between the time one is born and whether one becomes an "early-bird" who wakes up early, or an "owl" who wakes up late.

possible is mistakenly believed to be what is likely, without any rational attempt to challenge these assumptions; in this respect judgment is ruled not by reason but by emotion. These are the moments when one needs to calm down and engage in probabilistic thinking. Probability is the most efficacious measure to predict the future; this gives us an inner sense that the future can be "known" within the parameters of a statistical model. We have already discussed probabilistic thinking under cognitive-behavioral rescripting.

What does it actually mean to be temporally integrated? Essentially it means that living in the now is guided by the past, the present and expected future, and together with wisdom, self-agency and willpower coalesce as intricately embedded factors in our everyday life. Unlike the shallowness of one who lives primarily in the present, or the person whose life is trapped in the past, or the worrier who dreads tomorrow, or the dreamer who yearns for the day he will become very important, the integrated person is one for whom there is a depth of character and who is seen as wise, proactive, and multifaceted.

Those who are stuck in the past, without relief for a better future, tend to be pessimists. If the past is seen as negative then this will be the prologue governing the future; if, on the other hand the past is seen as completely wonderful, then the expectations for a wonderful future will likely be experienced as disappointing.

People who live in the negative past tend to be depressed. Their ruminations are considered to be attempts to magically resolve the past by reliving it in their minds, in what Freud called a *repetition compulsion.* The irrationality of this is apparent since past events are revived over-and-over in similar ways it was experienced, so that the past continues to be reinforced as bad; in fact, it often becomes worse as memories are negatively reconsolidated. Both the present and future are framed on this basis, which then becomes self-fulfilling prophecies. Hope is diminished, as darkening despair deepens within.

On the other hand, those who have created a Garden-of-Eden past with little mooring in a more realistic history, and who continually wish for what was imagined, are often described as dreamers and romantics. They are Pollyanna's whose denial of the negative leaves them living in a world of nostalgic discontent.

We have often discussed context, and especially the context of age; from a temporal perspective this has tremendous impact on one's integrative position. We have said that the emergence into wellbeing is more likely for the elderly, which makes sense given the primacy of wisdom and self-agency. For those in their youth and adulthood, there is less past and more future, while for seniors the past is long and the future is limited.

Considered among the top tasks for the elderly is coming to terms with their past and future. Many seniors report that they frequently think about the past. For example, an elderly patient of mine once told me about his tendency to think about past events with shame and guilt, emotions he suppressed at the time the event occurred. He told me about how well he dealt with these be conflicts for which he always had a rationale in his reframes. True, these were adaptive at the time; the failure with a client at work, or the blunder made at a board meeting, were rationalized not as failures, but as lessons well learned. In addition, they showed how assertive he was by speaking his mind, even when it led to undesirable consequences. His rationalizations, however, resulted in his repressing these images and feelings into his unconscious, which were tucked away only to begin emerging in the latter years of his life[78].

---

[78] Like all defense mechanisms rationalizations are geared to cope with the present, even though a price may be extracted in the future.

Many seniors ruminate on the past, as did this patient; his task was to now rescript his memory by facing and experiencing these painful feelings, rather than avoiding them by putting them back *into the* past; by dealing with these feelings, the past will no longer be present to impede integration.

Seniors are also dealing with physical and mental decline, setting the context from which the future is framed. In addition, friends and family are dying which acts as a constant reminder of one's own limited future. To deal with this gloomy prospect, such attributes as humility and spirituality, wisdom and self-agency become necessary and essential for feeling competent and attaining and maintaining emotional wellbeing.

Affectively, seniors live life more through enjoyment-joy than interest-excitement. This affective change allows seniors to focus more on the now for their happiness, since ambition and achievement, which are future oriented needs, are now less important.

There is an interesting account of two elderly friends, one whose internal reverie usually centered on past events. He was a storyteller who constantly told tales about his youth. Almost every event would bring about some association to his childhood; he lived in the past. Why he did so could be attributed to a number of factors, such as the past having many unresolved issues, or as a defense against the present and future. The other friend lived largely in the future. He reported that most of his thoughts were about the future; planning his next outing, thinking of the tasks ahead of him, or rehearsing a meeting he will soon have. Interestingly, as a man in his middle seventies, he recently said that he had been thinking a lot about the past. It is, of course, no surprise that thinking about such a limited future is no longer adaptive, or as important as it once was.

To rescript past memories, seniors need to feel the feelings (the felt-feel) whenever these memories come up: hold onto those feelings for several minutes, or until they become too unpleasant; then intervene using some of the affect-focused and cognitive-behavioral techniques already discussed; then let go and refocus. Remember that rescripting entails (a) awareness, (b) intervention and then (c) practice. The goal of practicing in this case is not to inculcate the rescripted skills but instead its opposite, namely to habituate these feelings into insignificance since we want to eliminate reactions rather than build them into the self. You should intervene whenever the memory comes up and then practice on a regular scheduled basis.

Younger adults live in a very different context than seniors. They are driven by success and achievement so that the present is largely contextualized into the future. Much of their life is anticipatory as they look at what is ahead of them. Unlike seniors, who tend to ruminate about the past, younger adults will more often dream of the future. True, the past, which is relatively recent and continues to play a primary role in their life, and for some it plays too much of a role that then limits future progress. For seniors, the future is known; for younger adults, the future is unknown. The unknown can activate fear and avoidance or excitement and attraction; again, past and present contexts (together with one's predisposition) are critical factors determining whether fear or interest will dominate.

The Selfother Self

Selfother self-scripts make up our social self. As referenced earlier, George Berkeley stated that for the self to exist it must be perceived by others. Self-awareness comes when we "know" that others perceive us; and it is not until we internalize others into the personal space of our inner self, that our self comes *to be*. This perception is attained when others respond to our own expressions of affect that calls into being our existence. The idea that our sense of self emerges within the context of others was highlighted by Francis Broucek.

The role that seeing and being seen plays in the development of the self now comes together in the form of the selfother-self. It evolved from Alan Shore's *selfmother-self*, and comes into being at the age when we become aware of our body, thereby differentiating our self from our mother; now there is self *and* there is non-self, i.e. the *other*. Through interpersonal relationships this *other-self* merges with one's own self to form the *selfother-self*. We must, however, not limit the selfother-self to just human relationships. The selfother-self also extends to our relationship with nature, the world of animals and plants, as well as our entire environment; this is part of the extended self. Nevertheless, it is our connection with other people, and especially our parents and significant others, that forms the crucible from which the self evolves.

As one differentiates from their mother, the process of individuation begins. Although there are many definitions of individuation, the most well-known is by Carl Jung who defined it as the mode which forms the self by integrating elements of the conscious and unconscious mind. I, instead, define it as the process by which an individual forms those unique personality features that distinguish one's self from others. Through individuation the person is developing the component parts of the self, namely the self-scripts that lead to the integration of the self. To summarize, first there is differentiation, then individuation, and then integration.

The failure to fully differentiate and individuate leads to many problems that are particularly characteristic of personality disorders, most notably the narcissistic and borderline personalities. Many cognitive distortions, such as misattributions and unrealistic expectations, are prominent. Shame is the primary affect involved as one vacillates between too much shame and too little shame. For example, the narcissist will shamelessly demand attention from others, yet be overwhelmed with *humiliated fury* when "rejected." Shame, as the master emotion, needs to be integrated into the self as pride, which cannot occur if there is a failure to fully differentiate.

Most people fall somewhere between full differentiation and no differentiation. An example of someone who fears too much separation and differentiation are those who are overly compliant and dependent. They tend to agree and support others to a fault, and come across as both submissive and conforming. On the other hand, there are those who fear merger (intimacy) as a loss of self; contrarians are a good example.

A contrarian is someone who usually acts in a contrary way, by taking an opposing side from whatever position another person takes. Contrarious define the phrase "to go against the grain." They never hesitate to inject a contrary point viewpoint: if you say "right" they say "left," if you say *banaaana* they say *ba'nahna,* if you say tomato they say *to'ma'to*. Contrarians will dismiss facts when contrary to their contrarian belief. This is often characterized by such definitive statements as "I don't believe that," or "that's wrong," rather than expressing curiosity or doubt, such as "that's hard to accept, but I'll look it up later." Contrarians tend to have a strong sense of certainty about their opinions.

Interpersonal self-scripts reflect the social roles one plays out in their social interactions, many of which were discussed earlier. They are observable and subject to outside social scrutiny; they are interactional in that each participant is impacting the *other* as well as being impacted on. Much of our social judgment stems from the selfother-self, which allows for empathy and the capacity to realistically judge what another person feels, which is called the *theory of mind*.

Intrapersonal scripts are essentially introjections of interpersonal interactions; these interactions are not objective, yet they are interactional since each inner voice mutually impacts the other voice. Since there is no external voice, only those created by the self, one can intentionally change the narrative to ones that entail positive scripts.

Special forms of selfother self-scripts are identity scripts. Identity scripts develop through our identification with others' attitudes, standards, and personality traits that become internalized as a part of the self. Our identity is known by the roles and labels we place on these attributes; thus, we have Erik Berne's identity scripts that he labels the Child, Parent and Adult, or we talk about real and false self-identity scripts such as the *Imposter Syndrome*. Identity shares the continuity and sense of sameness associated with the self, except that it changes when our identified label changes; for example, my professional identity changed when I retired from my clinical practice in psychology, yet my sense of self remained the same.

Among the most helpful scripts are those that describe the direction that inter-actions take, such as the *Dance Away Lover*. (Daniel Goldstine, 1977) Karen Horney described three choices one may take toward others, *moving towards*, *moving away* or moving against. Moving toward others is affiliative and prosocial; moving away is rejection; moving against is anti-social. There is a fourth possibility, namely not-moving in any direction, whether it is toward, away or against another. The reasons behind immobilization can reflect a number of states of mind such as indifference, indecisiveness, or hostility.

To assume that moving toward others is reflective of a behavioral style associated with a more integrated selfother-self can be a mistake, since it can instead reflect unresolved dependency or fusion needs. On the other hand, moving away can reflect a more integrated selfother-self, such as when the other person is hostile. In most cases we can rightly assume that a behavioral style characterized by moving against another is indicative of a failure to integrate.

Carl Jung identified two primary traits related to inner directedness vs. outer directedness, namely introversion and extraversion. The Meyers-Brig Test has popularized this polarity. Jung postulated that extroversion is more prominent among the young, but as we age we turn more inward; affectively this makes sense if we consider the dominance of interest-excitement in the young and of enjoyment-joy when we age. Some identify these propensities as either-or polarities, while others see them as reflective of a continuum based on degrees of one or the other; this latter view makes more sense prompting psychologists to coin the term *ambiversion* to describe those who show a relative balance between the two. In addition, since Jung postulated that a person's directedness changes over time shows that he believed these tendencies differed in degree, and not in kind.

Introversion often characterizes someone as shy and reticent, or pejoratively as a nerd or geek. These depictions are incorrect since introverts can be very sociable, especially with friends. Introversion is the tendency to be self-directed and self-reflective, whose focus is more on mental energy than on physical energy (Jung). Introverts often take pleasure in solitary activities such as reading, writing, using computers, hiking and fishing. An introvert is likely to enjoy time spent alone and find less reward in time spent with large groups of people.

Extraversion is the trait characterized by those who mainly gets gratification from others, instead of from within. Extraverts tend to enjoy human interactions and be enthusiastic, talkative, and gregarious. Extraverts are energized and thrive off being around other people, and bored or unhappy when alone. They take pleasure in activities that involve large social gatherings, such as parties, community activities, public demonstrations, and business or political groups. They also tend to work well in groups.

Hans Eysenck (1967) described extraversion-introversion according to the degree to which a person is outgoing and interactive with other people. These behavioral differences are presumed to be the result of underlying differences in brain physiology. He proposed that combinations in the degrees each trait was present, determined different personality types. Eysenck proposed that extraversion was caused by variability in cortical arousal: "introverts are characterized by higher levels of activity than extraverts and so are chronically more cortically aroused…" As a consequence of having this relatively high level of mental arousal leads introverts to seek lower levels of external stimulation. Conversely, the extravert seeks to heighten his or her arousal to a more favorable level by increased activity, social engagement and other stimulation-seeking behaviors.

Many of the interpersonal styles discussed so far are also reflected in our *intrapersonal* dialogues. Although our thoughts may at times seem like monologues, they are actually dialectic interchanges between our self and our internalized selfother-self; in other words, the introjected *other* actually represents a part of the self. For example, when thinking about an event in which one's boss was particularly critical and hurtful, the internalized dialogue may represent the parental-self (the "I") shaming the child-self (the "me").

Since many of our internal narratives are attempts to resolve conflicts, their focus is on issues involving such negative emotions as anger, fear, and especially shame. Shame is the absence of power, and thereby reflects what our dialogues are usually about, namely to feel more power. Anger themes reflect the shame underlying anger, while fear themes reflect the powerlessness of shame. It is therefore important to pay attention to your own inner dialogues and identify those scripts you are playing out. You can certainly intervene if you do not find them helpful, and change the theme and dialogue to more positive thoughts. Rather than these internal interactions being directed bottom-up, they can now be directed top-down by the selfother-self when using these techniques.

Chapter 9: Emotional Wellbeing and the Integrated Self

Emotional wellbeing is most often associated with health - physical, mental and social. Emotional health takes place when these three areas become integrated. However, wellbeing goes beyond one's emotional condition and instead impacts on the very quality and essence of life, which is to live it well. Just because one *feels* emotionally healthy does not necessarily mean that person is actualized and fulfilled and living in a state of wellbeing; this can only come through the integration of the self.

In addition, many assume that either they have it or they don't have it; yet we know that in truth we sometimes do and sometimes don't. Wellbeing is organic; it is not a static state of being, but a dynamic state of becoming. Implicit in this view is that wellbeing is always evolving. All of us go through times when we clearly do not feel any sense of wellbeing. We may feel exhausted and overly tired, had a bad day at work, argued with a close friend, or got a bad medical diagnosis. Yet this does not mean that one lacks wellbeing; it just means that one is going through a rough time that will pass with the passage of time, as has happened so many other times in one's life. Complexity theory tells us that these ups-and-downs are the naturally occurring cycles of life that, in the long run, usually takes us to an even higher plane of living.

Wellbeing is a part of Freud's concept of *Eros*, the life energy force, the inherent progressive nature built into all living things. If we stop for a moment and consider the natural course of evolution, we see that it takes us forward toward greater and more adaptive levels of living. Although Freud talked about a negative energy force, *Thanatos*[79], it is actually counter-intuitive to believe that this is built into the DNA structure of living things, whose essence is to grow and survive.[80]

Wellbeing evolves from positive affects and consists of positive self-scripts. In fact, negative affects and negative scripts are antithetical to wellbeing. When asked what emotional wellbeing is, one is likely to equate it with such positive emotions as happiness, serenity, contentment, and equanimity, emotions that stem from the affect enjoyment-joy. However, we can also think of wellbeing as an active engagement in life, if not a zest for living life to its fullest. This involves a sense of accomplishment and a feeling of being a part of the community with others, of living a life that is good, good for oneself and good for others; in this respect, wellbeing also stems from the affect interest-excitement.

Wellbeing is both a state of mind and a state of being. When we evaluate how competently we function, we use objective measures. To evaluate our performance at work we look at such variables as productivity levels and durability; when we examine our social life, we consider how often we are invited to social gatherings, how many friends we have, and the frequency with which we feel good or bad when interacting with family. Wellbeing, on the other hand, relies not on objective measures, but on self-evaluation questionnaires. We can ask others to rate a person's state of being, yet this too is highly subjective and lacks any means for validation. This is because wellbeing is based on our own *sense* of being and thus tells us how we feel about our inner self.

---

[79] Freud reluctantly called Thanatos the "death instinct." This controversial viewpoint was largely determined by the context he was living in, namely Nazi-occupied Austria.

[80] This statement obviously does not apply to the elderly, for whom there is cellular necrosis.]

As we know, functioning relies on the fulfillment of our affect-regulating prescripts, namely to decrease negative affect, increase positive affect, and maximize affective expression. Wellbeing reflects the regulation of our script-based prescripts, which is to magnify positive self-scripts, minimize negative self-scripts, and maximize the expression of self-scripts in optimal ways. It is when all three prescripts are fulfilled at the same time that we attain wellbeing; thus, to just magnify positive scripts, without minimizing negative scripts, does not lead to wellbeing. In a negative cost-benefit script, such as addiction, we see heightened positive emotions followed by such negative emotions as distress, anger, fear or shame, experiences that will impair one's sense of self. Nor do we see wellbeing when the expression of an affect is impeded; this can certainly be the case when someone is so fearful of their anger that they suppress it, leading to negative-regulating affect-scripts such as sarcasm or other pejorative actions.

As affect-regulation is fundamental to functioning well, the regulation and organization of self-scripts is essential for wellbeing. The regulation of self-scripts follows the prescriptive rules related to functioning, while the organization of self-scripts follows rules related to the formation of scripts into an integrated whole. Regulation and organization provide the order that maintains homeostasis and balance, and therefore stability. When there is a disruption to this homeostasis, there is then *dis*order. We feel this when we agitate, when a negative event and negative affect disturbs our equilibrium.

On the other hand, without any disorder there will then be stasis and thus a lack of growth and development. Yet, life has a way of throwing curve balls at us that rocks our level of stability, thus creating disequilibrium. This is a natural process of living. We move from order to disorder, and hopefully back to order in never-ending cycles. Our goal is to work toward regulating that which is dysregulated so as to attain a higher and more complex state of equilibrium that will then help us move more-and-more toward greater levels of wellbeing. As affect-regulation works to stabilize our functioning on an everyday basis, self-regulation helps stabilize our sense of self, a fundamental factor for attaining wellbeing.

Factors Related to Wellbeing

All people are not created equal. Some of us are unfortunately born with medical conditions, or an innate temperament that will limit, if not preclude, the development of wellbeing. Others suffer such traumatic indignities of abuse and neglect in early childhood that it is unlikely to be undone in later life. Yet, for those who are severely impaired there still is the opportunity to attain some degree of happiness; thus, for the vast majority of people, some degree of wellbeing is attainable. However, wellbeing doesn't just come to us; we have to work for it. Critical to this process is both effort and perseverance, proactive behaviors that are essential for attaining many of the essential components that make up wellbeing, such as self-efficacy, self-agency and willpower.

Learning from experience, and using that learning in adaptive and competent ways, is another fundamental attribute found in wellbeing; we call this wisdom. As we shall see, wisdom develops with age, so that a state of wellbeing is most likely to emerge, in a significant way, later in life. Wisdom comes from the proverbial *school of hard knocks,* which prepares us for dealing with the many tribulations that make up life.

Wisdom and self-agency represent two essential components of wellbeing. These are largely excitatory processes that develop through the cognification of interest-excitement, and is mediated by the dopaminergic system. The other necessary component for wellbeing emerges through enjoyment-joy; these are the emotional components of happiness and equanimity.

We shall examine these essential attributes of wellbeing in greater detail. Before doing so, let us first discuss some of the critical factors that influence, if not determine, the attainment of wellbeing.

Competency in Functioning

It goes without saying that the cognitive and behavioral skills we learned in life set the scaffolding upon which wellbeing can be built. The ability to directly control and manage both affects and emotions through such affect-focused rescripting techniques as relaxation, affect expression modification, or distraction provide a fundamental approach for directly minimizing negative affect. The skills learned in controlling negative thinking through refocusing, enhancing positive thinking through self-talk, and reframing a negative perspective to one that is positive, or at least is less negative, is critical not only in regulating affect but in building a broader perspective of one's self and one's life that can help lead to wisdom and equanimity. Finally, through the myriad of behavioral rescripting techniques we can develop those proactive and assertive behaviors that are crucial to the development of self-agency and willpower.

Learning these skills and strategies comes by way of our experiences in overcoming obstacles. All learning, in fact, requires effort, which is essential for learning new ways of dealing with new and difficult situations. Whenever there is something new and different, there is the factor of the unknown. Uncertainty, as well adversity, can create anxiety and distress, which in turn can impair the ability to learn valuable lessons from some of these events, lessons that help lead to greater wisdom and wellbeing. This negativity can be mitigated both by regulating and reducing the fear-terror and distress-anguish affects while, at the same time, increasing both interest-excitement, the critical affect for developing new learning, and enjoyment-joy, the affect that promotes the consolidation into memory of this new learning.

These positive affects also provide a buffer to adversity and uncertainty, thereby allowing one to better learn from these negative experiences.

Temperamental Predisposition

We have spoken about temperament as an inborn affect propensity, whereby certain affects are more sensitized toward activation and amplification. Ask any parent who has two or more children; from birth, they could immediately identify significant differences in, say, activity level, and notice that these observed differences are largely carried into their childhood and adulthood. There is also research on early infant behavior that seems to corroborate these observations. Of course, this is not always the case. We often do hear stories of the calm placid child who turns out to live a life of misery and suffering; and with equal frequency, we hear of the difficult and troublesome child who grows up to be a pillar of society. Yet, these stories stand out and get our attention because they are so unusual; overall, we can justifiably say that the probability of an even-tempered newborn attaining wellbeing is greater than for a deeply troubled newborn.

Autobiographical Memory

Autobiographical memory provides the template for the construction of one's self in space and time; this will ultimately provide one with a sense of coherency, and an "extended consciousness that places a person in an individual history over time, aware of a lived past and anticipated future." (Blinder, 2007, p.276) Blinder further points out that "autobiographical memories provide the content...[while] episodic memories provide the sensory and perceptual components of experiencing self-recollection." (278)

Autobiographical memory, as potentially remembered memory, begins to develop between ages three and four. At this time, a number of neurological functions come into play. As previously stated, the earliest memories are processed through the olfactory system, and then expands to include all other sensory data via the thalamic relay system. According to Blinder (2007), "from a multilevel coalescence of signals within the somatosensory system integrated through special thalamic lines into the insula, the more fundamental homeostatic and momentary events lead to the beginning of a self-process...[the] self is not the same as the conscious self because much of who we are as individuals takes place outside of conscious awareness."(pp. 276-277) The hippocampus matures as the left hemisphere begins its dopaminergic and synaptogenic development; at this same time there is greater inhibition of activity in the right hemisphere. In addition, the orbitofrontal cortex takes on a greater role in the regulation of affects as well as in the cognitive storage of information to be used by the prefrontal cortices. These neurological developments are accompanied by changes in affective and cognitive functioning. Cognitively, semantic language begins in earnest. Not only is interpersonal communication more verbal, but the *dialogical* self, consisting of our inner narratives, develops as well.

By age 8, when the two cerebral hemispheres connect, there is an increase in the communication between the implicit right-hemisphere's sense of self, and the more explicit left-hemispheric conceptualization of self. This is the beginning of the integration of the self, and of the development of higher-level prefrontal cortical activity. In adolescence, cognitive abilities allow for greater coherency in one's life-story, and therefore greater self-knowledge and understanding. By young adulthood autobiographical memories become further modified as one's personal narrative grows with the greater understanding of emotional nuances, together with ones expanding self-differentiation and personal knowledge and experience. "Mental *time travel* through subjective time that allows one to experience the past through self-awareness is the last feature of autobiographical memory to become fully operational." (Blinder, p. 278)

Our epigenetic history is written into our autobiographical history; what this means is that although there is an inborn temperament, events are critical for activating these genetically encoded programs. Both the sanguine newborn, who is subjected to a chaotic environment, or the overactive newborn that is treated to a stable environment, the situation will have a mediating effect on these inborn tendencies.

Psychology has gone back and forth between the nature-nurture "controversy." From the 1950s through the 1980s, learned experiences took precedence; during the 1990s through the early part of the 21st century, biology was dominant; recently there has been a move back toward a focus on learned experiences. This time, however, without the burden of either-or thinking, both genetics and experiences are co-equals in determining our functioning; therefore, nature gets actualized and modified by experience-dependent learning. Rather than thinking of nature vs. nature as a controversy, in which one or the other is most significant, we instead speak of nature and nurture as the nature-nurture complex, or as Tomkins puts it, the *nature-nurture accord*.

The idea that our autobiographical past, in particular our childhood, is of critical significance in setting the stage for wellbeing, is quite evident. Most of us look to our past to help describe our present condition. It is from our experiences in life that scripts emerge, scripts that enhance or impede our developing sense of wellbeing; in fact, both wisdom and functioning are essentially based on life experiences.

We have spoken of the continuity between the genetic temperament of the newborn and the disposition and temperament of the adult. We also emphasized the value of learning through adversarial experiences. There have also been a number of studies showing the same continuity between childhood experiences and later adult functioning. We have discussed, for example, the signature studies by Mary Ainsworth [Chapter 4, page 62]. These studies showed not only that parenting effects a child's developing scripts, whether positive or negative, but that scripts formed in childhood are maintained 40 years later in follow up studies: those exposed to secure attachments were more likely to develop stable relationships and states of relative wellbeing, while those exposed to insecure parenting were likely to have disturbed relationships and inner conflicts.

Evidently, most theorists focus on the significance of early childhood in forming our basic personality. As the study cited above indicates, along with a plethora of other studies, this is undoubtedly the case. Freud highlighted the significance of childhood in determining later development. He identified three childhood stages, the oral, anal, and phallic stages, by which certain critical conflicts arose, which if not resolved, would lead one to be stuck and fixated on the issues that were prominent at that earlier age. Given the demands to move on and not stay stuck, children developed defense mechanisms that were adaptive at that time, but became maladaptive as one grew into adolescence and adulthood. These defensive mechanisms reflect cost-benefit scripts, which with few exceptions, are maladaptive and make up what we call psychopathology.

Through these defense mechanisms, negative events get relegated to the unconscious in the form of repressed memories. When these defense mechanisms failed to successfully keep these memories under wrap, there is a tension build-up that leads to anxiety and suffering. Freud's remedy was psychoanalysis, an approach based on reviewing one's autobiographical past so as to gain insight into these conflicts and how they impact one's state of mind in the present, and thereby resolve these early conflicts. This came about by making the unconscious conscious, thereby giving the ego, the executive cortical part of the brain, the ability to work them through. Although Freud's psychoanalysis has been much maligned these past several decades, particularly his psychoanalytic therapy technique, there is a growing resurgence for some major parts of his theory, such as his proposition that resolving past conflicts is necessary and essential for the development of wellbeing.

The affect-rescripting model accepts the premise that autobiographical memories (from childhood) can interfere in learning strategies and skills for competent functioning, thus impairing the integration of the self and the development of wellbeing. In affect-rescripting therapy there is this working assumption: if a patient does not learn new and adaptive strategies, then defensive scripts from the past are likely interfering; in this scenario, rescripting the past is necessary. The corollary to this working assumption is that when a patient is progressing nicely, it is likely that the past is not present, and so there would be less of a need to thoroughly review the person's past. However, when it comes to wellbeing, it is essential that we deal with past scripts so as to allow them to be integrated into the self in a cohesive and coherent way; specifically, this means rescripting the past by minimizing the negative affect that saturates negative memories

Critical for the development of wellbeing is that one *not* repress negative experiences.[81] Yes, negative affects and negative scripts impede integration and thereby block the attainment of wellbeing; this is apparent since these negative experiences will remain as negative memories in our unconscious and so will likely continue to interfere with the integration of the self and the consequent attainment of wellbeing. Thus, it is necessary not to ignore or deny negative experiences, but to bring them into conscious awareness so they can be successfully rescripted.

Context

We have been discussing how significant the past is for the development of wellbeing. We must, however, look at the present as well, and in this respect, we need to consider the current context of our life. If one's life circumstances necessitated living at subsistence level, then one's focus would be on survival, not on living life well. Psychologist Abraham Maslow (1962) developed a theory based on his *hierarchy of needs*. In this model, there are five levels of needs, from the basic needs to a more complex and higher order of needs. The first level entails the need to fulfill our physiological needs, such as breathing and eating; the next level is personal security and safety against accidents and illness; at the third level is love and belonging; the fourth, esteem; and the fifth and highest level, self-actualization. To move up the ladder each lower level of needs must first be satisfied before one can move to the next level; as such, if one is stuck trying to survive, it is unlikely he or she can move forward to that highest level of wellbeing.[82]

The significance of context cannot be underestimated as a major factor that influences how well we function. We have already discussed how shame is more toxic when activated in a public setting than in a private setting, or whether fear is triggered in a threatening or supportive environment. Socio-cultural and political influences will also leave a mark on the context in which we operate in life. Do we feel like insiders or outsiders in our community? How does our home life affect our work life, and vice versa? What is the history behind an event? What are our prospects for the future? Of course, it is not just the external context, but the circumstances related to our physical and mental health. All of these, and many others not here mentioned, play an important role in influencing our state of being. Thus, we need a favorable context to function well and to establish a sense of wellbeing.

The reason why context isn't everything is because we have some control over how we perceive and respond to events and situations that contextualize our life. We have choices as to whether a situation dominates us or whether we can effectively minimize it. In this regard, we can say that perspective is "almost" everything as well. In many respects context and perspective are intertwined; we know that what is negative to one individual may be positive

---

[81] This is not to suggest that we do the opposite and dwell on a triggering event. It is important, in fact, that we *not* obsess about an event, but instead examine it from time to time.

[82] Maslow mentions wellbeing as a need at the security and safety level. He is referring to being well as it relates to having a sense of security and safety, and not to our definition of wellbeing, which is at the level of self-actualization.

to another; a work assignment may be seen as stressful and threatening to one person, while an opportunity or challenge to another. Perspective taking is in the realm of cognitive reframing, a skill both innate and learned. We know that optimists tend to have longer and more fulfilling lives than pessimists, who see and experience negatives everywhere. Our mind set is essential in determining our state of mind, which after all is what makes up our sense of wellbeing anyway.

Although temperament and context play a significant role in setting the mold from which we perceive life, learning is a greater factor for most of us. We earlier discussed how instructional learning is essential to our knowledge base. However, it is experiential learning that is most significant in determining our perspective on life. Since experiences are processed procedurally, it is most likely to become stored as primary schemas in lower level cognitive and emotional centers, and thus operate implicitly as the backdrop underlying how we view our circumstances. The information we gain through instructional learning becomes integrated only when we experience an affective reaction to this information. As stated earlier, since our perspective is largely learned, it can also be unlearned and modified; by so doing we can gain the upper hand over many situations that come our way.

Aging

To many, the idea that being old is accompanied by wellbeing seems like an oxymoron. After all, with age health and vitality decline, friends and family die, and one lives in the constant shadow of death and dying. Laura Carstensen (2000) calls this the "wellbeing paradox." Yet this is what both observation and research show. In fact, most surveys reveal that older adults report greater happiness and contentment than any other age group.

Does this mean that one cannot attain wellbeing until the autumn of life? The answer is yes and no. Like most concepts, it is relative. A woman of 30 can certainly feel a sense of wellbeing and display a great deal of optimism and happiness; and certainly, an octogenarian may be quite unhappy and pessimistic, with little sense of wellbeing. In general, however, the degree of wellbeing is higher for the elderly. The wisdom and self-agency gained through a life long lived, are fundamental components underlying wellbeing.

Wellbeing is not a steady state or end state, but is an ever-evolving process that emerges through time. Aging releases one from living life primarily through affect-regulation. Affects generally mute with time, meaning there will be less fear, anger, disgust and shame. The exception is distress, which due to the high level of physical problems among the aged is, unfortunately, indigenous to aging. Yet, through the coping skills learned and the wisdom gained, the elderly have often learned how to deal and minimize this distress. In fact, this is an age when selective denial can be judicious; for example, when a person observes a potentially serious symptom, worry can motivate that person to see their doctor; however, to continue worrying about that symptom after a medical appointment has been made serves no purpose, and in fact can worsen the condition.

We have said that with age, affects become more modulated; this applies not only to negative affects, but also to the positive interest-excitement affect. It is for this reason that we emphasize leading an active life into our retirement years. However, the energy efficient affect of enjoyment-joy is less likely to modulate, which is why wellbeing is most often associated with happiness and contentment.

Studies indicate that older adults feel more comfortable than younger adults when dealing with uncertainty and ambiguity; this is largely due to the wisdom gained. In addition, older adults are suppler in their assessments of problems, are able to perceive the social context of their situation better than younger adults, and are able to adjust their reactions accordingly. And perhaps, most importantly, when it comes to settling on a strategy of action, they display greater flexibility, guided in part by their ability to regulate their emotions. In Blanchard-Fields useful idiom, older adults develop a *feel*, something akin to emotional intuition, that lets them know when it is best "to do" and when it is best to "let it be." (Hall, p. 427)

Most theories of development focus on the stages of childhood, as did Freud. It was Eric Erickson (also a psychoanalyst) who took stage theory to a new level by extending it beyond childhood to include not only adulthood, but also old age. In his *Eight Stages of Man* (1950) Erickson provided a valuable outline, not only for child-adult development, but also for the development of wellbeing. His penchant for using polarity labels for each stage fits nicely into affect-script theory. Each stage represents a battle between two opposing scripts, one positive, and the other negative; that which prevails determines the development of the self, which he labeled the *emerging ego identity*. Erikson's basic premise is that each stage is characterized by an age-specific psychosocial task, which when resolved leads to an "accruing sense of ego strength," while failure leads to potential psychopathology. Although ego is technically a term related to the executive functions of the prefrontal cortex, it has also been used to describe the self as well.

Erickson's stages of ego development are as follows: (1) Trust versus Basic Mistrust (infancy); (2) Autonomy versus Shame and Doubt (around two years of age); (3) Initiative versus Guilt (around three years old); (4) Industry versus Inferiority four to six years old); (5) Identity versus Role diffusion (adolescence); (6) Intimacy versus Isolation (young adulthood); (7) Generativity versus Stagnation (middle adulthood); and (8) Ego Integrity versus Despair (late adulthood). As you can see the evolution of positive scripts emerge from scripts of trust, autonomy, initiative, industry, identity, intimacy, and generativity, which then leads to the final stage of ego integrity. Of course, if there is a constancy of negative self-scripts, the foundation for successful functioning will not be laid down, and the consequence will be despair.[83]

Erikson's state of ego integrity is akin to wellbeing. "Only he who in some way has taken care of things and people and has adapted himself to the triumphs and disappointments adherent to being, by necessity, the originator of others in the generator of things and ideas – only he may gradually grow the fruit of these seven stages." Erickson then lists some of the primary traits associated with ego integrity: "the proclivity for order and meaning," "a post-narcissistic love" of the world and not of one's self, an acceptance of the way things are and the way things were, and a sense of personal dignity and integrity in the way one lives life…The style of his integrity… becomes the 'patrimony of his soul,' the seal of his moral paternity of himself…Before this final solution, death loses its sting." Ego integrity, therefore, implies an emotional integration that permits participation by "followership as well as an acceptance of the responsibility of leadership." Ego-integrity comes about during our senior years. Wellbeing and wisdom go hand-in-hand and are fertilized by the process of aging. This will become quite evident in our discussion on wisdom.

Erickson rightly assumes that the development of ego-integrity, and by fiat that of wellbeing, lessens the fear and terror of death; I would add that it also may lower the fear of dying as well (which is often more fearful than death itself). One simple reason for this is that

---

[83] Erikson points out that often "disgust hides despair."

aging prepares us to accept death better because of the very nature of mental and physical decline; suffering is a great equalizer when facing death. More importantly, the attributes gained with wellbeing are critical factors as to why the fear of death lessens with old age.

Aging can be a process of chaos and disintegration. There are losses everywhere: loss of family, friends and colleagues and the decline in mental and physical health. Earlier stages have been punctuated between loss and gain. Now comes the final stage. There is a very limited future compared to an unlimited past as one struggles with a changing identity and declining image of self. As such, the integrity of our basic prescripts is upended so that the maximization of positive affect is instead lessened, the minimization of negative affect is instead challenged, and the expression of affect is narrowed. The antidote is to maximize affect expression and minimize the inhibition of expression. As both physical and psychological needs are changing, so too must self-schemas and behaviors become more realistic.

The task in later life shifts from affect-*regulation* to affect-*integration.* Integration requires congruence and coherency; without these, disintegration and chaos may follow. The integration of affects takes place largely through its cognification into more complex cognitions and emotions, as well as the development of wisdom and self-agency.

What Is Wellbeing?

Wellbeing is a dynamic state of being that emerges as our competency grows, as our inborn potentials are maximized, as we recognize and re-contextualize our present situation, and as we rescript our past and mature with age. These are some of the major pre-conditions that shape the winding and often turbulent road toward wellbeing.

Emotional wellbeing has many meanings. As stated in the opening paragraph of this chapter, we typically refer to wellbeing as it relates to physical, mental and social health. This relates not only to our condition but also to our quality of life. We need to keep in mind the dynamic and evolving nature of wellbeing, and the significance of the context we are living in. As a part of Eros, wellbeing is part of the naturally progressive nature of evolution.

Wellbeing reflects the fulfillment of our prescriptive goals. Maximizing positive self-scripts, minimizing negative self-scripts, and maximizing the expression of self-scripts in optimizing ways—and doing all of these at the same time—is essential for attaining emotional wellbeing. [See Appendix 16: Wellbeing Questionnaire]

We know that affect-regulation is fundamental for functioning well, and that the organization of self-scripts is essential for wellbeing. Regulation and organization give us order, equilibrium and stability; when disturbed, there is then disorder. Yet, we know that if there is no disorder, inertia will set in and, therefore, impede growth and development. We also know that events will occur that will upend this order and thus create disequilibrium. Remember that moving between states of order to states of disorder is the natural process of life. Rescripting works to regulate affect and organize scripts in order to stabilize the self, thus allowing for the emergence of wellbeing.

Wellbeing can perhaps be best described through its attributes and traits. Table 9.1 below lists thirteen important traits; it is the last three, wisdom, agency and willpower that make up the necessary and essential features that are inherent in wellbeing. First, however, let us look at the first ten attributes.

Table 9-1
Attributes Associated with Wellbeing
Robert Kayton

Attributes Associated with Wellbeing

- Happiness
- Humanistic
- Altruism
- Compassion
- Humility
- Spiritual Enlightenment
- Equanimity
- Optimism
- Moral Integrity
- Humor
- Wisdom
- Self-Agency
- Willpower

Happiness leads the list, because it is the most common feature we associate with wellbeing. When discussing the positive emotions, we defined happiness as an emotion based on enjoyment-joy; it is the *feel-good* emotion. Neurophysiologically it entails such neurotransmitters as dopamine, oxytocin, and especially the endorphins. It is often equated with optimism, which studies show improves not only our emotional wellbeing, but also our physical wellbeing, by improving the functioning of our immune system; as a by-product this can increase longevity. Happiness is most often described as both "living the good life," and of "living life well." When happiness rules, one has attained a state of wellbeing

Humanism is *human being centered* (Tomkins) and thus is basic to the humanist ideology. In humanism the individual person is intrinsically good and inherently of value and worth. Humanism is characterized by such features as empathy, nurturance and tolerance toward others and the maximization of positive affect, together with the minimization of negative affect, conflict and negativity.

Since these factors are necessary for integration and wellbeing, what then is the status of normatives who lack many of these integrative features; can they attain wellbeing? It certainly does not seem likely within the rubric of affect-script theory. However, we will see that normatives share many of the attributes necessary for wellbeing. It is important to keep in mind that wellbeing is not an end state, but a dynamic state of becoming so that few, whether normative or humanistic, will attain the deep fullness that fills the self with wellbeing. We also need to keep in mind that just because someone is a humanist, does not automatically mean they are happy, or that someone who is normative cannot find happiness. In fact, normatives tend to be very intimate with their family, friends and community.

Altruism is another characteristic essential to the humanistic tradition. Altruism is defined as an *unselfish regard for or devotion to the welfare of others* (Webster). Whether "pure" altruism truly exists is often debated in never-ending hypotheticals of little practical value. Let it suffice to say that like everything else, altruism is relative; it is therefore reasonable to say that the more altruistic a person is, the more likely that person will attain both greater wisdom and higher levels of wellbeing. Altruism is embedded in the selfother-self; however, if the selfother-self is deficient, then others become mirrors of one's self, so that rather than altruism we have its opposite, narcissism.

Narcissism is a condition characterized by excessive self-love, egocentrism, and a grandiose sense of self-importance, together with a lack of empathy for others who are seen and used for self-exploitation. In its most extreme and pernicious form we have the Narcissistic Personality Disorder, a serious defect of the self, most notably because of a defective selfother self; this is especially evidenced by the narcissists inability to emotionally connect with other people. This defect in the self obviously means that integration cannot take place.

Freud coined the term narcissism from the mythological character Narcissus, who fell in love with the image of himself reflected in a pool of water. Narcissism itself is considered a normal stage in early childhood, which nevertheless had to be overcome before the self or ego could grow and develop. Those stuck or fixated at this stage, become narcissists; those who instead learn ways to successful inhibit these urges, and instead sublimate them into other-directed behaviors, were capable of developing an emergent selfother self; thus, overcoming narcissism is critical to the development and integration of the self.

Some psychologists, unfortunately, confound what they call "healthy narcissism" with pride. Pride, the positive emotion discussed earlier, entails a realistic self-interest, mature goals and principles, and the ability to form deep relationships with others (the selfother-self). Many theorists believe pride is inborn and, for young children, is a fundamental ingredient in self-agency. Pride is the polar opposite of shame. In adults, a respect and love for the self is essential; however, there also needs to be a healthy love of others, not as reflections of one's self (as in narcissism), but because close attachments with other people enhance one's own self.

Compassion is a close cousin to altruism. It consists of a benevolent concern and consideration for others and requires the capacity to empathize. Empathy is based on affect attunement, the ability to mutualize one's experiences with another person's experiences. Empathy also gives us an understanding for what that person is going through, and how he or she sees the world, even though that viewpoint may differ from one's own. Empathy differs from understanding in that understanding is mostly cognitive, while empathy is emotional. This is why we often feel better when someone conveys that they "feel" our pain, rather than understand what we are going through.

Humility is a virtue essential to wisdom. Among the key features of wisdom and humility are, "an ability to acknowledge limitations and mistakes, and an openness to new ideas and new contradictory knowledge, a knack for avoiding self-aggrandizement, and ability to keep one's achievements in perspective, and that kind of self-aware self-perception that perceives both strengths and weaknesses." (Hall, 2010, p. 246) It is important to recognize that a humble person is not one who feels inferior to others, but is someone who recognizes their place in the greater scheme of things, who knows that what he knows is subject to error and is open to advice from others without personalizing it.

Spiritual enlightenment is another important feature of wisdom that gives meaning and worth to one's life. It entails a faith in life itself. Spiritual enlightenment, as used here, reflects more the secular sense of a oneness with some higher force, such as a god or the vastness of nature. As the existential psychoanalyst and holocaust survivor Victor Frankl wrote in his classic book *The Search for Meaning,* the essential and fundamental purpose of life could be found in the spirit of each person, in their quest for living life at every moment with a greater sense of being. It is a faith in something beyond the material world; it is also a personal attachment to an idea or thing that is exemplified by deep trust and commitment.

Equanimity is characterized by tranquility, as expressed by a calm composure that is accompanied with dignity and grace. One's attitude can be described as sangfroid, of taking life as it comes, of unconditional acceptance of self and others. One who has equanimity is one known for their self-control, level-headedness and level-handedness. Stoicism, namely patience, forbearance, acceptance and tolerance, is a prime characteristic. Equanimity is based on enjoyment-joy.

Optimism is characterized by hopefulness, a positive outlook on the future, and is often accompanied by a cheerful and buoyant enthusiasm for life. It is one of the essential features of wellbeing, and is largely based on interest-excitement.

Morality evolved from the social affects of shame-humiliation and disgust/dissmell. It is interesting that these moral affects are negative, since morality is not just about what is bad, wrong and unjust, but also about what is good, right and just. As you can see positive morals and negative morals are polarized between good or bad, right or wrong, just or unjust.[84]

Moral integrity refers to the reliability, authenticity, and genuineness in one's moral position, which ultimately boils down to differences in ideological postures. Most would say there are universal morals that apply in most contexts, and which are shared by normative and humanist alike. These include many of the tenets found in the Ten Commandments.

Humor is both healing and engaging. Some of you may be familiar with the story of Norman Cousins, a renown American political journalist and author who, while hospitalized for a serious illness, found that comedy, wit and slapstick were antidotes to his medical condition. Since then there have been a number of neuroscience studies that have verified the immunological benefits of laughter.

Wisdom, Self-Agency and Willpower

There is a concept called *mental presence* in which thoughts and emotions are tied to action. A number of studies found this to be a significant predictor of happiness. We could say that mental presence is more related to self-agency, while the "presence of mind" is related more to wisdom. It is through a combination of wisdom and self-agency that the self becomes integrated. Wisdom helps us govern our self, while agency is the self as integrated. Wisdom gives us perspective and emotional maturity, while agency gives us willpower and self-efficacy. These are so fundamental to what it means to have emotional wellbeing, that wellbeing itself is often equated with wisdom, while self-agency is intrinsic to its experience and meaning. Both share the emergent properties that come with age and experience. We could say that wisdom is the mental state that evolves over a lifetime of experiential learning. It provides us with those higher and more complex attributes we associate with executive functioning, such as judgment, planning and decision-making. Self-agency is a state of being that provides the fortitude and willpower to carry out wisdom wisely.

---

[84] Since these differences are bipolar, each exists in the absence of the other; this means that positive morals exist because there is no shame or no disgust, while negative morals exist because there is no pride or love. However, in truth, morality is often a relative-variable, meaning that differences are in degrees rather than in kind. A possible explanation for these different models is that the bi-polar and fixed point of view is based on the more extreme affects of humiliation or dissmell, while the relative-variable viewpoint is based on those of lesser intensity, namely shame or disgust.

Wisdom is the accumulation of stored knowledge that is based on experiential learning. Wisdom allows us to look at our past, see the present for what it is, and anticipate the uncertainty of our future. In this respect, our perspective of our self and our self in the world is guided by wisdom. Wisdom is conscious self-reflection; as the Oracle of Delphi implores one to "know thyself," this self-knowing self evolves through insight, both of one's self and of other people; those who are wise are those who are enlightened.

Wisdom gives us the emotional resilience and ability to cope with adversity, ambiguity and uncertainty. Wisdom is also context-based: what is wise in one situation can be folly in another. We learn best through adversity, since failure motivates us to find solutions to problems. This is the journey we take on the road to wisdom.

As Vivian Clayton so eloquently said, *knowledge tells [us] how to do something, wisdom tells us whether we should do it or not.* This is what the serenity prayer tells us when it says: *I will learn to accept the things I cannot change, the courage to change the things I can, and the* **wisdom** *to know the difference.* In this respect wisdom can be equated with our prefrontal executive functioning. These functions consist of a set of cognitive abilities that control and regulate our functioning. They include the ability to initiate and stop actions, to monitor and change behavior as needed, and to plan future behavior when faced with novel tasks and situations. They form the concepts that are necessary for judging, planning, organizing and deciding wisely. Wisdom is our highest level of cognitive attainment. We shall see that rescripting both enhances our wisdom-based knowledge and actuates the use of it wisely.

Gaining knowledge through experience is what leads to wisdom, which is why we equate wisdom with aging. However, just because someone is older does not automatically make that person wiser, and in addition, having wisdom does not mean that one lives life wisely. Nevertheless, maturity is critical for wisdom to develop, as evidenced by several studies that show that the elderly earn the highest wisdom scores in many different categories. Julia Carstensen (2000) credits this response to something she called "socioemotional selectivity theory," whereby the elderly are able to better tailor their social interactions to avoid stress, thereby increasing their state of wellbeing; as a result, they make thoughtful and wiser decisions.

Self-agency leads to willpower, which then becomes a part of self-agency. Agency is the self as integrated. It is a dynamic state of being, of being engaged in life and living that life well and to its fullest. This means maximizing positive self-scripts, which move us toward others, and minimizing negative self-scripts, which turns us away or against others. Negative scripts disengage and alienate us from life, while positive scripts connect us to life.

Self-agency refers to the explicit and conscious *awareness* of self as the doer of one's actions, together with the implicit, preconscious *sense* of self as the doer. The self as doer entails conscious volition, whereby one is conscious of one's own intention to voluntarily enact behaviors.

Agency is the process of purposely and deliberately choosing, either consciously or unconsciously, to engage in some action or activity, caring through that action on one's own, with the result of a particular outcome that one has envisioned. This describes the willpower inherent in self-agency. Thus, agency entails the ownership of one's behavior, while willpower is the enactment of that power. Purposeful deliberation entails volition, intent, self-initiated effort and action, resolve and determination, and the perseverance to carry through with one's intended actions. It also means that each person is responsible for his or her own thoughts, feelings, emotions and behavior.

An act of agency departs from previous patterns of behavior and is a means to which a person can alter his or her own state of being by engaging in certain actions. Effort, especially deliberate effort, is an essential part of agency: "those acts that require greater alterations from habitual patterns of behaving require more agency (namely greater deliberate effort) than those that represent repetitive behaviors." Thus, behavior that entails little effort falls into the category of a habit, not of agency; exercising, when one does so regularly, involves little agency, while preparing to exercise after a period of inactivity requires considerable effort and agency. In the former, the neural synaptic connections, developed and maintained through practice, has made that activity a relatively low-grade energy factor; however, starting up a new behavior forces the brain to forge new synaptic pathways that involves substantially greater amounts of neural energy.

The idea that agency requires effort is a double-edged sword. Many of us complain that practicing takes too much effort, or that it is "easier said than done." In response, we can say "so what." It is true that we need to expend greater effort and energy when undertaking a new and different action. To encourage yourself to take effortful action say to yourself the words *I Will Practice*; say it with passion, placing emphasis on a different word each time it is repeated. This encourages variant repetition, which is more successful for learning than fixed repetition, and highlights three different facets: "I" refers to the active knowing self as agent, "will" to the power of will, and "practice" to the dedication of doing.

Thus, agency provides us with a sense of self-efficacy, the feeling that we are masters of our life. This leads to what is perhaps the chief component of self-agency, namely willpower, or the power of will. *Will* is defined as "the capacity or faculty by which a human being is able to make choices and determine his or her behaviors in spite of influences external to the person." (APA Dictionary, 1993) It comes from within the person, from the self. If this means there is self-direction, then it also means there is free will. Whether this is true or just an illusion is the stuff of great debate, especially when it comes to the unconscious.

Michael S. Gazzaniga wrote a paper entitled, *Free will is an illusion, but you're still responsible for your actions* (2012). Accordingly, he claims that neuroscience reveals that the concept of free will is without meaning. He takes a mechanistic view that *brain determinism* obviates the idea of free will, because it is the brain and not the mind that determines our actions. He also emphasizes that responsibility is a function of social rules and norms, not of free will.

Grawe (2007) presents a brief but interesting section entitled *Act of will from a neural perspective*. He presents several research studies (Libet, 1978; Haggard and Eimer, 1999), which demonstrate that "our volitional choices appear to be preceded by unconscious processes that set the stage for the subjectively experienced decision to lift the finger." He goes on to say that "The act of will (decision) ends with the subjective experience instead of beginning with it." (p.106) This suggests that we do not have conscious will. However, Grawe points out that if we consider our unconscious to be as much a part of the self as is the conscious, then it still is one's self that makes decisions. This points to the need for the integration of the self, for the emergence of scripts that incorporate our unconscious world with the world we are aware of. Grawe sums this up when he says, "as soon as I accept that my self encompasses more than the part I am aware of, I can accept that my decisions, in the moment that I subjectively make them, were already predetermined by the implicit parts of my self." (Grawe) In other words, each of us needs to take agency of our implicit self, as well as our willpower.

Free will is thought to reside in the higher centers of the brain, especially the orbito-frontal and prefrontal cortices, which controls the lower primary centers. Consequently, unless physically limited, each of us can be thought to have free will, or at least to function as if we do. From a purely practical point of view, believing in free will is better than believing that our behavior is determined by other forces; it shifts the locus-of-control from the external to the internal. The many benefits attained through an internal locus-of-control schema, as compared to an external locus-of-control schema, have been well documented in psychology.

Unlike inscripts, behavior is learned. We humans have the ability to modify nature to best fit our needs. Thus, events do not determine our behavior; instead our *self* does. Self-will represents an evolutionary change, an alteration of functions that entails a higher and more complex level of functioning. This is the knowing self (the "I") as the executive director of the known self (the "me"); we are our own CEO.

Underlying self-direction is the importance of purpose and meaning. This has been a central theme in religion, philosophy, and existential psychology and was a hallmark of Viktor Frankl's classic book. The search for meaning is an evolving process that operates as an overall guiding principle in life. The meaning of life changes with time, place, and context. At a fundamental level, there is the survival and fulfillment of our prescripts; while at higher levels, meaning and purpose moves us toward greater levels of wellbeing.

We have spoken about will, but not the *power* embedded in will*power*. This is self-empowerment, the strength and control one gives to oneself. Like Napoleon crowning himself emperor, one can anoint and decide that he or she has what it takes to fulfill one's will. The power of will is carried out purposefully and with conscious intent. Behavior is volitional, and characterized by perseverance and effort. Responsibility for choices and decisions reside within one's self. These attributes define the willpower in self-agency.

Chapter 10: Integrative Rescripting

When we discussed function-focused rescripting, our focus was on each core self-script. For integrative rescripting, we look at the totality by which each self-script integrates with all other self-scripts. When working on cognition we are simultaneously working on emotion and behavior. The essential principle is that by working on each specific function, in combination with all other functions, and practicing these exercises over-and-over again, we are strengthening the bond that cements these areas of functioning into an integral whole.

Although integrative rescripting relates to emergent self-scripts, this does not mean that we abandon function-focused rescripting. Instead, we now add to our strategic goal of integrating the self by working on those essential self-scripts that define the emergent self. These self-scripts are characterized by the property of extensionality, and by definition represents the integration of those extended elements into the contextual framework of the whole. As discussed, when we talk of temporal integration, we speak of autobiographical self-scripts in which past and future scripts are melded into the present, while our focus in spatial integration is on intrapersonal and interpersonal scripts that become unified as the selfother-self.

The emergent-self is, therefore, a more complex organization of scripts that extends the self through time and space; these emerging self-scripts coalesce into an ever-changing and ever-expanding self. When we say that someone is "one-dimensional" we refer to a person whose self is restricted and narrow, who fits the model of a relatively simple and predictable system. One who is said to be "multi-dimensional" is described as being well-rounded and having depth, which fits the complexity model of emergence

This is not to say that the structural components of the self lack any depth. Certainly, cognition and emotion are complicated and quite intricate. Yet, when we describe a person as intellectual or emotional, we are describing one modality of functioning that more or less minimizes all other functional modalities. Dimensionality comes only when all four structural components (affect, cognition, emotion and behavior) become integrated and melded together as a whole, instead of being differentiated as intellectual or emotional. This helps lead to the emergence of the integrated self, which takes place when each component is defined by its extensionality and its connection to all other components.

By definition, extensionality is integration. Integrative rescripting is one of the many ways to augment this process. The goal is to increase the integrative complexity of both autobiographical self-scripts and selfother self-scripts, and when bound together with the growth of our structural self-scripts, leads to greater wisdom and agency, and therefore an enhanced sense of wellbeing.

When we discuss function-focused rescripting, our model follows a linear process based on affect-regulation via the excitation-inhibition polarity. Our strategy is to inhibit negative functions and excite positive functions. By so doing we end up changing both affect-scripts and cost-benefit scripts, as well as integrating these modalities together. Our techniques focus on each specific component while, at the same time, integrating others as well. For affect we focused on the body, for cognition on our thoughts, for emotion on our feelings, and for behavior, on our actions. In this step-by-step manner we learn, store, and then consolidate these skills into our internalized repertoire of strategies that will then enhance our basic self-scripts.

Most therapeutic models take place in three phases, awareness, intervention and practice. In function-focused rescripting this means first identifying ones affects, cognitions, emotions and behaviors. Intervention takes place by first using both affect-focused and cognitive-behavioral techniques, and then practicing these skills over-and-over again. These three phases also apply to integrative rescripting, namely to be cognitively aware of all our self-scripts, intervene by using integrative strategies (such as narrative dialogs, doing the opposite of the urge, and "as if" mimicking) and then to practice these techniques over-and-over again.

In integrative rescripting, the goal is to first become aware of your self-scripts by bringing the implicit-self into consciousness, and then intervening, both structurally and temporally to fuse all self-states together into a unified whole. This might include using the opposite of the urge and "as if" processing, as well as a variety of other strategies, and to then practice, practice, and practice again, both by reviewing your insights and then acting with wisdom and agency. Practice is arguably the Achilles heel in psychotherapy: without doing, awareness fades.

For integrative rescripting, the strategy shifts from affect-regulation to the regulation and reordering of scripts. Rather than the linear dynamics underlying our functional self, our attention will turn to techniques that enhance self-emergence.

Integrative rescripting is an eclectic model that uses and integrates many well-known experiential and psychodynamic therapies; this is in contrast to function-focused rescripting that uses focused and directive techniques, such as cognitive-behavioral therapy. Experiential therapies focus on the subjective experiencing self. Foremost is gestalt therapy, whose major tenant is *the sum is greater than the sum of the whole,* and whose focus is holistic and multidimensional. Role-playing, such as found in psychodrama, are specific techniques in the grab-bag of strategies used in gestalt therapy.

Existential psychotherapy is an approach based on the principle that inner conflicts are due to an individual's confrontation with the realities of existence that includes the inevitability of death, freedom and its attendant responsibility, of essential isolation, and finally meaninglessness. (Yalom) Other models include guided imagery, mindfulness, as well as a host of body-focusing models.

As experiential therapies focus on one's experiences at the moment, psychodynamic therapies use insight-oriented talking therapy in which the self becomes a part of the narrative process. Among the goals of psychodynamic therapy are to enhance one's self-awareness and understanding of the influence of the past on present behavior, and to make the unconscious conscious through the process of transference.

Key to integrative approaches is that all the modalities of functioning be addressed together. Among experiential strategies, the individual is to experience, in the *now,* those affects, emotions and actions involved in both one's biographical schema and one's social schema. The same applies to the insight-oriented psychodynamic spheres. Insight is not just a cognitive phenomenon, but is also a highly charged emotional experience, as epitomized by the "ah-ha" or eureka experience. Insight without affect is relatively useless since it lacks the fuel to motivate change. However, not only is the lack of motivation an impeding factor, but the lack of knowledge is as well. The one major problem with both experiential and insight-oriented therapies is that they lack the tools needed for change; that is why more structured techniques, such as cognitive-behavioral therapy, are used. I was originally a psychoanalyst and thus was required to go through my own personal analysis; I certainly gained a great deal of insight but found that I had not significantly changed. I had bought into the propaganda of many analysts that insight would automatically lead to change, but instead found that I lacked the tools to implement change; this led me to get trained in cognitive-behavioral therapy.

As we have discussed, affect-regulation underlies both our functioning and sense of wellbeing. Scripts evolved primarily for the purpose of affect-regulation so as to minimize negative affect, maximize positive affect, and express all affects in adaptive ways, and to attain all three at the same time. On a practical basis, this means exciting inhibitory affects and inhibiting excitatory affects through affect-regulating scripts. Scripts are made up of scenes that consist of cognition, emotion and behavior all geared to operate as a unit in regulating their triggering affect. The more effective these scripts are in regulating affect, the more competent a person will function.

The integrated-self is the basis for wellbeing. The self is the highest and most complex script that encompasses all other scripts. Its main function is to organize and manage self-scripts which in turn regulates affect-scripts. Unlike the excitation-inhibition principle underlying affect-regulation, the organization of self-scripts follows the convergence-divergence polarity. Since the self is a script, it too follows these prescriptive regulation goals, except in this case the focus is on regulating and managing scripts rather than affects; thus, our objective is to minimize negative-scripts, maximize positive-scripts and maximize the expression of all scripts. To do so requires that, at its core, affect-regulation is successfully managed. This allows the self to fulfill its second major function, which is to organize and reorganize self-scripts top-down, so as to allow for the bottom-up emergence of a higher and more complex self. This is the essence of the integration of the self and the attainment of emotional wellbeing.

Because of the analogical connection between self, scripts and affect, we must consider all three for integrative rescripting; this is why functioning is such a necessary component for integration and wellbeing. Function-focused rescripting uses a combination of affect-focusing and cognitive-behavior strategies to enhance one's ability to regulate affects for optimal functioning. When these skills are learned, stored and consolidated into memory, and then integrated throughout the brain and mind, they become ingrained as new ways of thinking, feeling and doing that now operate implicitly as new habit patterns.

Certainly, negative scripts are learned and become stored and consolidated in memory. However, negative scripts impede integration since the very nature of negative affects and negative scripts is disruptive to cohesive and coherent functioning; they promote disintegration rather than integration. Just think what happens when terrified or enraged; your attention is taken over by these affects.[85] In fact, it is the activation of negative-affect that leads to states of chaos. And true, from chaos we develop higher levels of complexity, which in the long run can be beneficial; however, unless there is the consolidation and integration of positive-affects and positive-scripts at the core levels of the brain and mind, the foundation for recovery and further growth will likely be impaired.

This is why we need to continually work on affect-regulating scripts, not just during the learning phase of function-focused rescripting, but also during the final phase of integrative-rescripting. In principle, when there is disorder, when symptoms re-emerge such as following a difficult, if not traumatic event, one needs to go back to basics and shore up these skills. It

---

[85] It is true that intense excitement or joy may preoccupy one's attention, and if maintained too long it can become negative as evidenced in mania; although it feels good, its consequences are negative.

is not only necessary but also expedient, given that negative-affect will, in most cases, capture one's attention over positive affect.[86] What you will likely find is that over time, as these skills continue to integrate, recovery to states of equilibrium and growth will be faster and fuller.

During these periods of disorder, we need to remind ourselves that wisdom comes from adversity. The message is that there is an automaticity of change reflecting the natural order of life, whereby perpetually ongoing cycles from chaotic disorder to states of order and equilibrium reflect a normal process; it is therefore important not to get stuck in the illusion of the moment. The simple prescription is to intervene, using function-focused rescripting when the tolerance level for chaotic disorder is reached; if not, then it is important to ride it out, to let it be.

Worry and depression interferes with this naturally unfolding progress, the so-called life force that is built into the DNA of all living beings. Of course, there is the other side of the coin, namely getting stuck in the rigidity of too much order. In this case the goal is to shake things up, to excite rather than inhibit. The maxim here is that when there is too much change and chaos, then we work for sameness and stability, whereas when there is too much sameness and stasis, we work toward change. This is the strategy of doing the opposite-of-the-urge. This strategy of course is not to be taken as dogma, but applied judicially to states that are counterproductive.

Viktor Frankl, the existential psychiatrist we earlier mentioned, first introduced the paradoxical maxim of doing the opposite-of-the-urge.[87] As earlier discussed, affect-regulation itself is based on this principle, namely to excite inhibitory-affects and inhibit excitatory-affects. Thus, for vegetative depression we work to engage in excitatory activities, just as when agitated we work toward inhibitory activities. Fear is excitatory, so we encourage inhibitory relaxation techniques, while shame, as an inhibitory-affect means that we work to increase excitement and action. Doing the opposite-of-the-urge will act as a corrective factor that will lead to greater balance and homeostasis; this in turn will help pave the way toward integration, especially when used to minimize, if not eliminate, negative affects and negative scripts.

Psychology often couches phenomena in terms of polarities. Tomkins' bipolar labels of affects, such as fear-terror or enjoyment joy, reflect differences in the degree of affect-intensity. Self-states are also presented as polarities, such as the implicit-explicit self, the physical-mental self, or self-scripts of the past and self-scripts of the anticipated future. Often these are presented as differences in kind, rather than differences in degree. By doing the opposite-of-the-urge, we can integrate these discrete states into a merged or interconnected whole. On the one hand, we can work toward merger by incorporating one state into the other, such as by making the unconscious conscious, or by melding the past and future into the present. When working to integrate physical, mental and behavioral self-scripts, our strategy is to organize these scripts into a coherent, cohesive and harmonious whole. As to the selfother-self, we work to increase intrapersonal narratives and to increase interpersonal experiences of the self-with-others.

To do the opposite-of-the-urge is quite apparent when we talk about behavior; if the urge is to avoid, then its opposite is to engage. We can also apply this to thinking-the-opposite by using such cognitive techniques as counter-thinking, disputation and reframing. However,

---

[86] Like pain, negative affects are more critical for survival, and thus more likely to get our attention.
[87] Frankl called his treatment approach *logotherapy*.

many a patient has asked me how they can get themselves to feel the opposite of how they feel, to feel happy instead of sad, confident instead of fearful. The simple answer is that this will come as one thinks or acts differently. Yet, there is another way to jump start this process and that is to feel "as if" you are happy or confident. This, of course, can also apply to thinking and doing as well.

This "as if" concept was first introduced by the philosopher Hans Vaihinger, who wrote a book called *The Philosophy of "As If."* In his model, we live life through "as if" constructs. We behave *as if* we knew the world will be here tomorrow, *as if* we are sure what good and bad are all about, *as if* everything we see is as we see it, and so forth. We use them "as if" they are true. He called these partial truths *fictions*. Alfred Adler picked up on this concept, which he called *fictional finalisms*; these *finalisms* are teleological since the fiction lays in the future, yet influences our behavior in the present. Since we live life *as if,* why not live our life as if we are happy and integrated, as if we are living life well.

There is growing evidence that when we feel and act "as if" we are happy, oxytocin is actually released in the brain. It is like being a method actor who gets into his or her character and becomes that character in thought, feeling and action. When we imagine being someone whom we admire, and get into feeling this experience, we are tricking our brain which does not distinguish between what is going on inside the brain or what is going on outside the brain. It is our mind that makes this distinction.

We know that mimicking is the most fundamental mode of learning. By mimicking "as if" you are wise, "as if" you have agency, and "as if" you have willpower, and when you practice this over and over again, there is then a high likelihood that you will become wiser and more empowered. Knowing what you now know about wisdom and agency, and what they entail, you can take on the mantle of these traits and help inculcate them into your own self.

To directly use the "as if" strategy, it is best to do so while practicing positive scripts "as if" you are feeling, believing and acting positively; of course, it is best to do so analogically, so that the affective feel, schematic thoughts and scripted behaviors are coherent. For example, to say the affirmation "I will exercise," say it "as if" you are excited and passionate, while at the same time literally going through the motions. To maximize and enhance integration it is best to practice this exercise using *variant repetition*. If you practice a skill the same way over-and-over again, it will tend to habituate and decrease over time. Instead it is best to vary when, where and how you practice, since learning is enhanced and thus more likely to be stored, consolidated and integrated into memory.

An example of the "as if" strategy comes from a story of a triple amputee that was written up in New York Magazine (January, 2017):

> *It wasn't that Miller was suddenly enlightened; internally, he was in turmoil. But in retrospect, he credits himself with doing one thing right: He saw a good way to look at his situation and committed to faking that perspective, hoping that his genuine self might eventually catch up. Miller refused, for example, to let himself believe that his life was extra difficult now, only uniquely difficult, as all lives are. He resolved to think of his suffering as simply a "variation on a theme we all deal with — to be human is really hard," he says. His life had never felt easy, even as a privileged, able-bodied suburban boy with two adoring parents, but he never felt entitled to any angst; he saw unhappiness as an illegitimate intrusion*

into the carefree reality he was supposed to inhabit. And don't we all do that, he realized. Don't we all treat suffering as a disruption to existence, instead of an inevitable part of it? He wondered what would happen if you could "reincorporate your version of reality, of normalcy, to accommodate suffering." As a disabled person, he was getting all kinds of signals that he was different and separated from everyone else. But he worked hard to see himself as merely sitting somewhere on a continuum between the man on his deathbed and the woman who misplaced her car keys, to let his accident heighten his connectedness to others, instead of isolating him. This was the only way, he thought, to keep from hating his injuries and, by extension, himself.

As you may or may not have noticed, these integrative strategies work for both emergent integration and structural integration. It is also critically important for integrating the implicit with the explicit, of making the unconscious conscious so that greater insights might be attained. In what is called *psychoanalytical complexity*, insight is an emergent phenomenon that takes place when multiple parts integrate at the same or proximate moment in time to form the eureka experience. Many of us are familiar with how Einstein came up with his discoveries when he was no longer thinking about the problem. Research shows that learning takes place through the dopaminergic system and through the affect of interest-excitement; the storage, consolidation and integration of this new information takes place through the inhibitory neurotransmitter acetylcholine, which mediates the affect of enjoyment-joy. Knowing this, for example, I always made sure to take a break after researching some topic (top-down directive), aware that when I again begin to write, it likely had become more integrated bottom-up. This process was also addressed in the Acknowledgement section of the book when I suggested that you first read through the book without trying to understand everything, and then read it a second time more carefully since there will have been some bottom-up incorporation of this material.

In integrative-rescripting, we look to integrate top-down processing with bottom-up processing. Topographical integration (conscious and unconscious) refers to the reciprocal interplay between top-down organization and bottom-up self-organizing emergence, each of which are going on at the same moment in time. Like trying to balance yourself on a bicycle, there is constant feedback going on as you decide to shift your balance to the right and then self-correct if the sensory-motor feedback is that this shift was too much. In this regard, your body signals your cortex, via the thalamic-limbic pathway, while your brain adjusts and signals back to your body instructions to move either to the right or to the left. So too does our conscious mind work top-down, only to be immediately modified bottom-up. Learning to ride a bicycle entails a great deal of top-down concentration and effort; when consolidated and integrated as a habit, riding a bicycle is now implicitly bottom-up and automatic.

What we will look at now are several strategies that directly focus on integration and self-agency. Like affect regulation techniques, these strategies focus on self-regulation, and require conscious and intentional practice, with greater attention focused on yourself, on others, and of yourself in relation of others (part of the selfother-self). Tune into your body, then your thoughts and feelings. Now that you are aware of affect-rescripting strategies, use this knowledge proactively. Keep in mind that your goal is both affect-regulation and self-integration, which operates within the parameters of both the excitation-inhibition polarity and the convergence-divergence polarity.

As we have already said, the basic formula for change is awareness, intervention and practice. What this means is that you first identify and quantify your negative functioning, and then immediately intervene with some by corrective action, and to do this every time there is dysfunction. It is not only your self that you need to observe, but also your surroundings. Context refers to all the exigencies of life in the present. These include your present circumstances, which are framed in the context of the past and future. Likewise, the past exists within the "meaningful" now, as does your expectations for the future. This speaks to the importance of temporal integration, since these dimensions also co-evolve together. For example, your current context consists of health, work situations and the relational scenes and events that are ongoing now. However, this context is constantly being modified by past events and those anticipated in the future. At every moment in time, your past is being reframed within the context of the now and what may be tomorrow, and filtered through the lens of your remembered-past. Thus, you will need to understand your current situation and its context, relate similar past events to this context, reframe and rescript these events into a more positive construction, and then plan and initiate actions you will do now and in the immediate future.

In focusing on the now, listen to your body talk. When we use the term *sense-of-wellbeing*, the word *sense* speaks of sensation. Sensation is sensory-motor, and so is your *sense* of something; and to sense something is to sense and internally experience your self. Since your body is also the locus of affect, it tells you what is going on at your core-self in terms of embodied images.

As you listen to yourself think, talk and act, ask yourself if you are rationalizing in order to avoid agency. Remember that there are always valid reasons why a person does or does not do something. Are you justifying how you live? Don't buy into the belief that such rationalizations represent the only truth; as Carl Jung once said, "today's truths are tomorrow's deceptions." A rationalization is a logical and rational argument that is, however, used as an excuse to maintain an undesirable script. Perhaps most, if not all explanations are rationalizations; nevertheless, we need to keep in mind that some rationalizations are maladaptive while others are adaptive.

Listen to your language. Do you hear yourself engaging in maladaptive cognitive styles of thinking? If so, then correct them. Are you thinking about what you should or shouldn't do? What you can and cannot do? Are you engaged in black-and-white thinking? Are you catastrophizing or overgeneralizing? Are you personalizing or externalizing? Are you engaging in magical reasoning, emotional reasoning or mind reading? All of these are clues that you are not engaging in self-agency.

Change the passive to the active voice. The term *will* embodies action and intent, whether used as a future tense verb ("I *will* go to the store") or a noun ("the *will* to power"). Using the active voice has power in and of itself, and promotes self-agency.

Language both expresses our beliefs, and magnifies them as well. There is a large body of evidence supporting the idea that our thinking and talking amplifies our affective schemas, and consequently the affect itself. By modifying your narratives (internal and external) you inhibit and thereby regulate the negative affects associated with those thoughts; for example, when talking or thinking negatively, do so very slowly, monotonically and in a near-whisper so as reduce the intensity of the underlying negative affect. On the other hand, when you challenge your thoughts and ideas, do so vigorously and intensely. Doing the opposite follows the principle to inhibit excitation and excite inhibition.

Listen to your inner narratives. These often take the form of a dialogue between you and yourself, or you and another internalized person. Internal narratives have been called the "left-hemispheres interpreter," (Michael S., Gazzangia, 2012) and works to integrate many constructs into a meaningful story of the self. These inner dialogues represent various scripts that are being played out internally. Identify the theme, such as that in a damage-repair script. Like all cognition, these running dialogues also shape the scripts they represent. Consequently, you can rescript these dialogues into ones that entail greater self-agency. You are in charge of your thinking, and so take charge. You learned the scripted dialogue and so you can change it for your betterment. For example, if you are musing about telling another person off, stop yourself and instead try to understand, and then empathize with that person's position.

Observe your behavior. Look at the consequences, intended or otherwise. Are your actions adaptive? Do they enhance or detract from your goals? Are they assertive and proactive? If not, then change your behavior and act in a proactive, realistic and adaptive manner. If you say, "that's easier said than done," respond to this statement by a counter statement such as, "so what, it just means I have to put more effort than just saying it." And remember, agency requires effort.

These tasks, when practiced frequently, enhance the ongoing process of integration. We will soon examine a few more techniques that directly deal with integration and agency. These strategies will help accelerate the self-organizing process of complexity.

There are a number of approaches that focus on structural integration. The connection between brain structures and mental structures is essential for integration. The brain is a physical organ; we can observe and touch the anatomical (corporeal) matter that makes up the brain. The mind is a function of the brain; its structure is in terms of organized patterns that characterize its functions. We know that lower structures in the brain, such as in the limbic system, mediate primary mental functions, while higher levels in the brain, such as the prefrontal cortex, mediate complex mental functions. By integrating both top-down and bottom-up structures, both the brain and the mind will come to operate in a more integrated manner.

An example of structural integration can be seen in Freud's tripartite model of Superego Ego, and Id.[88] These terms refer, not to anatomical structures, but to mental structures, which are functions that operate in a structured and organized manner; they are, in other words, scripts. The Superego consists of both one's conscience, the internalized mediator of right and wrong, and the idealized-image of who and what one should be (i.e. the Ego-Ideal). Violations of conscience elicit guilt, while failing to live-up to one's ideal-self leads to shame. Ego refers to the executive functioning of one's complex cognitive-self, whose major function is *reality testing*, that is judging and deciding what is feasible and what is not. The Id is the repository for all our undifferentiated impulses and urges; in many respects, Id shares many features with affects.[89]

When these functions operate independently from each other, then the Ego, that is executive-self, is likely disintegrated; thus, one may know that some action is risky, which is a function of the Ego, yet go ahead and do it anyway, a function of the Id. In this case the I is in control; affects are dysregulated, so that after the act is done one may feel guilty as the

---

[88] The *id-ego-superego* are not anatomical entities, but functions of the mind.
[89] It has been stated that Freud's original term for Id was *affects*, and only later did he change it to the Id. I have not yet been able to verify the source.

Superego now dominates. When the Id[90] and Superego are integrated into the Ego, we likely will not engage in unwarranted, risky or ethically questionable behaviors simply because they are self-evidently wrong. Such judgments and decisions are now expressions of a well-integrated self.

A specific metaphor technique to promote the integration between the brain, body and mind can be found in Appendix 17, which depicts parts of the brain that correspond to parts of the body by way of the *homunculus image*. While imagining this brain-body map you are to move a part of your body as you mentally connect the image corresponding to that part of the brain.

Rescripting the Autobiographical Self

Rescripting the autobiographical self is both retrospective and prospective. *Retrospective rescripting* involves correcting and changing scripts from the past, while doing so in the present, while *proscripting* entails rescripting expectations of the future. Again, this is done in the present, which like retrospective rescripting, is essentially to live that future now; this serves the purpose of integrating the past and future with the present.

Temporal integration can be summarized as follows: *we are what we were, and become where we go.* By emotionally rescripting the past we change who we are, and by doing and living our future, we become that future now. Remember, a script is different from the script that was, as well as the script that will be. At this level, our self is made up of scripts from the past and anticipated scripts of the future. There is a well-known dictum, from the eminent psychoanalyst Franz Alexander, which says that when a patient is talking about the past, relate it to the present, and when one talks about the present, relate it to the past; I would extend this to the future as well. I have always valued that maxim since it is so geared toward integrating past, present [and future] in the narrative therapeutic interchange.

In retrospective rescripting the very act of invoking scripts from the past will automatically change them through the process of recall and reconsolidation, as discussed earlier. This change offers us the opportunity to rescript the past. By invoking the dynamics of "doing the opposite of the urge" and acting "as if" it is different, we can re-write the past and change the emotional memory itself.

The continuance of past memories in PTSD is because the recollection of the trauma recreates the context in which that event took place. One is transformed back to the original event with all the startle and terror associated with that event. When a current event triggers associated memories that are not traumatic, the affect has been diminished sufficiently that it is no longer salient; if, however, a present event triggers an affect associated with a previously traumatized event, then that affect will become the most intense and salient. The use of EMDR (Eye Movement Desensitization Reprocessing), a technique designed for trauma, is partly based on the relaxation response being induced while the memory of the traumatic event is being recalled, thus changing the context to the now; thus, when a memory is brought up, it is not in the context of the traumatic situation, but in the calming and supportive environment of the therapist's office.

Where there is past, there is also a future. Adler's *fictional finalisms* refer to how the future shapes the present; it also shapes our memories of the past. In *proscripting,* one is to imagine and experience the future differently than one usually does by imagining oneself

---

[90] As stated by Freud, "where Id is there shall Ego be.".

doing what is the opposite-of-the-urge, feeling and acting "as if" it is different, of reframing the situation, utilizing knowledge wisely, and assuming the mantle of agency and willpower.

Like retrospective rescripting, proscripting about the future changes one's perspective of the future from what it once was. Again, the context is different. When a person thinks about an upcoming event while euphoric she will likely feel optimistic, whereas when she thinks of it while depressed she will more likely feel pessimistic and worry about all that may go wrong. She also may feel dread as she begins to prepare a speech, while feeling joyful when it is completed. On a broader level, a younger person's view of the future will be quite different than that of an elderly person; again, context is (nearly) everything.

In addition to the cognitive-behavioral tactics discussed, the integrative approach to proscripting is to first identify scripts that are the most adaptive and constructive, and then engage in those scripts in the present. One often does this naturally, especially when planning for the future. For example, when filing away items one does so by imagining how one would find them in the future. As implied by the concept of fictional finalisms, the future actually helps determine the present; it also helps determine one's memory of the past, such as when filing those items before.

Rescripting the Selfother-Self

The goal for rescripting your selfother-self, is to enhance both the quality and quantity of your social interactions, and to enhance those socially oriented qualities that characterize wellbeing, such as humanism, altruism, and compassion. It should be noted that you not only want to improve your social relationships with others, but to improve your relationship with your own selfother-self, a relationship that can be identified both through your actions, and through your self-talk (internal narratives).

Doing the opposite-of-the-urge means reaching out to others when the urge is to withdraw or attack, while acting "as if" you are adept at socializing. Volunteering to do social service activities, such as working in a soup kitchen or in a children's ward, are rewarding in many ways and has been shown to promote wellbeing; interestingly, getting paid seems to lessen those benefits.

Chapter 11: Disorders of the Self

Thus far, we have been focusing on the *to be* part in Shakespeare's soliloquy. In closing, it may be of value to briefly look at the *not to be* alternative, namely the state of (relative) non-being, or the non-self. The non-self reflects a state of emptiness, of nothingness, of a soulless non-being living as though a zombie or robot. This is a state made up of undifferentiated, amorphous and fluid self-scripts that manifest themselves as disorders of the self.

All segments of the self are impaired. The structural self is fragile and therefore lacks integrity, while the functional self is incapable of acting competently. There is a highly constricted autobiographical self whose temporality narrows into the moment. And finally, the selfother self evaporates as infantile narcissism comes to dominate. As is evident, the self is unintegrated and thus lacks an emergent self.

Disorders of the self may entail a fragmented self, such as seen in cases of arrested development, or of a self that failed to fully develop, as evidenced by the personality disorder, especially Borderline Personality Disorder. Another type of personality disorder consists of multiple selves, or multiple self-scripts as seen in Multiple Personality Disorder. Then there is the imaginary self that takes flight from reality, as we see in psychosis. We also have the disintegrated self, a regressed self-state resulting from disease or injury; this condition underlies the ravages of dementia that in the last stages personifies a non-self, self-state.

Features that are juxtaposed to those we find in the rescripted self characterize disorders of the self. At the core level, there is an inability to effectively regulate affects in ways that maximize positive affect and minimize negative affect; thus fear-terror, shame-humiliation, anger-rage and distress-anguish predominate, while interest-excitement and enjoyment-joy are relatively absent. As a consequence, incompetence and failure are evident in all areas of functioning. Cognitively we find that judgment, decision-making, learning, memory, language, reasoning and critical thinking skills are impaired. Without the capacity to regulate affect there is an inability to self-regulate, and so emotions will be dysregulated. Symptoms include feelings of emptiness, inappropriate behaviors, a personality that appears "flaky" and unstable, and thoughts that are sometimes delusional or disconnected. In fact, Borderline Personality Disorder is now classified as an Emotional Dysregulation Disorder. Since self-scripts and their executive functions are limited in directing actions in appropriate ways, we find serious behavioral problems. The structure of the self is so compromised that chaos, instead of stability, will reign.

With the functioning-self so destabilized, the emergence of an integrated self is impossible. The disordered-self lacks most of the features associated with wellbeing. Without a self, there is minimal agency and willpower, since the exigencies of the moment take over. Wisdom is seldom, if ever, evident as judgment and reality testing are severely tested. Humanistic altruism and empathy are largely absent, as self-centeredness predominates. Humility, humor and moral integrity will also be lacking. With an impaired selfother-self, narcissism will rule and thereby limit one's ability to develop fulfilling relationships; with a defective autobiographical self, unpredictability, superficiality and fragility will dominate.

Borderline Personality Disorder (BPD): The Fragmented Self

There are several types of personality disorders: antisocial personality, avoidant personality, narcissistic personality, obsessive personality, schizotypal disorder, and borderline personality. According to the Diagnostic and Statistical Manual (DSM-V, 2011) the essential features of a personality disorder are "impairments in personality (self and interpersonal) functioning and the presence of pathological personality traits."

Impairments in self-functioning include the following: identity diffusion and thereby an unstable self-image, feelings of emptiness, dissociation under stress, and a lack in self-direction and self-agency. Impairments in interpersonal functioning include a lack of empathy, hypersensitivity to perceived criticism, and difficulties in establishing intimate relationships. Those with this disorder are characterized by negative affects, emotional lability, anxiousness and depression, disinhibition, impulsivity and hostility. We could also add that a sense of morality and ethics, namely a functioning conscience, is also lacking.

Borderline Personality Disorders (BPD) share all these traits, but specifically represent a character structure that exists at the *border,* or at the *line,* between a "state of self" and a "state of non-self," of a *real-self* and a *false-self*. As such, it is not much of a jump to understand why a major and defining feature of a borderline relates to boundary issues, such as the failure to set or observe customary social norms. Most often this is expressed though socially inappropriate behaviors, such as being too personal with another person, or making hurtful statements, or commenting negatively about another person's appearance. Instead of clarity, boundaries are amorphous and suited, not for others, but solely for oneself; obfuscations operate in the service of narcissism.

BPD represents a broken, unstable and fragmented self, which is euphemistically characterized by the moniker of the "as-if" personality, that is someone who doesn't seem to be "all there," who seems like a "shadow" self. They seem to be empty inside, void of any substance. Fragility, insecurity and fears of abandonment and separation predominate, since others were used as anchors for maintaining a sense-of-self.

BPD is largely viewed as an emotionally unstable personality, an affect dysregulation disorder that is characterized by intense and uncontrollable emotional reactions that often seem disproportionate to the precipitating event or situation. In this regard, the inability to regulate affects successfully is due to a split within the self.

As a reflection of a fragmented and either/or self, *splitting* is a prime interpersonal behavior. Splitting is defined in the DSM-IV as "a pattern of unstable and intense interpersonal relationships characterized by alternating between extremes of idealization and devaluation." This split represents a split in the selfother-self, between the *all-good self* and the *all-bad self* that then gets projected onto others. Splitting creates instability in relationships because the *other* can be viewed as either all good or all bad, depending on one's distorted and maladaptive assumptions.

Splitting can also be expressed in interpersonal triangles that involve one's self and two other people; in this "jealousy" scenario, one person comes to be regarded as a friend, the other as an enemy; splitting these two people apart is a divide-and-conquer strategy; for example, a borderline may tell person A about negative statements person B said about her. Unfortunately, divorced parents will sometimes engage in splitting behavior that divides their children from their ex-spouse, thus using a "borderline" tactic.[91]

---

[91] This does not mean that one is a BPD. It is here being used descriptively, not diagnostically. All of us have gone through stages of borderline functioning during self development, and thus retain some of the

Lying, or exaggerating to the point of lying, is another common feature of the borderline. Oft-times they cannot even recognize they are being untruthful; this lack of self-awareness represents a split between their false-self and their real-self. Lying is often a defense against shame and guilt, which distorts reality and erodes trust from others.

Self-damaging behaviors may include frequent attempts at suicide or self-inflicted cutting behaviors. These self-destructive actions may be deliberate or impulsive, and can become habitual. A patient of mine once described his cutting behavior as a need to feel his emotions, to feel his self, which seemed to be "caged inside" him; to hurt himself certainly elicited sensations and feelings, albeit pain.

Borderlines suffer severe distortions in self-image, display considerable identity diffusion, and have difficulties knowing what they value and what they believe. They are often unsure about their long-term goals, and have difficulty maintaining relationships and jobs. This confusion in knowing who they are, and what they value, leads them to experience themselves as empty and desolate.

Dissociation entails the "I" detaching from the "me," of the *observing-self* as separate from the *experiencing-self*. It can also mean that the self is detached from the immediate environment, a separation (not loss) of one's self from reality, unlike the loss of reality that takes place in schizophrenia. These alterations can include: "a sense that the self or the world is unreal (depersonalization and derealization); a loss of memory (amnesia); forgetting one's identity or assuming a new self (fugue state); and fragmentation of identity or self into separate streams of consciousness (Multiple Personality Disorder, which has been reclassified as a Dissociative Identity Disorder); and complex post-traumatic stress disorder."[92]

Multiple Personality Disorder (MPD) presents an interesting challenge as to whether there are completely separate selves, or whether there are different self-scripts that compete for dominance. Many believe there are separate selves, each with their own identity and set of self-states. I define the self as a megascript that consists of all other self-scripts. Consequently, each state represents a self-script that has failed to coalesce with other self-scripts. Each has a different identity, which we know is not what the self is. MPD, therefore, entails separate self-scripts that cannot integrate as part of the self.

Schizophrenia: The Imaginary Self

Schizophrenia is a psychotic disorder. Psychosis is "a symptom or feature of mental illness typically characterized by radical changes in personality, impaired functioning, and a distorted or nonexistent sense of objective reality." (American Medical Dictionary) Reality testing is impaired since there is an inability to distinguish objective reality from subjective experiences.

Distinguishing features include hallucinations and/or delusions. Hallucinations may occur in all five senses, but is most commonly associated with auditory or visual distortions, such as hearing voices or seeing things that are not there. Delusions relate to false beliefs, such as a paranoid's fear of a conspiracy, or the belief that one is Napoleon. Behavior and

---

features used.

[92] Wikipedia, An accurate description

communication can be highly inappropriate and incoherent, often consisting of neologisms (made up words) and other nonsensical speech patterns.

Psychosis may appear in a number of mental disorders, including mood disorders such as bi-polar disorder, whether it is in the depressive or manic state, or in personality disorders. In addition, there are brief psychotic disorders that may be induced by trauma, or psychosis due to a medical condition, substance abuse, and even a shared psychosis as seen in cases where there is a *folie à deux* (two), *or even a folie à plusieurs* (many), as evidenced by the mass witch hysteria of Salem or the mass adulation of a dictator.

Schizophrenia is the most common and well-known form of psychosis. According to the DSM-III, there are several types the Schizophrenia that includes catatonic type, disorganized type, paranoid type, residual type, and undifferentiated type. In schizophrenia, the self is fragmented and disintegrated, with the distinguishing characteristic that it also imaginary. It is more than a fake or false self, it is an unreal, illusory and made up self. In paranoid schizophrenia, the self may become Jesus, or the target of a grand conspiracy.

Dementia: The Disintegrated Non-Self

The rescripted self refers to a person who has achieved both competency and success in life, and who has attained a state of being characterized by happiness and wellbeing. Rescripting leads to the rescripted self. There are two levels in the rescripting process; at the basic level is the functional self, a self that is based on affect-regulation scripts, while at a higher and more complex level there is the emergent self, which evolves through the integration of its self-scripts.

As you may remember, the reason the functional self is also called the structural self is because its self-scripts are sufficiently organized so as to provide order and stability; disintegration lessens this bond that will lead to a dysfunctional self, and therefore instability and disorder. Since the functional self is primary to that of the evolving emergent self, then emergence itself would be impaired. Instead of integration, there is disintegration with the consequence that there be incompetency rather than competency, misery rather than wellbeing.

What is the state of the *dis*integrated self? In a word, we can say it is the opposite of wellbeing, namely despair, anguish and the absence of wisdom, self-agency and willpower whereby the locus of control is external to the self, which then leads to feelings of vulnerability and powerlessness. In addition, there is a high level of incompetency and a failure to function effectively; in other words, the disordered and deconstructed self characterizes dementia.

Dementia, as a medical term, came from the French physician Philip Pinel, who in 1801 had a patient who lost her memory, speech, and ability to walk or use common objects like a fork or a hairbrush; Pinel called this process "demence" to mean incoherence of the mental faculties.

In 1907, the German physician Alois Alzheimer published a paper on a patient of his who, like Pinel's patient, suffered a "failure of memory, paranoia, and loss of reasoning powers, incomprehension, and stupor." Using an optical microscope, he looked at her brain and described a disease process whereby the brain was shrunken, full of fluid, displayed structural damage in the form of neurofibrillary tangles, and had bone structures growing in the brain tissues. These turned out to be the four principle features of a brain with Alzheimer's disease.

Alzheimer's dementia constitutes 60 to 80 percent of all dementias. In order of frequency the next most common form is Vascular or Multi Infarct, then Parkinson's dementia, followed by Frontal Temporal, Lewy Body, Pick's Disease, Huntington's, Korsakov's and Progressive Aphasic Dementia. The remaining types of dementias are very rare and are not often seen.

Is it Dementia or is it Senility?

Dementia is not senility; senility is a function of the aging process (and is euphemistically called "age-based" dementia), unlike the pathological disease we call "dementia;" Unlike senility, dementia can also be found among younger adults, or be associated with specific kinds of diseases.

Most people experience mild cognitive changes and memory loss as they begin to move into their 50s. One of the clearest indicators of dementia is the speed and intensity of progression. Regular mental decline associated with aging is usually a slow and gradual loss of memory and attention span. Dementia, however, is often characterized by rapid, sudden, and severe changes in memory and cognitive ability. These can include the following:

Speech skills: Occasionally forgetting words is usually a sign of normal cognitive changes, while frequently forgetting words, many pauses in speech, difficulty understanding speech, or a tendency to call things by the wrong name can be a sign of dementia.

Memory loss: Those with normal age-related memory loss will usually be able to recall specific events, while those with dementia-related memory loss will be unable to recall specific instances, even when prompted.

Short-term memory changes: Significant declines in short-term memory, such as an inability to remember recent conversations or events, are not a normal sign of aging and can indicate dementia.

Trouble with familiar tasks: Normal cognitive decline can cause some problems following directions or remembering how to get somewhere, but getting lost in familiar, frequently visited locations or forgetting the way home could be signs of dementia.

Social skills: Loss of social skills isn't a normal part of aging, nor is a loss of interest in socializing, decreased ability to speak to others, or increased socially inappropriate behavior.

Difficulty with complex tasks: Extreme difficulty planning or organizing events, paying bills, following recipes, writing letters, or traveling to new locations.

Decreased concentration: The inability to stay focused, to attend to detail, to concentrate for relatively short periods of time, to display very slow recall speeds and reaction times, as well as a decreased ability to learn and memorize new information.

Problems with coordination: Decreases in motor functions and motor coordination, sometimes manifested as trembling, shaking, or difficulty walking.

Decreased reasoning skills: Neglecting safety, personal hygiene, exercise, or nutrition. Decreased judgment involving money, like making unnecessary purchases or giving away large sums of money.

Psychological Changes in Dementia

Changes in mood: Frequent mood swings, increased sensitivity to change, and increased anxiety and agitation.

Personality changes: Loss of interest in previously enjoyed activities and changes in personality and behavior.

Hallucinations or paranoia: In later stages of dementia, sufferers may believe that even close friends or family are dangerous or "out to get them."

The Six Stages of Dementia[93]

Learning about the stages of dementia can help with identifying signs and symptoms early on, as well as in assisting sufferers and caretakers in knowing what to expect in further stages. The earlier dementia is diagnosed, the sooner treatment can begin; there is ample research showing that that early treatment can slow the progression of this terrible disease.

Stage 1: Age Associated Memory Impairment

This stage features occasional lapses of memory, most frequently seen in forgetting where one has placed an object or forgetting names that were once very familiar. Oftentimes, this mild decline in memory is merely normal age-related cognitive decline, but it can also be one of the earliest signs of degenerative dementia. At this stage, signs are still virtually undetectable through clinical testing.

Stage 2: Mild Cognitive Impairment

Clear cognitive problems are manifest at this stage. Among its characteristics are: getting lost easily, noticeably poor performance at work or accomplishing tasks, forgetting the names of family members and close friends; difficulty retaining information read in a book or passage, losing or misplacing important objects, and difficulty concentrating.

Stage 3: Mild Dementia

At this stage, individuals may start to become socially withdrawn and show changes in personality and mood. Denial of symptoms, as a defense mechanism, is commonly seen in stage three. Behavioral changes include a declining knowledge of current events; a decrease in recalling recent events; difficulty remembering things about one's personal history; decreased ability to handle finances or arrange travel plans, or trouble traveling to familiar places; and difficulty recognizing faces and people; and avoiding challenging situations in order to hide their symptoms or to prevent stress or anxiety.

---

[93] Largely taken from the Global Deterioration Scale for Assessment of Primary Degenerative Dementia. Stage 1 was originally Pre-Dementia, which I eliminated since technically, it is not a stage of dementia

Stage 4: Moderate Dementia
Those in stage 4 need some assistance in order to carry out their daily lives. The main sign, at this stage, is the inability to remember major details such as the name of a friend or relative, or one's home address and telephone number. The person may become disoriented about time and place and will have trouble making decisions.

While moderate dementia can interfere with basic functioning, those at this stage do not need regular assistance with basic functions such as using the bathroom or eating. They also still have the ability to remember their own names and generally the names of spouses and children.

Stage 5: Moderately Severe Dementia
When the individual begins to forget the names of their children, spouse, or primary caregivers, they are most likely entering stage 5 of dementia and will need full time care. In the fifth stage, individuals are generally unaware of their surroundings, cannot recall recent events, and have skewed memories of their personal past. Among its other symptoms are delusional behavior, hallucinations by some, obsessive and compulsive behaviors, agitation and aggression, difficulty sleeping, and wandering around because of the loss of orientation. It is at this stage that the loss of willpower and self-agency become more prominent; the self is near-death.

Stage 6: Severe Dementia
Along with the loss of motor skills, people progressively lose their ability to speak, as the brain deteriorates to the point where the brain-body connection is lost. This is the stage where the self is truly dead; instead of self, there is only body.

Without a self to govern one's self makes Pinel's description of the "incoherence of the mental faculties" quite palpable. Incoherence is the opposite of coherence and thus speaks to the absence of integration and, the consequent state of disorder and irrationality. We could say that the self is *unscripted*, living a life by the seat of one's pants whereby inscripts and affects are unregulated by learned scripts. This is Id, where Ego once was. Not even the basic prescripts survive, such as maximizing positive affect and minimizing negative affects. It is often said that the anxiety in dementia lasts only while there is a self to understand what is going on; once the self is gone, so is the anxiety; this is partly because with the autobiographical self is gone; so too is the ability to contemplate the future. In addition, there is a relative lack of depressive ruminations since the past cannot be recalled; there is only the moment, which can be distressing, frustrating, angering, disgusting, or frightening. Hallucinations and delusions may also be present as seen in late-stage Parkinson's dementia.

Conclusion
It is evident that *to be* is better than *not-to-be*, although all of us are destined to lose our self, especially when death comes to visit. Are states of non-self treatable? Although successful treatment is very limited and cannot prevent loss, it may be able to slow down its progression. Unfortunately, studies on the relationship between pre-dementia and dementia are scant, although anecdotal examples are evident. For example, two people I personally knew developed Parkinson disease nearly at the same time. One individual deteriorated much faster than the other, and in fact died of the disease sooner than did the other. Although many factors were likely involved, the fact that the person who did much better was certainly more "put-together" than the one who declined more rapidly. The pessimism, frustration, fear and

anger were noticeably worse than the person whose attitude, toward his disease was more sanguine and accepting of his condition. This suggests that the more fully rescripted-self may be more resilient and less prone to deterioration than a person whose self had not equally evolved. This is illustrated when we refer to the structural self and the integrated self, labels that denote resiliency and strength.

We can define nonbeing as the absence of being, of the state of non-self; in other words, the state of nothingness is the opposite of the state of something, which brings up the question whether phenomena exist outside consciousness? Or, in George Berkeley's famous paradox, "if a tree falls in a forest and no one is there to hear it, does it make a sound?"[94] These mind games play well among existentialists, especially for Jean-Paul Sartre's "Being and Nothingness" (Altona, 1959). To fully comprehend nonexistence is beyond our capacity to even imagine, since the very act of imagining, is in itself, a state of being. We try to understand the concept of nonbeing through such metaphors as, "without light there is only darkness;" or "the non-self is a state like sleep or coma." Yet, even in these conditions, there is also self. Perhaps we can best understand non-self by equating it with death itself.

An important question to look at is whether there is any treatment available for dementia. A promising approach comes from Gunther Wolfram of Germany. (Washington Post. December 30, 2017, p.10) It is based on the findings that, unlike short-term memory which is severely impaired, long-term memory is relatively intact. As we discussed earlier, this is the basis why autobiographical therapy is often the treatment of choice for the elderly. In Wolfram's approach, however, it is important not to just discuss and review the past, but to re-experience it. As a consequence, they created an environment that largely simulates the circumstance that was dominant in the past. Not only were environmental cues prominent, such as the décor and objects of the past, but also the tools of the trade of that senior to reactivate memories. According to Wolfram, the "dementia residents often have this challenge of being unable to structure their own lives and nor really knowing what to do with themselves." By providing a familiar context from the past that is likely to be remembered and thus re-experienced, provides the opportunity to stabilize their lives.

Rescripting can help by using many of the coping strategies we use in function-focused rescripting. Cognitive approaches require a cognitive-self; if intact, then some basic cognitive interventions can play a role in strengthening cognition. Knowing that short-term memory loss could be due to attention problems, or hearing problems, or a neural disease, would be critical in knowing how to treat these problems.

To remember something entails encoding a perceived event into a construct that can then be stored and consolidated into memory, making it subject to recall. Memory requires learning, and learning can be enhanced by increasing one's concentration abilities and then reviewing and repeating the information. Memory consolidation tactics can also be very helpful, especially mnemonics, which consists of using patterns of associations to assist in remembering something.

A relatively well-known mnemonic technique looks at a person's style of learning in sensory terms that is specified as auditory, visual or kinesthetic. Visual learners (the most numerous) relate most often to the written word or to pictures, such as diagrams; auditory learners relate more to the spoken word; while kinesthetic learners use procedural learning via doing. The goal is to fit the techniques to one's primary learning style.

---

[94] Some say the answer is that the tree makes a *noise* when it falls, but not a *sound* which by definition would require a listener.

Of course, as one's dementia progresses, there are functional incapacities that render many of these tactics inoperable. Using behavioral conditioning techniques will at least help organize behavior. Prevention, deterrence, or symptom inoculation are also valuable options. However, at the last two stages, the self has withered away. Some say that at death the spirit or soul may live on, which is interesting since sometimes spirit and soul are used as synonyms with the self. However, when the physical-self dies, so does the self die. It is likely that the self extends beyond death only in the minds and hearts of those left behind. As stated by Jean-Paul Sartre, "Death is a continuation of my life without me."

Appendices

Appendix 1: Affect Recognition Worksheet

As often as possible, fill out the worksheet below, using the Likert SUDS Scale in which 0=lowest and 7=highest.

Affect Recognition Worksheet			
Date	**Time**	**Event** **Affect(s)**	**SUDS Level**

Appendix 2: Graduated Desensitization Worksheet

Graduated Desensitization Worksheet

Affect: _____

Date	Time of Day	Duration	Beginning SUDS Level	Ending SUDS Level

Appendix 3: Diaphragmatic Breathing

Begin by lying on your back, either on the floor or on your bed.

Place your left hand just below the rib cage and just above your stomach, and your right hand on your chest.

Make your left hand move up and down as your diaphragm moves in and out, while your right hand remains relatively still.

Practice this until you are able to expand and contract your diaphragm with minimal movement of your chest.

Once you have this movement "in hand:"
- Inhale by taking a deep breath through your nose as you expand your diaphragm (or as your left hand moves up),[When very low energy, hold your breath for a count of three]...and
- Exhale through your mouth as your diaphragm contracts (or as your left hand moves down).

Continue this breathing...inhaling fully through your nose as your diaphragm expands.......and then fully exhaling through your mouth as your diaphragm shrinks. Do this between one to two minutes at a time.

Practice this as frequently as you can until you feel confident that you have mastered this breathing technique and do not have to use your hands as a guide.

Once you feel comfortable with this way of breathing, practice it while sitting up, while standing and while walking. Practice diaphragmatic breathing between 10-20 times a day, or whenever upset.

Appendix 4: Progressive Muscle Relaxation

OUTLINE FOR PROGRESSIVE RELAXATION (PMR)

1. Basic Technique
    A. Separately tense your individual muscle groups.
    B. Hold the tension about five seconds.
    C. Release the tension slowly and at the same time, silently say, "Relax and let go."
    D. Take a deep breath.
    E. As you breathe slowly out, silently say, "Relax and let go."

11. Muscle Groups and Exercises
    A. Head:
        1. Wrinkle your forehead;
        2. Squeeze your eyes tightly;
        3. Open your mouth wide;
        4. Push your tongue against the roof of your mouth;
        5. Clench your jaw tightly.
    B. Neck:
        1. Push your head back into the pillow.
        2. Bring your head forward to touch your chest;
        3. Roll your head to your right should
        4. Roll your head to your left shoulder.
    C. Shoulders:
        1. Shrug your shoulders up as if to touch your ears;
        2. Shrug your right shoulder up as if to touch your ear;
        3. Shrug your left shoulder up as if to touch your ear.
    D. Arms and hands:
        1. Hold your arms out and make a fist with each hand;
        2. One side at a time: Push your hands down into the surface where you are.

Appendix 5: Basic Autogenic Training

BASIC AUTOGENIC TRAINING

Get into a comfortable position, either sitting or lying, and close your eyes. Take a deep breath, and exhale fully and completely. Remember to breathe properly throughout the exercise. Let the day's experiences and thoughts pass through you and out of you. Do not hold onto your thoughts; allow them to go. Watch them flow by as if on a movie screen, or like billboards passed on the highway.

Repeat this mood phrase to yourself three times: "I am at peace with myself and fully relaxed." Remember to breathe properly, and on the exhalation breathe away any tension.

Concentrate on feeling heaviness in your arms and legs. Right-handed people begin with the right arm; left-handed people with the left. Right-handed people begin: "My right arm is heavy. My right arm is heavy. My right arm is heavy." Left-handed people begin: "My left arm is heavy. My left arm is heavy. My left arm is heavy." Pause between each phrase—this is not a race. Take your time, and let any worries or thoughts that may enter your consciousness flow through you, and out of you. Feel the heaviness in your arm. Proceed to the opposite arm and repeat the phrase to yourself three times: "My left arm is heavy," or "My right arm is heavy." Feel the heaviness in your arm.

Then proceed to the legs, saying to yourself: "My right leg is heavy. My right leg is heavy. My right leg is heavy." Feel the heaviness in your leg. Remember to breathe naturally, and take your time, pausing between each phrase. Then the other leg: "My left leg is heavy. My left leg is heavy. My left leg is heavy." Feel the heaviness in your legs.

Then say to yourself: "My neck and shoulders are heavy. My neck and shoulders are heavy. My neck and shoulders are heavy." Feel the heaviness in your neck and shoulders. Take a deep, calm breath, and exhale fully and completely.

Concentrate on feeling warmth as you relax the smooth muscles in the walls of the arteries. Right-handed people begin: "My right arm is warm. My right arm is warm. My right arm is warm." Left-handed people begin: "My left arm is warm. My left arm is warm. My left arm is warm." Feel the warmth in your arms; be aware of the pulse, and the flow of blood through your entire body. Go on to the other arm.

Then let go of the tension in your legs, saying to yourself: "My right leg is warm. My right leg is warm. My right leg is warm." Feel the warmth in your right leg. Continue with the other leg and repeat the phrase to yourself three times. Feel the heaviness in your legs. Remember to breathe slowly and naturally, and let any thoughts flow out of you.

Move on to your neck and shoulders, and say to yourself: "My neck and shoulders are warm. My neck and shoulders are warm. My neck and shoulders are warm." Feel the warmth in your neck and shoulders, and feel the warm blood flowing through your body. Just allow yourself to remain relaxed, don't try to force the feeling, and be aware of any sensation of blood flow or temperature change. Remember to breathe naturally and calmly.

Slow and calm your heart by saying to yourself: "My heartbeat is calm and regular. My heartbeat is calm and regular. My heartbeat is calm and regular." Some people may experience discomfort when they turn their attention to their own heartbeat. If you feel nauseated, lightheaded, or notice any other disturbing sensation, change the phrase to: "I feel calm. I feel calm. I feel calm."

To slow your breathing say to yourself: "My breathing is calm and regular. My breathing is calm and regular. My breathing is calm and regular." Feel the air completely filling your lungs when you inhale, and on the exhalation feel the warm air leaving your lungs. Pause between each phrase, and say the phrases to yourself slowly and calmly.

Concentrate on warmth in your abdomen, saying to yourself: "My abdomen is warm and calm. My abdomen is warm and calm. My abdomen is warm and calm." If you have serious abdominal problems, bleeding ulcers, diabetes, or are in the last trimester of pregnancy, change the phrase to: "I am calm and relaxed. I am calm and relaxed. I am calm and relaxed."

Move on to your forehead, repeating to yourself: "My forehead is cool and calm. My forehead is cool and calm. My forehead is cool and calm." Feel the excess blood flowing out of your head. Remember to breathe the calm, full breath; allow any extraneous thoughts to flow through you, and out of you.

When you have completed the last phrase, rest for a moment. To bring yourself back to a normal state of alertness repeat the phrase to yourself: "I am refreshed and completely alert. I am refreshed and completely alert. I am refreshed and completely alert." Take a deep, full breath, flex your arms and legs, and stretch. You may wish to repeat the last phrase several more times. Slowly open your eyes.

Appendix 6: Defensive Beliefs

The Questionnaire below[95] lists some of the general defensive assumptions and expectations that one develops in order to live life in ways that regulates affect through defensive and protective assumptions. As you will note, these are idealisms based on wishes rather than reality. To live according to these beliefs and expectations will lead to the ultimate fulfillment of our prescripts, namely that at all times negative affect will be minimized, if not eliminated, positive affect will be maximized, and we will always be able to express our affect, assured that others will love and approve of us unconditionally.

As you read and rate each belief, you likely will be immediately aware of their absurdity. This is because the task itself requires higher cortical levels of evaluation and judgment. Try to suspend this complex level of thinking since what we are trying to identify are lower level secondary beliefs that usually operate at an implicit and nonconscious level. It is at this level that you would best benefit from identifying which expectations, and to what degree these assumptions direct how you feel and how you act.

General Defensive Beliefs

Rate the strength or validity for each belief or expectation

1	2	3	4	5	6	7
Not at all	Hardly	Somewhat	Fifty-Fifty	More so than not	A lot	Completely

[ ] I must be loved unconditionally
[ ] I must be approved of unconditionally
[ ] I must be in complete control of everything
[ ] I must be right all the time
[ ] I must be perfect all the time
[ ] I must always be and know what's fair
[ ] I must know all the why's, how's and what's of life
[ ] I must always have the best of intentions
[ ] I must always like what one does

---

[95] Taken from Albert Ellis, the putative father of cognitive therapy.

Appendix 7: Maladaptive Styles of Thinking

Maladaptive Styles of Thinking[96]

1	2	3	4	5	6	7
Not at all	Hardly	Somewhat	Fifty-Fifty	More so than not	A lot	Completely

ABSOLUTISTIC THINKING: a rigid and compulsively driven mode of thinking.

[ ] **Imperative Thinking**: commands, rules and exhortations; "should," "must," "have to,"

[ ] **Certaintistic Thinking:** absence of probability; "can't," "never," "always," "forever" .

[ ] **Dichotomous Thinking**: polarized, either-or, thinking; yes-no, good-bad, right-wrong.

EXAGGERATED THINKING: blowing things out of proportion.

[ ] **Catastrophizing:** predicting the worse possible outcome.

[ ] **Awfulizing**: taking the worse possible perspective.

[ ] **Overgeneralizing**: making blanket assumptions based on singular events.

CONSTRICTED THINKING: narrowing the focus out of proportion.

[ ] **Selective Perception**: noticing only one of many features.

[ ] **Minimization:** discounting or oversimplifying information so things appear insignificant. e.g., "it was nothing."

MISATTRIBUTION: attributing a motive, or cause of some event, to another.

[ ] **Personalization**: relating external event to oneself: "he did this because of me."

[ ] **Internalization**: attributing responsibility to oneself: "I caused this to happen."

[ ] **Externalization:** attributing responsibility to others; "others made me do that."

ARBITRARY INFERENCE: conclusions based on illogical reasoning or inadequate data.

[ ] **Magical Reasoning**: superstitious reasoning; "if I'm good, things will turn out right."

[ ] **Emotional Reasoning:** " I feel or sense it...therefore...it is true"

[ ] **Mind Reading**: knowing another's motives or thinking.

[ ] **Fortune Telling**: knowing future outcomes.

[ ] **Labeling**: blanket categorizing of self or others

---

[96] Largely taken from Aaron Beck, the other putative father of cognitive therapy, and Eric Burns

Appendix 8: The Practice of Mindfulness

The Practice of Mindfulness

Keep your back straight, in an alert yet restful position. This is a posture of dignity, rather than rigidity. Let your hands comfortably repose together in your lap or separately on your knees. Allow your eyes to close gently. Allow your breath to come and go naturally—to breathe itself—do not force it. And as you inhale and exhale, notice your breathing. Pay attention to the feel of your breathing.

Now take a few moments to check for possible tension in various areas of your body eyes, forehead, jaw, neck, shoulders, chest, hands, pelvis, knees, and feet. Bring a gentle awareness to each place, letting it relax and soften.

Begin to notice where in your body you can feel the movement of the breath most distinctly while still allowing the breath to remain natural. This may be in the abdomen, chest, or at the tip of the nostrils. It is important to choose only one of these areas and maintain it as the "primary anchor" of mindfulness because it serves as the basis for calmness to arise.

Now bring awareness to the beginning of an "in" breath, sustaining mindfulness there as much as you can until the end of the "in" breath. Do the same with the "out" breath. You may find it helpful to make a silent mental note of "in" or "rising" as you experience the in-breath, and "out" or "falling" as you experience the out-breath. This technique of mental noting strengthens your practice by clearly connecting awareness with the physical sensations of the breath. It also helps in focusing your attention more precisely.

After a few breaths, your mind will probably wander to one of the six sense doors (the five physical senses and the mind). As soon as you are aware of this, acknowledge where you are present in that very moment with a silent mental note about whatever is actually happening—wandering, thinking, hearing, pain, itching, coolness, sadness, happiness, smelling, fantasizing, etc. This wandering of the mind is normal. It's important to be compassionate and patient with yourself. Just remain relaxed, yet alert, and be willing to begin again and again.

Gently bring mindfulness back to the primary anchor of the breath, experiencing each breath as fully as possible and continuing to note "in/out" or "rising/falling."

Appendix 9: Affirmation Self-Statements

It is critical that you believe, or can learn to believe in them. If you use any examples, feel free to modify them as you wish. You can use the list presented below, or develop your own. Keep them brief, direct and believable. Practice saying each statement 10 times out loud, and 10 times to yourself. State them with conviction and determination. After repeating each 20 times, then move on to the next. Practice these repetitions at least three times per day. Affirmation training is similar to body building. the more you practice, the more you build up these positive self-statements in your mind.

1. I'm responsible and in control of my life.
2. Circumstances are what they are and I can choose my attitude toward them.
3. I am setting priorities and making time for what is important.
4. Every challenge that comes along is an opportunity to learn and grow.
5. I accept the natural ups and downs of life.
6. I love and accept myself the way I am.
7. I deserve the good things in life as much as anyone else.
8. I am open to discovering new meaning in my life.
9. It's never too late to change.
10. I am learning, one step at a time. how to cope better.
11. I am capable of dealing with life's stresses.
12. I am learning to love myself.
13. I am learning to be comfortable with myself.
14. I respect and believe in myself apart from others' opinions.
15. I can accept and learn from constructive criticism.
16. I'm learning to be myself around others.
17. I appreciate my achievements.
18. I am learning how to balance work, relationships and play in my life.
19. I am learning that there is more to life than success.
20. The greatest success is living well.
21. I'm a unique and capable person just as I am.
22. I am satisfied doing the best I can.
23. It's O.K. to make mistakes.
24. I'm willing to accept my mistakes and learn from them.
25. I'm willing to allow others to help me.
26. I am open to receiving support from others.
27. I am willing to take the risk of getting close to someone.
28. I am learning to relax and let go.
29. I'm learning to accept those things I can't control.
30. Nobody's perfect. I am learning how to be easier on myself.
31. I'm doing the best I can.
32. It's O.K. to be upset when things go wrong.
33. I'm O.K. if I don't always have a quick answer to every problem.
34. It's O.K. to make time to rest and relax.
35. I do the best I can and I'm satisfied with that.
36. It's O.K. if I'm unable to always foresee everything.
37. I'm learning to be honest with others, even when I'm not feeling pleasant or nice.
38. I will learn to accept the things I cannot change; the courage to change the things I can, and the *wisdom* to know the difference [The serenity Prayer]

Appendix 10: Anxiety Inoculation[97]

This approach uses a series of coping self-statements to deal with a specific anxiety-producing situation, such as giving a speech or attending a social event. Self-statements are to be prepared in advance, and used to handle four phases of a stressful situation: preparing, confronting, coping if overwhelmed, and assessing how well you handled the event.

Anxiety Inoculation Worksheet

Preparing For Situation
  Purpose: Focus on specific preparation for task, combat negative thinking
      emphasize planning and preparation
  Examples: What do I have to do?
      I can develop a plan to deal with it.
      Just think about what I can do about it.
      Remember, stick to the issues and don't take it personally.

Confronting and Handling Stressor
  Purpose: Control stress reaction, reassure yourself that you can handle the situation, reinterpret stress as something you can use constructively, remind yourself to use these coping responses, remain focused on the task.
  Examples: "I can meet this challenge"
      I can convince myself to do it.
      One step at a time.
      Don't think about my stress, just about what I have to do.

Coping with Feelings of Being Overwhelmed
  Purpose: This stage does not always occur, set up contingency plans, prepare for possibility of becoming extremely stressed. prepare to deal with worst situation when feeling out of control and overwhelmed , encourage self to remain in situation, stay focused on present, accept feelings and wait for them to decrease, learn to have some control even if worst happens
  Examples: When stress comes, just pause.
      Keep my focus on the present; what is it I have to do?
      Label my stress on a 0 to 10 scale and watch it change.
      I should expect my stress to rise sometimes.
      Relax and slow things down.

Evaluation of Coping Efforts and Self-Rewards
  Purpose: Evaluate attempt, what helped and what didn't, look back at experience to see what has been learned, recognize small gains, don't belittle progress, praise self for trying, keep trying, don't expect perfection, what you would have done differently or better
  Examples: It wasn't as bad as I expected.
      I made more out of stress than it was worth.
      It didn't work. That's okay.

---

[97] Taken from Meichenbaum's "Stress inoculation" technique

The Rescripted Self: Competence and Wellbeing

Appendix 11: Reframing Worksheets

Re-labeling Worksheet -1[98]

Fill out the reframed positive label that can be attributed to the behavior. See the next page for a master copy

A Person Who:	Negative Label	Positive Label
changes their mind a lot	wishy-washy	
expresses their opinion	egotistical	
is emotionally sensitive	sick, fragile	
is selective in choosing a mate	afraid to commit	
gets depressed sometimes	Neurotic	
isn't good at a game	stupid, inferior	
isn't orderly	Sloppy	
pleases others	low self-esteem	
believes what others say	Gullible	
loves another strongly	dependent	
gets anxious	week, coward	
is nontraditional	troublemaker	
is helped by another	manipulated	
is not working hard on the task	Lazy	
is sure of something	conceited	
stands up for personal rights	argumentative	
thinks before making decisions	indecisive	
takes risks	harebrained	
sticks to projects	compulsive	
gets excited	hysterical	

---

[98] McMullin, Rian E. (1986)

Robert Kayton

Re-labeling Worksheet 2: Master Copy

A Person Who:	Negative Label	Positive Label
changes their mind a lot	wishy-washy	flexible
expresses their opinion	egotistical	honest, assertive
is emotionally sensitive	sick, fragile	open, caring
is selective in choosing a mate	afraid to commit	patient, careful
gets depressed sometimes	neurotic	understandable
isn't good at a game	stupid, inferior	hasn't practiced
isn't orderly	sloppy	spontaneous
pleases others	low self esteem	likable
believes what others say	gullible	trusting
loves another strongly	dependent	loving
gets anxious	week, coward	traumatized
is nontraditional	troublemaker	independent
is helped by another	manipulated	cared for
is not working hard on the task	lazy	relaxed
is sure of something	conceited	self-confident
stands up for personal rights	argumentative	gutsy
thinks before making decisions	indecisive	careful
takes risks	harebrained	brave
sticks to projects	compulsive	determined
gets excited	hysterical	exuberant

Appendix 12: Disputation Exercise

Like all cognitive approaches, you need to be passionate and emphatic.

1. *What is the evidence for my thought?* Most maladaptive beliefs and cognitive styles are not evidence based. They may be based on superstitious thinking, or on how you feel. Reality testing is based on facts, not fictions. Thus you need to look at objective evidence. Ask yourself whether your belief would hold up in a court of law. Circumstantial evidence usually does not.

2. *Is this always true?* Look for exceptions, especially when engaging in absolutistic, all-or-nothing thinking. Percentage evaluations can often be helpful, such as is it true 100% of the time, 50%, 5%?

3. *Even if true, what is the worst thing that can happen?* This is sometimes call top-down analysis and is often helpful with catastrophic or awfulized thinking. It is essentially a "so what" query, whereby you continually ask yourself what is the worst thing that could happen, all the way down to the primary concern. For example, "If I fail this test...then I will get a failing grade...then I will start to lose confidence...then I will get failing grades in all my subject... then I'll be thrown out of school…then I will not be able to earn a living... then I will be rejected by friends and family...then I will be all alone…then I will die." This can help you get to the bottom line irrational fear.

4. *How likely is it that it will happen?* Doing a probability check on these dire and extreme assumptions helps put these fears in perspective. In the example above, the likelihood of death, or being all alone, all because one fails a given test, is as improbable as it is absurd. You can then do a probability check on how likely it is that it will not happen. For example if you assume the probability of dying because you failed is 1 out of a thousand (.005) then the likelihood you will not die is 99.995%.

5. *What can I do if it does happen?* This is a question if the fear has a higher probability of occurring, especially when based on past experience, or if there is enough evidence to suggest it may occur. An employee, who fears losing her job because there are layoffs taking place, may have good reason for her concern. The goal then is to think in a planning and coping fashion.

6. *What alternative ways can I think about that?* This is a direct suggestion to reframe your perspective so as to consider more constructive ways to think. Perhaps your boss's gruffness had nothing to do with you, and instead with issues he might be dealing with at work or with his family. This is a good way to deal with misattributions and mind-reading. It is also good for challenging absolutistic thinking

7. *What good things can occur?* This can be thought of as a part of the above query. If my boss avoids me then maybe I could get my work done on time. Or my friend canceling lunch gives me the opportunity to go to the gym, or get some tasks finished.

8. *Does this way of thinking help me?* This challenge looks at the utility of thinking the way you do. If it does help, then examine whether the benefits outweigh the costs. However, you should consider the costs in terms of its consequences. Thinking that your boss does not like you, may help you not to rely on his good-will; yet, you will want to consider whether this thought can turn into a self-fulfilling prophesy. For example, if you believe he does not like you, then you may end up avoiding him, which can then lead him to feel rejected by you, so that he may end up rejecting you out of hurt and anger.

9. *Do I really want to continue doing this to myself?* This is similar to the above query. It is helpful to see how this thinking interferes with living life well.

Appendix 13: Counter-Thinking[99]

Although similar to disputation, countering does not involve challenging questions. Instead, you simply present a different and more adaptive thought to counter the negative thought you have. It is essential that you say the negative belief in a slow, monotonic, and monosyllabic way. This will help to lessen the negative affect. For each counter-belief be passionate by exaggerating your facial, vocal and bodily movements. This will help bind and condition positive affect to each positive statement.

Negative Statement	Counter Statement
1. I feel powerless and helpless.	1. I am powerful and in control of myself.
2. Often I feel like a victim of outside circumstances.	2. I am in control of how I deal with outside events.
3. I don't have the money to do what I really want.	3. Money isn't everything as long as I can take care of necessities.
4. There is seldom enough time to do what I want.	4. I can make time to do what I want.
5. Life is very difficult, it's all struggle.	5 Life is sometimes difficult and sometimes easy.
6. If things are going well, watch out!	6. If things are going badly they will likely get better.

---

[99] Bourne, 1990

Appendix 14: Narrative Rescripting

A. Use a log sheet to record your inner dialogues, just as people use dream logs. One can do it as an evening review of the days ruminations or try to take note of your inner dialogues at scheduled times or whenever you become aware of your "daydreaming."

B. Identify the dialogue and the scripts that are being enacted. For example, my thoughts are about the neighbor and I'm talking to the police or mediator and am giving my psychological and professional assessment of a scene of great rancor. I replay this intense scene as enacting a damage-repair scripts with those in authority. I sound like a brilliant expert on interpersonal and intrapersonal psychology. I also always win. If feel better. Perhaps this helps at working through the that shame-anger scene. These thoughts continually reinforced greater pride than shame-anger. They also help by cognifying the negative affect into thoughts which through the inner damage-repair dialogue I can begin to rescript that scene into a positive script. I can use reframing or other such techniques

Appendix 15: Daily Log

This worksheet is a familiar cognitive therapy task for people to help identify and understand your reactions to events.(Burns,   ) In the first column you are to list your feeling. The reason for this is that consciousness is triggered by affective and so most often our awareness of a happening, a scene, is first activated by the emotional response. Again, this is not always the case, especially for those who live life in a highly cognified script. To increase your understanding of your emotional reaction you could then add additional columns, such as underlying affect, schematic core belief and/or expectation, cognitive style, as well as behavior.

An offshoot approach would be to use a timer to remind you to focus in on your emotion. Since the timer, rather than affect, triggered your attention you may need to do a body focusing scan to get what your feelings are. This approach would be helpful to those of you who are more attuned to your to the world around you than to your inner world. This likely applies to the Type A worker who is overly focused on work or to the extravert who is mostly social; or the athlete whose focus is on her sport. A momentary time-out in order to look inward, may be an added benefit to identifying your emotions. It is also critical to self-awareness as we shall discuss at length in the next section on the emergent dialogical self.

Daily Log Worksheet

Affect/Emotion	Date	Event	Interpretation	Thought

Appendix 16: Wellbeing Questionnaire

Wellbeing Questionnaire
Robert Kayton

Rate from 1-7 the level of satisfaction you feel for each of the following items.
1=extremely unsatisfied; 2=very unsatisfied; 3=somewhat unsatisfied; 4= neutral
5=somewhat satisfied; 6=very satisfied; 7=extremely satisfied

[ ] Relationships
[ ] Work
[ ] Ability to play and just let loose
[ ] Relaxing and enjoy things
[ ] Do you laugh much?
[ ] Creative and stimulating activities
[ ] Engagement with life
[ ] Health
[ ] Depression
[ ] Anxiety
[ ] Stress
Ability to Handle:
    [ ] Health problems
    [ ] Loss of family member
    [ ] Loss of friend
    [ ] Uncertainties
    [ ] Boredom and lack of stimulation
    [ ] Conflicts with others
[ ] Sense of purpose and meaning
[ ] Optimism
[ ] Pride
[ ] Altruistic
[ ] Make mistakes
[ ] Taking personal responsibility when things go wrong
[ ] Spending alone time with yourself
[ ] In control of your life
[ ] Past
[ ] Present
[ ] Future
[ ] Wisdom
[ ] Perspective
[ ] Assertiveness
[ ] Sex life
[ ] Plan ahead
[ ] Prioritize
[ ] Decisiveness
[ ] Perseverance
[ ] Self-limitations
[ ] Listen without interrupting (and other narcissistic questions)
[ ] Directness with others

Appendix 17: Brain-Body-Mind Integration Techniques

The Homuncular Image: Let us use a metaphor technique to promote the integration between the brain, body and mind. Imagine your body as a robot, and that your self is to be the governor, the executive ego. First, conjure up an image of the body-brain map. Some of you may be familiar with the homunculus image of parts of the brain that correspond to parts of the body. This is depicted in the illustration seen below.

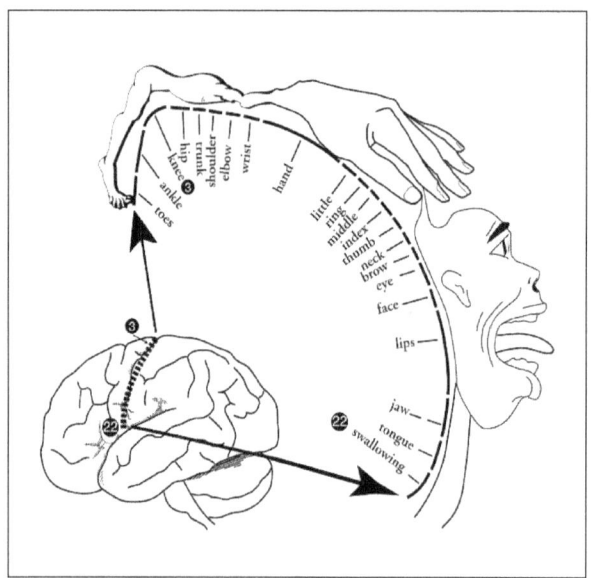

    Begin to move different parts of your body as you imagine their connection to those specific areas of the brain. And as you continue to coordinate your movements with the brain-body map, attune to the sensations that accompany these movements. Thus, when you move your finger or your jaw, look at the homunculus illustration and focus on your sensations. Practice making these associations stronger; it is as though you are wiring your robotic self to be more integrated. Practice making these connections between the body and brain.

Brain-Mind Integration Imaging: Now picture the right and left hemispheres of the brain, as well as the lower limbic and higher pre-frontal levels of the brain. [See Diagrams A and B on pages 18 and 19] As you engage in different mental activities, imagine each mental activity corresponding to its appropriate area of the brain. For example, as you are planning an activity, image your left prefrontal cortex being activated, while when feeling scared imagine right amygdala being activated. Now imagine that you, as the personal "I", are calling the shots. This is the conscious, executive (left prefrontal cortex) self. You can then begin to make conscious decisions by ordering your body to enact certain behaviors. I propose that as you do so you will promote the structural integration of body, brain and mind.

Integrating the Experiencing Self with the Doing Self: Grab the back of your neck with one of your hands and begin to massage it rigorously. First focus on the sensations in your neck and as you do your experiencing self will become dominant. When this is evident spend a little more time enjoying this. You will not be completely unaware of your hands, however, since your experiencing neck massage will help regulate the intensity and location of your neck rub. This means that the hand is the part of the observing self that is operating top-down; however, the experiencing self that is focused on neck sensations is sending signal bottom-up to the brain and from their top-down to the hands directing its movements.

When you have relaxed enough, now shift your focus to your hands, the doing part of the body. As you begin to focus on your arms and hands the sensations from arm and hand will begin to dominate and come into relief. Now the neck sensations recede into the background. Interestingly you will find that the sensations of your hand and arms begin to merge with the sensations in your neck. They are becoming integrated top-down and bottom-up.

Glossary of Terms

Action Potentials: The change in electrical potential associated with the passage of an impulse along the membrane of a muscle cell or nerve cell; it precedes activity thus allowing the neuron can inhibit its tendency to fire when activated.

Action Tendencies: An inclination towards a certain action, as when bacteria move toward nutrients and away from toxins.

Affects: The fundamental processes underlying our emotional and psychological life. Affects are innate neurobiological function that make up the physical experiences of an emotion. Affects refer to what some call "basic" or "inborn" emotions."

Analog-amplifier: Affects act as analog amplifiers by amplifying its source, such as making a scary dog even scarier; this in turn will amplify the fear-terror affect even more, so that it appears as though affects are self-amplifying.

Affect-Integration: Affect-integration underlies self-regulation and ultimately underlies self-integration. It specifically refers to the coherence of affects both with other affects and with cognition and behavior that forms a harmonious, balanced and cohesive whole.

Affect-Regulation: The fundamental process determining our capacity to function competently in life. At its core is the *excitation-inhibition* polarity, which operates to balance levels of excitation with countervailing levels of inhibition; most often this entails affect-inhibition.

Affect-Rescripting Therapy (ART): The same as *rescripting therapy*; it was the term earlier used.

Affect-Scripts: Scripts that directly regulate affects.

Affect-tolerance training: The goal is to excite negative affect until it habituates.

Affluence scripts: Optimizing scripts that are governed by higher ratios of positive to negative affects.

Altruism: An "unselfish regard for or devotion to the welfare of others."

Analog Principle: An analog is a near duplication, or copy, of its original source.

Autobiographical Self-Scripts: Scripts that make up the temporal self, which is extended in time that consists of all the stored emotional memories and scripts accumulated during one's lifetime. It is our personal story, our saga and our legend.

Autostimulation: An infant's purposeful act of thumb sucking; it is arguably the first act of self-agency.

Auxiliary Affects: Shame-humiliation and disgust/dissmell are *auxiliary affects*, either to the basic affects themselves (such as shame-humiliation, which we shall soon see is triggered by the partial interruption of positive affect), or to the more basic biological drives (i.e. disgust/dissmell), and thus are not innate analogs of external stimuli. In other words, they are not triggered by differing rates and densities of neural firings, but are activated by other variables, especially those that relate to the social world. As such these auxiliary affects evolved in social mammals, and thus can be thought of as making up the social and moral affects.

Backed-Up Affect: The socialization of affects may lead to "pseudo-affective expressions," or *backed-up affect*. This is particularly observed in the facial expression of the *stiff upper lip*, or in suppressed vocalizations when one bites their lip. Tomkins believed that the inhibition of affect is what makes up *stress*.

Behavioral Modification: The alteration of behavioral patterns through the use of positive or negative reinforcement.

Central Nervous System (CNS): The CNS consists of the spinal cord and brain.

Conditional reinforcement: Conditional reinforcement links a stimulus to a response.

Cognification: The analogical transformation of affects into cognition, as when the affect enjoyment-joy is cognified into happy thoughts, anger-rage is cognified as angry thoughts.

Convergence-Divergence Principle: The principle underlying the integration of the self that looks at the ratio between degrees of similarity and degrees of difference among self-scripts.

Cost-Benefit Scripts: Cost-benefit scripts are primarily defensive scripts based on inhibiting negative affect and minimizing negative affect scripts, often at the expense of the positive. 21

Damage-repair script: Scripts whose purpose is to repair the damage incurred by shame. The most recognizable scenes entail shame-anger-guilt-rapprochement.

Classical conditioning: Classical conditioning deals directly with the autonomic nervous system and is mediated by lower pre-limbic areas of the brain (such as the reticular activating system and the cerebellum). Many of you are familiar with the Pavlovian experiment demonstrating that when a bell-ring becomes associated with food, that bell-ring will then come to elicit the salivation response that is naturally elicited by food. Learning takes place when the two stimuli are associated together in time and space.

Consciousness: The subjective state of awareness in which affects, emotions and memories are active and operating at any given moment of time. Consciousness is activated, when affect is activated.

Contrarian: Someone who usually acts in a contrary way, by taking an opposing side from whatever position another person takes.

Declarative learning: Learning that is top-down and takes place explicitly through the use of symbols and syntax; it includes semantic (factual) and episodic (autobiographical, event-based) processing, and requires conscious attention. Most academic learning takes place declaratively in the form of instructional teaching.

Denial: A defense used to disavow the presence of negative affect. There are two primary types: *Pollyannaish denial* is to make the negative positive, *Counterphobic denial* is to do the opposite of what will induce fear.

Dialogical self: The self as consisting of our inner narratives.

Differentiation: The process by which an infant separates self from the selfmother-self.

Disorganized/disoriented relationship: A relationship in which a mother's behavior is duplicitous and unpredictable, leading the child to display both disorganized and disoriented behaviors, ranging from startle to fear to shame to distress to anger.

Embodied images: Cognition at this primitive level is highly *affect laden* and codified in sensory-motor images via touch, smell or taste. Sensory data gets stored, probably at cellular levels, in the muscles and tissues of the body. Because these bodily images are so primal, they form the foundation for all higher levels of mentation. It is at this level that non-semantic schemas that underlie our core beliefs, begin to develop.

EMDR (Eye Movement Desensitization Reprocessing): A technique designed for trauma, is partly based on the relaxation response being induced while the memory of the traumatic event is being recalled, thus changing the context to the now. It uses such devices as lights and electrical stimulation that innervates right and then left hemispheres.

Emotions: Emotions are ideoaffective complexes that merge affect and cognition.

Eros: (a) The life energy source, (b) The sexualized passionate love between two people.

Exposure/response prevention: A behavioral technique in which a person subject himself to the negative event until the negative affect subsides.

Extraversion: The trait characterized by one who mainly gets gratification from others, instead of from within.

Fairness Fallacy: Most people believe there is a universal truth as to what is fair and what is not fair. Unfortunately, this could not be further from the truth. Fairness is in the eyes of the beholder, and follows what could be described as the reverse golden rule; instead of *do unto others as you would like others to do unto you,* the fairness fallacy instead says, *others should do unto me as I would do unto them.*

Felt-Feel: The "felt-feel" of an emotion is the affective sensation itself; when cognified, the experience is more that it "feels-like" a given affect.

Fictional finalisms: How the future shapes the present; it also shapes our memories of the past.

Fixed Action Patterns (FAP): Fixed action patterns refer to an automatized sequence of specific movements, a fixed set of reflexes that represent a furthering of motor sequencing actions.

Excitation-Inhibition Polarity: The principle underlying our ability to function competently in life; it operates to balance levels of excitation with countervailing levels of inhibition; most often this entails affect-inhibition.

Extraversion: Extraversion is the trait characterized by one who mainly gets gratification from others, instead of from within.

Free will: The power of self-direction.

Function-focused Rescripting: A structured, strategic, and top-down approach, whose primary purpose is to expeditiously regulate affect, first through body-focused rescripting, then through the restructuring of negative cognitions and emotions, and finally to the modification of negative behaviors.

Hierarchy of needs: Maslow's stage-based model of development in which there are five levels of needs to be fulfilled before attaining wellbeing, from the basic needs to a more complex and higher order of needs.

Humanism: "Human-being centered" is what makes up humanist ideology, which is opposed to the *rules centered* normative ideology.

Ideoaffective Complex: An emotion is socialized affect, whereby the innate and automatized nature of affect is transformed, through experiential learning, into emotions, which make up the cognitive-emotional nexus, or more technically the ideoaffective complex.

Ideoaffective scripts: Cost-benefit scripts, and thus defensive scripts, are technically called *ideoaffective scripts* since they are largely based on emotions.

Ideological scripts: These scripts are more highly organized complex scripts than are cost-benefit scripts. They relate to one's ideology, ones relatively coherent set of fundamental beliefs about the world and how to live in it. There are two basic bimodal ideologies, the *normative* and *humanistic*, which correspond in politics to conservative or liberal, right or left.

Individuation: The process by which an individual forms those unique personality features that distinguish one's self from others.

Inscripts: The innate fixed action-pattern built into each affect.

Insecurely avoidant attachments: In this mother-child dynamic, the child failed to show distress at separation, and in fact maintained the greatest degree of separation and the least degree of attachment than any of the other behavioral tendencies.

Instrumental, or operant conditioning: This is a behavioral technique that is mediated the amygdala and the hippocampus, parts of the limbic system that function at a higher level than structures activated in classical conditioning. Unlike classical conditioning, which focuses on the pairing of stimuli in time and space, instrumental conditioning focuses on the response and its consequential reinforcement.

Integration: When parts cohere in a cohesive way.

Integrated Self: The integrated self as *a personality in which the constituent traits, behavioral patterns, motives, and so forth are used effectively and with minimal effort or without conflict. Those with integrated personalities are thought essentially to know themselves, and to enjoy and live life fully.* The dictionary also goes on to say that the integrated personality is the same as the well-integrated self.

Integrative-Rescripting: Entails integrating the components of the structural self, together with the autobiographical self and the self-other self. Although many techniques are used, the "as if" and "do the "opposite of the urge" strategies.

Intellectualization: To detach the affect charge associated with a cognition by cognifying that affect.

Introversion: The tendency to be self-directed and self-reflective, whose focus is more on mental energy than on physical energy.

Mental presence: When thoughts and emotions are tied to action. A number of studies found this to be a significant predictor of happiness. We could say that mental presence is more related to self-agency,

Mirror neurons: Neurons that synchronize movements and brain activity between the doer and the observer. two people or animals. It is the basis underlying empathy.

Misattributions: Making false assumptions.

Modeling: A genetically inherent tendency toward imitation, and is thus the first mode of social learning.

Modularity: Refers to the "property of any system that permits its subsystems degrees of freedom of combination and recombination."

Narcissism: A condition characterized by excessive self-love, egocentrism, and a grandiose sense of self-importance, together with a lack of empathy for others who are seen, and used, for self-exploitation.

Neural Networks: A nexus of multiple combinations of neural connections.

Neurogenesis: The formation of new neurons from stem cells in the brain.

Neurotransmitters: Chemicals that help regulate brain activity by signaling some neurons to fire and others to hold their fire.

Normative: The ideology that is rules-based.

Overcompensation: To diminish negative affect by exaggerating opposing thoughts and behaviors.

Parasympathetic Nervous System: The inhibitory and energy conserving system of the Autonomic Nervous System, which carries signals that act to conserve energy during periods of rest.

Patterns of Neural firings: Patterns of neural firings that vary according to its rate (speed/time) and its density (number of neurons) that are increasing, decreasing, or steady. These three neural patterns replicate the dynamic stimulus patterns taking place in the external world and determine which affects get triggered, how they get expressed, and what feelings are experienced.

Peripheral Nervous System: The peripheral nervous system is divided into the *Somatic Nervous System* (SNS), the *Autonomic Nervous System* (ANS), and the *Diffuse Enteric System*.

Potentiation: The "enhancement of one agent by another so that the combined effect is greater than the sum of the effects of each alone."

Prescripts: Innate drive of affects geared to *maximize positive affect, minimize negative affect*, and *maximize the expression of all affects* (whether positive and negative).

Procedural learning: Implicit and subconscious and takes place at the lower levels of the brain, and is thus bottom-up. Information is acquired, not through cognition, but through action, which some call "muscle memory." It is the first mode of learning, and continues throughout life.

Posticipation: "The linking of the past with the future."

Projection: To attribute ones feelings and thoughts (in terms of wishes or fears) onto another person.

Proscripting: One is to imagine and experience the future differently than one usually does.

Protoscripts: Consists of inscripted fixed action patterns.

Protoself: The protoself develops in vitro. Although some believe that the self begins very early in fetal life, it is in truth the protoself that begins to form, and that takes place late in fetal development. It is at this inscripted level that affect-induced action patterns are evident.

Pruning: The process by which synapses lose their neural connections.

Reaction formation: A script in which one not only *does* the opposite, as in counterphobic denial, but also *becomes the opposite* by incorporating oppositional behavior into the self; in other words, a reaction formation script can evolve from defensive subscripts like counterphobic denial or overcompensation.

Reinforcement: There are three types of reinforcement: *positive* reward, which reduces negative behavior and increases positive behavior; *negative* reinforcement entails the absence or withholding of reward that will diminish positive or negative behavior; and *punishment*, which increases negative behavior and decreases positive behavior. There are several important reinforcement principles.

Repression: Acts to detach negative cognition from its associated negative affect.

Rescripting Therapy: The comprehensive method used to rescript the self by combining function-focused rescripting with integrative-rescripting.

Rescripted Self: A person who has achieved both competency and success in life, and who has attained a state of being that is characterized by happiness and wellbeing.

Resistant and ambivalent relationships: The child of an overanxious mother will be wary of any separation, as evidenced by minimal, if any, exploratory behaviors. Unfortunately, these toddlers gained little comfort from being close to their mother, and instead showed anxiety and distress.

Scene: The basic unit of a script that consists of an event that triggers patterns of activity in the brain and body that then excites an affect, which in turn activates the cognitive-emotional system that finally leads to behavior.

Scripts: Scripts are learned cognitive sets of rules and schemas that order and govern our lives in the service of affect-regulation and self-regulation.

Secure attachments: The toddler's comfort zone for closeness with the mother, and the exploration of the toy-filled environment, was by far the greatest.

Self: The self is a *general mega-script that encompasses the totality of all self-scripts.*

Self-agency: Refers to the explicit and conscious *awareness* of self as the doer of one's actions, together with the implicit, preconscious *sense* of self as the doer.

Selfother Self-Script: Selfother self-scripts make up our social self, and consists of both interpersonal self-scripts and intrapersonal self-scripts. The selfother-self is extended in space.

Self-organizing complexity: Complexity is an emerging process that proceeds from a relatively simple organized system to a relatively complex organized system. emerging complexity is what governs script formation.

Self-Script: Scripts that organize affect-regulating scripts into a more cohesive and coherent whole.

Self-states: A relatively stable configuration of self-states that exists at a particular time as a *state of mind.*

Schemas: An outlook or assumption that an individual has of the self, others, or the world, that endures despite objective reality.

Spatialization of time: The model that time is relative to space.

Specious present: The one-dimensionality of the present.

Socioemotional selectivity theory: whereby the elderly is able to better tailor their social interactions to avoid stress, thereby increasing their state of wellbeing; as a result, they make thoughtful and wiser decisions.

Splitting: A pattern in unstable relationships, often seen in Borderline Personality Disorders, characterized by alternations between the extremes of idealization and devaluation., a split in the selfother self and with others between the all-good self or other, and an all-bad self or other. that then gets projected onto others.

Sublimation: The channeling of one's charged affect into socially acceptable behaviors.

Sympathetic Nervous System: That part of the Autonomic Nervous System that is excitatory and carries signals that help organize, mobilize and energize resources during periods of real or perceived threat.

Synapses: Specialized junctions through which neural signals are transmitted from one neuron to another neuron.

Synaptogenesis: The growth of new neural networks and connections.

Temperament: The inborn personality traits based on innate affect sensitivity levels, such as the inhibited type or the uninhibited type.

Thanatos: Freud's so called "death instinct, namely the negative energy force, as opposed to its opposite, Eros.

Theory of mind: The capacity to realistically judge what another person feels.

Transformational representations: Signs, symbols and words.

Triune Brain: The tripartite division of the brain that illustrates the principle that *ontogeny recapitulates phylogeny,* namely that the development of an individual person's brain follows evolutionary stages a sequence that corresponds to the evolution of the human brain itself, from the reptilian brain to the early mammal brain to the neomammalian brain.

Wellbeing: Often equated with happiness and the end product of Eros, it reflects the fulfillment of our prescriptive goals. Table 9-1 on p.253 lists its important attributes.

Will: The capacity to make choices when our behavior is self-directed, through self-awareness and volition.

Willpower: Entails self-agency and personal responsibility.

Wisdom: The mental state that evolves over a lifetime of experiential learning. It provides us with those higher and more complex attributes we associate with executive functioning, such as judgment, planning and decision-making. Those who are wise are those who are enlightened.

References

Abramson, Lauren. (1998) Unpublished personal communication.
Allman, John. (2000) *Evolving brains*. New York: W.H. Freemand & Co.
Ainsworth, Mary D. (1992) *Developmental Psychology*, 28, 759-775.
Ainswoth, Mary D, et. al, (1962) *Patterns of Attachment*, Psychology Press
Aronoff, Joel, Rabin A.A. Zucker, Robert A. (Eds.), (1987) *The emergence of personality,* Springer Publishing Co.
Bakal, Donald B. (1999) *Minding the Body.* New York: The Guildford Press
Blinder, Barton J. (2007) *Autobiographical Memory: Who we are and what we know,* Psychiatric Annals, 37-4
Blackslee & Blackslee, (2007) *Where mind and brain meet.* Scientific American Mind, V18, No. 94.
Bloom, F.L & Lazerson, A. (1988) *Brain, mind, and body.* New York: W.H. Freemand & Co.
Bowlby, John. (1969) *Attachment and loss*. Vol. I, *Attachment*. New York: Basic Books.
Bowlby, John. (1973) *Attachment and loss*. Vol. II, *Separation*. New York: Basic Books.
Bourne, Edmund J. (1990) *The anxiety and Phobia Workbook,* New.
Bretherton, I. *The origins of attachment theory: John Bowlby and Mary Ainsworth* Bretherton, Francis F, Broucek, (1991), *Shame and the Self*, The Guildford Press.
Berne, Eric, (1969), *Games people play,* Mass Market Paperback
Burns, David D., (1999) *The Feeling Good Handbook,* Plume.
Ellis, Albert, ((1977), *A basic clinical theory of rational emotive therapy.* In A. Ellis & R. Grieger (Eds.) New York, Springer.
Ellis, Albert., & Harper, R.A. (1975), *A new guide to rational living,* Wilshire, Inge (1992) *The origins of attachment theory: John Bowlby and Mary Ainsworth.* Developmental Psychology, 28, 759-775.
Cartenson, Laura, (2000), *The aging mind: Opportunities in cognitive aging*, National Academy Press
Castaneda, (1985), *The Teachings of Don Juan.* Mass Market Press
Cozolino, Louis J. (2002) *The neuroscience of psychotherapy: Building and rebuilding the human brain.* New York: W.W. Norton & Co.
Damasio, Antonio R. (1994) *Descartes Error.* New York: G.P. Putnam's Sons.
Damasio, Antonio R, (2003) *Listening to Spinoza,*
Darwin, Charles. (1965) *The expression of the emotions in man and animals.* Chicago: The University of Chicago Press
Davis, Martha, et.al., (1990), *The Relaxation and Stress Reduction Workbook,* New Harbinger
Demos. E. V, (Ed.). (1995). *Exploring Affect: The Selected Writings of Silvan S, Tomkins.* Cambridge: Cambridge University Press.
Demos, E.V. Personal communication, 2006.
Dowling, John E. (1992) *Neurons and networks: An introduction to neuroscience.* Cambridge: The Belknap Press.
Eimer, Bruce N. (2002) *Hypnotize yourself out of pain now!* New Harbinger Publication
Ekman, Paul. (2003) *Emotions revealed.* New York: Henry Holt & Co. of New Jersey.
Gazzaniga, Michael S. (2012) *Free will is an illusion, but you're still responsible for your*

actions, The Chronical Review.
Gazzaniga, Michael S, (2018), *The Consciousness Instinct*, Farrar, Straus & Giroux,
Goldstine, Daniel (1977), *The Dance Away Lover*, Random House.
Grawe, Klaus. (2007). *Neuropsychotherapy: How the Neurosciences Inform Effective Psychotherapy* (1st ed.). Routledge.
Hall, Calvin S, Gardener, Lindsey, Campbell, John S, (1997), *Theories of Personality*, John Wiley & Sons
Hebb, Donald (1949). *The Organization of Behavior.* New York: Wiley & Sons.
Hoffer, Nancy Josephine (1997) Affect, coping, attachment, and alcohol consumption: An application of Tomkins' theory. Ph.D. dissertation, Long Island University.
Jerome, Richard (2019). *The Time-Bending Science of smell,* Time Magazine, Special Edition, "The Science of Memory: The Story of our Lives."
Kagan, Jerome, & Snidman, Nancy (2004), *The long shadow of temperament,* Harvard University Press
Leahy, Robert L. (2003) *Cognitive Therapy Techniques,* The Guildford Press.
LeDoux, Joseph. (1996) *The emotional brain.* New York: Simon & Schuster.
LeDoux, Joseph. (2002) *Synaptic Self,* Viking Press
Llina's, Rodolfo R. (2001) *i of the cortex: from neurons to self,* Cambridge: MIT Press.
Lewis, H.B. (1971) *Shame and Guilt in Neurosis.* New York: International University Press.
Masterpasqua, Frank and Perna, Phyllis. (1997) *The Psychological Meaning of Chaos,* American Psychological Association
Meichenbaum, Donald, (1985), *Stress Inoculation Training*, Pergamum Press.
McMullin, Rian E. (1986) *Handbook of cognitive therapy techniques.* New York: W.W. Norton & Co.
Nathanson, Donald L. Ed. (1996). *Knowing Feeling: affect, script, and psychotherapy.* New York: Norton.
Nathanson, Donald L (1992). *Shame and Pride: Affect, Sex, and the Birth of the self.* New York: Norton.
Nieburg, Dianh, H. (2000) *Excitement and joy: The role of the positive affects in development and wellbeing.* Ph.D. Dissertation, Pacifica Graduate Institute, United States, California
Oatley and Jenkins (1996) *Understanding Emotions,*
Omaha, John. (2004) *Psychotherapeutic Interventions for Emotional Regulation.* New York: W.W.Norton & Co.
Pine, Fred. (1990) *Drive, ego, object & self: a synthesis for clinical work,* International Press
Rosenberg, J.L. (1985) Atlanta: Humanics Limited.
Rosenthal, Norman E. *The emotional brain.* (2002). New York: Citadel Press
Schore, Allan. (1994). *Affect regulation and the origin of the self: the neurobiology of emotional development.* New Jersey: Lawrence Erlbaum Assoc.
Schore, Allan (2003A). *Affect Dysregulation & Disorders of the Self.* New York: W.W. Norton.
Schore, Allan (2003B). *Affect Regulation and the Repair of the Self.* New York: W.W. Norton
Schaller, Joseph George (1999) Affect and autism: Contributions from the work of Stanley Greenspan and Silvan Tomkins. Psy.D. Dissertation, Widener University

Schulkin, Jay (2007) *Effort: A behavioral neuroscience perspective on the Will*, Lawrence Erlbaum Associates
Sedgwick, E. K. & Frank, A. (1995). *Shame and its sisters: A Sylvan Tomkins reader.* Duke University Press: Durham and London.
Siegel, Daniel J.(1999) *The Developing Mind: Toward a Neurobiology of Interpersonal Experience.* New York: The Guildford Press.
Siegel, Daniel J (200) *Parenting from the inside out.*
Siegel, Daniel J. (2007?) *The mindful brain.*
Solomon, M & Siegel, D.J. (2003) *Healing trauma.* New York: W.W. Norton & Co. Spitz, Rene' (1065). The first year of life, New York: International Universities Press.
Stern, Daniel N. (1985). *The interpersonal world of the infant: a view from psychoanalysis and developmental psychology.* New York: Basic Books.
Sullivan, Harry Stack. (1953) The Collected Works of Harry Stack Sullivan Vol.1. New York: W.W. Norton & Co.
Sullivan, Harry Stack. (1953) The Collected Works of Harry Stack Sullivan Vol 2. New York: W.W. Norton & Co.
Tomkins, Silvan S. (1962) *Affect, Imagery, Consciousness. Vol. 1: The positive affects.* New York: Springer Publishing, Co.
Tomkins, Silvan S. (1963). *Affect, Imagery, Consciousness. Vol. 2: The negative affects.* New York: Springer Publishing, Co.
Tomkins, Silvan S. (1987). Shame. In D.L. Nathanson. (Ed). *The many faces of shame.* pp. 133-161. New York: Guildford Press.
Tomkins, Silvan S. (1987). Script theory. In J.Arnkoff, A.I. Rabin, & R. A. Zucker (eds). *The Emergence of Personality*, (147-216). New York: Springer Publishing.
Young, Jeffery E. Klosko, Janet S., Weishara. Margorie E. (2003) *Schema Therapy: a Practitioner's guide.* New York: The Guildford Press.

www.ingramcontent.com/pod-product-compliance
Lightning Source LLC
Chambersburg PA
CBHW060233240426
43671CB00016B/2928